THE CHRISTIAN GUIDE
TO PARENT CARE

D0905245

THE
CHRISTIAN GUIDE
TO
PARENT CARE

Dr. Robert J. Riekse
& Dr. Henry Holstege

Tyndale House Publishers, Inc.
Wheaton, Illinois

Unless otherwise noted, Scripture quotations are from *The Living Bible,* copyright © 1971 owned by assignment by KNT Charitable Trust. All rights reserved. Scripture quotations marked NIV are from the *Holy Bible,* New International Version. Copyright © 1973, 1978, 1984 International Bible Society. Used by permission of Zondervan Publishing House.

Library of Congress Cataloging-in-Publication Data

Riekse, Robert, date
   The Christian guide to parent care / Robert Riekse and Henry Holstege.
     p.   cm.
   Includes bibliographical references and index.
   ISBN 0-8423-0544-0
    1. Aging parents—Care—United States. 2. Caregivers—United States. 3. Adult children—United States—Religious life.
I. Holstege, Henry, date   II. Title.
HQ1063.6.R54   1992
306.874—dc20   92-3123

Printed in the United States of America

98 97 96 95 94 93 92
 9   8   7   6   5   4   3   2   1

We dedicate this book to our parents,
Gilbert and Esther Riekse,
who have been lifelong inspirations
and positive living examples of parents
who have had rich Christian journeys
throughout their long lives,
and
Henry and Betsey Holstege,
whose lives provided love and guidance in the Christian life
and whose deaths give continued assurance of the life to come.
We also dedicate this book to our wives,
Ellen Riekse and Lois Holstege,
who made this book possible
through their support, encouragement, and tolerance,
and to our children,
of whom we are very proud
and who give us insights into the ongoing cycle of life.

CONTENTS

ACKNOWLEDGMENTS

We gratefully acknowledge Dr. Wendell Hawley, senior vice president at Tyndale House Publishers, for recognizing the need for this book and encouraging us to write it.

We are most appreciative of Dan Elliott for his kind, careful, and professional management of the overall editorial process that brought the book to completion.

We also gratefully acknowledge the anecdotal research and writing assistance of Angela Elwell Hunt.

The proofreading and stylistic suggestions of Ann Annis were important and greatly appreciated.

And the manuscript would not have taken form without the typing and retyping of Maxine Comer, to whom we are also grateful.

INTRODUCTION

My retired parents will soon sell their house and move 650 miles to live near me and my family. I am pleased that they like us enough to move here. But my sister said something chilling on the phone the other day: "I'm glad Mom and Dad are moving near you. You'll be so good at caring for them in their old age."

That sounded like a prison sentence.

—Pennsylvania man[1]

My mom is in her nineties and lives with us. Though my husband and grown kids volunteer to help, I feel she is my responsibility. This situation is making me feel physically and emotionally exhausted, but I can't stop.

—New York woman, age sixty-two[2]

My mother-in-law sees everything as negative. She complains that everyone is better to her than we are. We love her and work hard to make her comfortable. How can we get her to see the bright side of things?

—Georgia man, age forty-five[3]

My mother has Alzheimer's. She has no money, no insurance. I feel I'm not doing enough, but she throws caregivers I hire out of the house.

—Pennsylvania woman, age forty[4]

More and more my father needs my help. How can I help without taking away his dignity?

—Illinois woman, age fifty-four[5]

> I wish I could be soft and understanding, taking things in my stride, humoring my mother's foibles. . . . But I am short-tempered, frazzled from all the responsibilities. I am the 'sandwich' generation, caught between kids and parents. I want to do the right thing.
> —New Jersey woman[6]

Jennie always thought of herself as a loving daughter. Until recently, most of Jennie's worries and joys centered on the normal routines of life. Her job in the local bookstore was a big help in paying college tuition for her sons, and she enjoyed meeting people. Jim, her husband, was even beginning to talk about retirement. On the whole, life was very good.

But Jennie's mother began to change. At first her mom seemed merely forgetful, but then she became confused and did some really strange things. Jennie's dad didn't know what to do, so he called on Jennie for help.

Medical tests determined that Jennie's mom suffered from Alzheimer's disease. She would not get better, and she needed monitoring every day, all day. Jennie's father wasn't up to the job. He had recently suffered a heart attack, and Jennie was careful to shield him from stressful responsibilities.

Jennie and Jim held a family conference with her dad. If Jennie could drop in and fix the meals and help her mom dress, they might get by. But that night, after their discussion, Jennie couldn't sleep. A thousand questions bothered her.

- Would she be expected to quit her job to care for her mom?
- If her dad's pension wouldn't cover the medical expenses, would she and Jim be expected to use their savings to pay the bills?
- Who would watch over her mom at night?

- How could she take care of her own family and her parents?
- How could she encourage her father to stay as independent as possible?
- Could she guide her parents financially? Should she interfere?
- Did her parents expect to move in with her?
- Could she ever put her parents in a nursing home? Would she have to?
- How could she talk to her parents about these things?

Jennie's situation is not unusual. Contrary to what many people think, care for the elderly in our society comes primarily from family members. "It is a myth," says sociologist Roberta Greene, "that government or other sources of help are the major providers of assistance to older people and their families: 80 percent of the care older people receive usually is from a family member. The other 20 percent may be getting a variety of care, ranging from being rather healthy and going to senior centers for activities and meals, to actually needing very intensive health care services in the community or a nursing home."[7]

Professor Nancy Schlossberg stresses that families usually provide support, and the family members who usually do the caring are the daughters and daughters-in-law. They are the kin-keepers, she says.[8]

According to a report from the Older Women's League, on average a woman will spend seventeen years caring for children and eighteen years "helping" an aging parent.[9] The report also states that

- 75 percent of caregivers for the elderly are women
- 55 percent of caregivers work outside of the home
- 37 percent of women will care for a frail adult

- 1.8 million women now simultaneously care for both children and parents
- Caregiving daughters outnumber sons three to one[10]

Children of aging parents struggle with a range of issues and problems. It is difficult to know and do what is best for our parents. Some who undertake care for an aging parent assume that guiding a parent will be simple, but "kin-keeping" is not another form of parenting. The roles are not easily reversed.

"There is such ambivalence," says psychologist Marilyn Bonjean. "Think of the term *adult child*. How can you be both? And how can you deal with someone who has been an authority figure who is becoming frail?"[11]

Caring for an aging parent can become all-consuming because the situation generally does not improve. For many, death is the only way out of this tough situation. As Christians we have the assurance that death is the beginning of heavenly life, but the journey to the end of earthly life is not an easy one for elderly parents or their caregiving children.

If you are caring for an aging parent, or if you suspect you will be filling such a role in the future, this book is for you. We want you to understand that you are not alone. We want to point you to helpful resources that can make a tremendous difference in how you cope with being a caregiver. And we want you to understand the limits of your responsibilities and resources as you help your parents continue to grow older.

As Jennie and Jim discovered, the pressure of caring for aging parents comes when most adult children are just beginning to get away from the demands of raising their own families. Jennie and Jim were planning their own retirement and considering how they could help their boys establish homes when they were ready to settle down.

Like Jennie and Jim, you may be in the "sandwich generation." You are a middle-aged child who is coping with supporting your maturing children as well as your aging parents. You may feel pressured by the needs of the generation ahead of you as well as the generation behind you. At times it may seem as if your entire life is devoted to caring for others.

If you have felt that you are at the end of your rope, you are not alone. The task can seem impossible, disheartening, and hopeless. But there are people and resources to help you.

This book is designed to help you as you try to cope with the range of issues and problems you face in trying to help your parents as they grow older in modern America. The book offers a broad array of practical approaches to the problems faced on a regular basis by older people and their adult children who are trying to help them. It also deals with the feelings adult children often experience in caring for elderly parents—frustration, anger, and guilt. It looks at biblical mandates as they apply to today's realities and demands. Throughout the book, issues, questions, and problems are looked at from a positive, loving, Christian perspective.

For example, is it my obligation to have my widowed father move in with me and my family when he can no longer get by in his own place? How does the process of aging affect my mom's ability to continue to be independent? What are the results of normal aging? What is not normal or unusual? Where can I go for help with my folks? How can I help my parents get by financially? What kind of resources and services are available in most communities to help older people? Who is eligible for these services? What kind of housing options are available to people as they get older? What can Christians do to help older people who have special problems? When is it time to put your mom in a nursing home? How can you do this without being overwhelmed by guilt?

These are some of the real-life situations this book deals with. It combines some of the best research available with the collective experience and perspective of the authors to offer practical, positive guidelines to improve the lives of adult children and the older people these children are trying to help.

> Middle-agers need their aging parents, though they may not know it, or even believe it. To grow older themselves, the younger ones need the lessons that can be learned from caring for their parents.
> —Oregon woman, seventy-eight[12]

PART ONE

PART ONE

CHAPTER ONE
What's Happening in American Families?

January: "Hello, Mom. How are you feeling this morning? Dizzy again! Did you take those pills the doctor gave you yesterday? You can't find them! I put them in the front of your medicine cabinet, next to your high blood pressure pills, just to the right of your arthritis medicine. Remember to take the red ones before you take the new ones.

"I can't come over and visit with you, Mom, because I promised Jill that I would come over to baby-sit her kids so she could go to her class at the community college. You know she is trying to get a better job since Gary lost his, and she thought some classes might help. I'll come over as soon as I can, but Pete expects dinner when he gets home. Try to lie down, and I'll be over later. Bye."

May: "No, Jill, I can't afford to give you my old car. I know times have been hard for you since Gary lost his job. Times have been kind of hard for me, too. Since your dad retired, my income has dropped more than half. And with Grandma needing more and more medicine that she really can't afford, I'm having more and more trouble each month paying my bills. I've been trying to get more hours at work, but things are a little slow right now. If Grandma has to go into a nursing home, I don't know what we'll do. She simply can't afford it, and I don't earn enough to pay for it.

And if she has to come here to live, I'll have to quit my job to take care of her. I just don't know how things are going to turn out."

July: "But, Maxine, can't you come over to help me with Mom? I'm checking on her twenty-four hours a day. I hear all her complaints, all her troubles, all her problems. Sometimes she isn't too tough to be with, but I feel like I'm responsible for her all the time. I've spent the last five nights over there—the toughest part is during the night when she has to go to the bathroom and calls me until I come to help her.

"I know you're busy with your job all week and being coordinator of the Sunday school. And I know that your kids take a lot of time, but I need a break. I need a few days off. Can't you help me?"

September: "But Mom, Maxine and I don't think you can keep living in this old house. Since you don't drive anymore, you are a prisoner in the house and in this old neighborhood. Sure, we are happy to pick you up for church. But with both of us working, it's hard to pick you up when you have to get to the doctor. I know you enjoy those Golden Circle meetings at church every Tuesday morning, but I work during the day and I can't take you. I wish you would ask your friends to pick you up. Too bad Gary doesn't live closer. He has more time because he doesn't have a full-time job anymore.

"Well, at least think about it, Mom. This house is too old and too big. And you're too isolated."

October: "Remember when I said, 'The last place we'll ever put Mom is in a nursing home!'? Well, lately I've been thinking about that old saying 'The spirit is willing, but the flesh is weak!' That's the way I feel after eight months of taking care of Mom. I'm beat! I know I've been really grumpy around the house. I certainly haven't been a wife to Pete lately, if you know what I mean. The kids are running out of patience, too. They help when they can, but Mom isn't always a happy person to be around. Most of the time she doesn't feel very well, so you can see why she gets depressed and short-tempered.

"The doctor doesn't hold out much hope for any improvement in Mom's condition. In fact, he said that it won't be too long before she'll need the kind of around-the-clock care that I just can't give her. He said we had better begin to think seriously about a nursing home. Can you believe it? When he said those words I was actually relieved! The words I thought I would dread the most actually gave me a feeling of release!

"But then I started feeling guilty again. How could I abandon Mom to a nursing home? Isn't it my job to care for her as long as she lives? And if I did think about a nursing home, how could I find one that will take good care of Mom?"

THE GRAYING OF AMERICA
Do any of these scenes sound familiar? Similar words are coming from the lips of thousands of men and women every day. Because more people are living to old age today than ever before, more people are faced with caring for aging parents.

In 1987, 29.8 million Americans were older than sixty-five—12.3 percent of the population. Just three years later in 1990, according to the U.S. Census Bureau, there were over 31 million persons sixty-five and older, which was 12.6 percent of the population.[1] By 2050 it is estimated there will be over 68 million older people, which will make up 23 percent of the total population.[2] In 2050 more than 5 percent of the population will be over eighty-five.[3]

The older segment of the population is growing faster than any other part of our population. We often think that it is unusual to find a man or woman over one hundred years old, but, according to projections, by the year 2000 there will be 100,000 of them. By 2050 there will be a million hundred-year-old people. If television personality Willard Scott were to read the names of all the centenarians with birthdays on any given day in 2050, there wouldn't be any time for the rest of the program.

Life expectancy is increasing for many reasons, including reduced infant and child mortality rates, the prevention and cure of many contagious diseases, technological advances in medicine, and the improvement of a general standard of living.

"Sixty-five is nothing today," says Avalie R. Saperstein, director of social services and therapeutic activities at the Philadelphia Geriatric Center. "People at 65 today are very healthy."[4]

Long life is a gift of God, and we do well to rejoice in it. But as people continue to get older, they are likely to have chronic health conditions that limit the things they can do. Many of these conditions are so severe that the older person requires help with shopping, getting to doctor's appointments, cooking, dressing, cleaning, getting out of bed, and getting to the bathroom. Obviously, not all older people need all these kinds of help, but as people continue to age, most of them need more help with the demands of everyday living.

How do we handle our parents when they need our help? How do we manage in the general daily routine?

CARING FOR AGING FAMILY MEMBERS

American families in general have always taken responsibility for the care of their older members.[5] This applies to the traditional mom-dad-and-the-kids families, widowed families, single-parent families, and "empty nest" families. Some people who care for aging parents must take care of their spouse's health problems as well. And sometimes the family that opens its doors to Grandma is also sheltering a divorced daughter who has moved back home with her baby.

When the history of the present generation of middle-aged people is written, to paraphrase Winston Churchill, it might be said that never before in recorded history have so many been called upon to do so much for so many more. We are faced with huge responsibilities and tasks as we are called upon to care for the growing number of older parents.

Caring for aging parents may become a major life effort for you. It is a task you probably didn't foresee, and it is an effort for which you may not be prepared.

THE SANDWICH GENERATION

Jim McEuen is raising two children and caring for his elderly mother. He carefully balances his time and attention between his kids and his mother. "That's the cost of being in the 'sandwich,'" he told a reporter for the *Washington Post.* "You try to balance, but sometimes you can't." But then he laughs. "Look at the metaphor: 'Sandwich generation.' What's in the middle? Chopped meat."[6]

In spite of all the changes that have occurred in American families, the responsibilities that come with caring for aging parents typically fall upon the daughter or daughter-in-law in the family.[7] This woman is likely to have a full-time job, and she is more likely than in years past to be divorced. She probably has children who continue to need some form of financial or emotional support, and she may have a husband who needs her help because of health problems he is developing as he grows older. She probably has only one or two siblings to share the burden of caring for and worrying about Mom and Dad.

Perhaps the most significant change in the American family is the increase in women working outside the home. Currently, according to *Newsweek Special Edition: The 21st Century Family,* 66 percent of all mothers work outside the home, a figure double that of 1955.[8]

Diane Krevoiln lives in Connecticut with her husband, three children, and her eighty-year-old mother. On a typical weekday morning, Diane is up at six to wake her mother, who must get ready for her adult day-care program.

Diane gets herself ready for work, checking in occasionally to help her mother along. She wakes up the children at seven, dresses and feeds them, makes their lunches, signs notes for school, and is out the door by 7:45.

Her mother catches a bus at 8:20. Her husband drops off the kids at the bus stop on his way to work.

After work, Diane usually takes either one of the kids or her mother to an appointment, gets home by five, makes dinner, helps with homework, gives baths, and puts the kids to bed. Then she does the dishes, cleans the house, and collapses into bed.

"You have to do a lot of planning to pull it off," says Diane. "It doesn't leave any time for spontaneity. It affects career decisions. My husband was out of work, and it meant we couldn't move to follow his career. Sometimes it's overwhelming."[9]

LOVE BINDS US TOGETHER

Though there have been distinct and disruptive changes in the American family, one thing that has not changed is the way we feel about caring for elderly family members and the lengths to which we will go in order to care for them. Most American families feel deeply responsible for elderly parents. In fact, the biggest problem most people have in helping their aging parents is not deciding *if* they are going to help, but deciding *how* to help in a way that will be best for all concerned.

Families do not routinely dump their aging family members in nursing homes. Many adult children sacrifice their personal interests, physical and mental health, and even their family relationships in order to give twenty-four-hour care to sick or weak elderly parents. If and when a decision is made to move a parent to a nursing home, most adult children cannot do this without assuming a load of guilt. Even while they are caring for their elderly parents, too many adult children feel guilty because they think they aren't doing enough for their parents.

American families are usually close-knit. Most family members maintain contact with each other on a regular basis. Family members, young and old, generally spend holidays together. Some studies indicate that 80 percent of Americans sixty-five and older are visited at least once a week by one of their children. About 60 percent are visited by one of their children every forty-eight hours, and at least half are visited once a day by one of their children. And adult children who live too far to visit telephone regularly.[10]

Nearly seven out of ten people sixty-five and older who live alone have at least one child who can reach them within an hour, says Mary Grace Kovar, a demographer for the National Center for Health Statistics. And about one-quarter of those people live within ten minutes of one or more of their children. "Middle-aged people with aging parents keep track of them," she says.[11]

WE DO NOT CHOOSE PARENTS

We did not choose our parents. They were given to us by God. Whether or not they have been especially loving, whether or not they adequately transmitted the Christian faith, whether or not they gave us special financial assistance, we need to honor and care for them. As the situation grows more taxing, this may not always be easy. It may be very difficult.

Our families give us an ideal opportunity for us to demonstrate our love for others. Our care for our parents can be an example to the world that loving care begins with our own family. The challenge is difficult, but if we are faithful and rely upon God's strength and grace, we can leave a remarkable impression on those who are watching us.

According to newspaper reports, the Chinese government is attempting to have adult children of elderly parents sign contracts promising that they will help their aged parents when necessary.[12] Most Americans feel strongly about caring for the needs of their elderly parents. But this does not mean that tensions between aging parents and their adult children do not exist. It does not mean adult children do not have feelings of guilt in their care of aging parents. They do.

Because the thought of expensive and time-consuming care for frail, elderly parents can be so threatening, it is easy to overlook the possibility that your parents will remain in fairly good health and be independent, active, and self-sufficient for many years. For the families of active older people, elderly parents are often a source of wisdom and a storehouse of family history. Their wisdom can benefit the family, the church, and the community. The psalmist illustrates the desire of the old to contribute:

> O God, you have helped me from my earliest childhood—
> and I have constantly testified to others of the wonderful
> things you do. And now that I am old and gray, don't for-
> sake me. Give me time to tell this new generation (and
> their children too) about all your mighty miracles.
> (Psalm 71:17-18)

CHAPTER TWO

Understanding
the Aging Process

Age Wave Incorporated is a San Francisco organization that markets products designed from an older person's perspective. Mark Goldstein, an Age Wave representative, spoke to twenty administrators from St. Jude Hospital in Fullerton, California:

"We're going to give you a chance to be seventy years old," Goldstein told his audience. He passed out dark glasses, glazed a bit on the lens to simulate the effect of cataracts. His listeners were directed to wear ear plugs and nose clips, and were told to breathe as normally as possible through a straw to simulate the decreased lung capacity that comes with age. The group pulled on rubber gloves to simulate arthritic fingers.

"Wearing the gloves and dark glasses, we then attempted to sort out a confusing array of variously colored tiny pills that would represent our daily medications," says Dana Parsons, a participant. "Suddenly our world didn't look the same. The bright colors of life grew dim; shapes and sizes were less distinct, sounds and voices were more muffled; drawing a full breath was a chore. So much for having fun."[1]

Leon Trotsky said, "Old age is the most unexpected of all the things that happen to a man." It isn't always the older people who are surprised by old age; their children are surprised as well.

Have you ever looked at your parents and been surprised at a sign of old age? Have you suddenly noticed the change in texture of your parents' older skin? Have you noticed that your mother seems to walk with the shuffling gait of an older person? That your father misses what you say unless you speak directly to him? Does your mother's handwriting suddenly seem spidery and not at all like the robust scrawl you're accustomed to seeing?

Your parents have probably looked in the mirror and thought, "My goodness, I'm old." J. G. Saxe wrote a poem about a man who comes to terms with his advancing years:

> *I'm growing fonder of my staff;*
> *I'm growing dimmer in the eyes;*
> *I'm growing fainter in my laugh;*
> *I'm growing deeper in my sighs;*
> *I'm growing careless of my dress;*
> *I'm growing frugal of my gold;*
> *I'm growing wise; I'm growing—yes—*
> *I'm growing old.*[2]

THE ROLES WE SURRENDER

With the realization that age is advancing, a person also realizes he or she must surrender certain roles in life. Most often these roles are valuable; they give a person identity. Your parent may have been a church member, a husband or wife, an uncle or aunt, a friend, a worker, a volunteer, a driver, consumer, athletic fan, and a home owner. One of the most crucial and important roles your parent has played is that of being your mother or father. It is a role your parent has treasured.

Your parents probably added roles to their lives until sometime in middle age. After middle age, as you and your siblings grew up and left home, your parents surrendered some roles: no longer were they youth sponsors and scout leaders. The house grew quiet.

When your folks retired from active employment, they surrendered other roles. Your parents began to realize they had few roles left.

Old age, they realized, is really about loss. Old people generally lose their roles, they often lose their homes, and sometimes they lose their children. At some point, a person will lose a spouse. This is a critical loss. It is the only life event that rates a maximum 100 on the Social Readjustment Scale in the *Journal of Psychosomatic Research*. (By comparison, being fired from work rated 47 on the same scale.)[3] Although this critical loss can occur at any time in marriage, when older people lose a spouse, not only do they lose a friend, confidant, and lover, but they lose the cherished role of husband and wife. Most never remarry.

RETIREMENT: MILESTONE OR MISERY?

Your parents have probably retired or are fast approaching retirement. Routinely celebrated as a milestone of American life, retirement has made many a marriage and family miserable. We tend to identify ourselves with our jobs: "I'm a banker." "I'm a salesman." "I'm a teacher." When retirement comes, that identity often vanishes. Small wonder that retirees frequently identify themselves by saying, "I'm a *retired* teacher."

"I'm not sure that most people who ever had real jobs can be happy not working," says psychiatrist George Guest. "And many of them keep right on working, one way or another. People may say that somebody is working too hard, but I don't believe that. The mere fact that you want to work tells you something."

The people who do best in their older years are those who do something beyond traveling, growing roses, or painting pictures, says Guest. "Who needs the roses or your piano playing? What do you do after you've seen the world? The big letdown is not being needed. . . . You see a lot of old doctors, writers, and politicians, don't you? That's because they keep working."[4]

Our jobs or careers provide us with opportunities to interact with other people. Not all work-related associations are positive, but for the most part they are stimulating and interesting. How many times have you heard people say that being involved in their work was "the best medicine" as they recovered from serious illness or tragedy? Work situations also give people the opportunity to join professional, business, or work-related groups that add to feelings of belonging and contribute to self-esteem.

Retirement, on the other hand, severs relationships. The friendship group established at work is gone, and the retired worker may find himself at home with nothing to do. He feels unwanted, underappreciated, and unimportant.

DEATH: AN UNWELCOME GUEST

Other significant losses can occur after retirement at sixty-five. Death can be an unwelcome visitor. As a person continues to grow older, death will continue to cause significant losses. An older person will eventually lose his sisters and brothers, his friends, and perhaps even his children. All of these are devastating losses to the older person, and they result in a decreased ability to cope with life and all its changing situations.

Someone once asked seventy-year-old baseball wizard Casey Stengel how he was doing. He sighed. "Not bad," he answered. "Most people my age are dead."[5]

According to studies on aging, by the time a woman reaches eighty-five, more than half her similar-age friends that she has known for twenty years are dead.[6] For eighty-five-year-old men, more than three-fourths of their similar-age friends of more than twenty years are dead. People of this age are not likely to make new friends. The losses come at a time when friends are very important to help cope with the changes an older person faces.

THE CAR: A KEY TO INDEPENDENCE

Your parents may not only be struggling with the loss of roles and familiar people, but with the loss of independence. It is a traumatic experience when an adult must give up a driver's license. Whether it is for physical problems such as poor eyesight or Alzheimer's disease or for reasons of practicality, when the driver's license or car is gone, so is the person's independence.

This is particularly true for Americans who live outside major metropolitan areas. Driving is our national means of personal transportation. Need something from the grocery store? You hop in the car and go get it. Want a late-night snack? Drive over to the 7-Eleven and pick up some snacks. Would you like to spend a lazy afternoon shopping? Drive to the mall and wander around to your heart's content. The key to convenience and independence is having access to an automobile.

Florence is eighty-six and has been driving her large, older car for years. She affectionately calls the car "Bubbles," but her daughter refers to it as "the tank." Florence has her own apartment in her daughter's home, and she relishes her independence. Every morning she backs her car out of the driveway and drives to the mall to join the mall-walkers, a small group of friendly older folks.

Florence has rammed the car into the garage wall more than once. She has hit the family's other cars while backing out of the driveway and never even realized it. Her family breathed a sigh of relief when "Bubbles" broke down and went into the shop, but Florence paid for the repairs and was driving again in two days. She flatly refuses to consider retiring either the car or her driver's license.

Like Florence, thousands of older Americans refuse to face the reality that it is unsafe for them to continue driving. Like Florence's daughter, thousands of middle-aged children worry about their parents driving in traffic. Aged parents' reflexes are no longer quick, their eyesight is often poor, and they may not be able to hear a warning signal or the crunch of metal when they back over something.

Although it is difficult, it is important to lovingly confront parents who simply can no longer handle driving. They need to be offered opportunities for alternative transportation before they injure themselves or someone else. This can be a tough situation, but it needs to be faced before the family is faced with a far greater tragedy than a cracked wall or a dented fender.

SELF-CONCEPT AND SELF-ESTEEM

As you care for your children, you draw upon your own experiences as a child to help you understand what your children feel when they are tired, frightened, lonely, embarrassed, and irritable. But when you care for your aging parents, you do not have a reservoir of similar past experiences from which to draw. You may not understand why it is such a "big deal" for your dad to sell the car and learn how to take a city bus. It may seem silly to you that your mother spends hours pouring over old photograph albums. You keep telling your father to "take it easy, you've earned a rest," when he wants desperately to go out into the backyard and build a tree house for an older child who's long past the age for tree houses.

Philip Dormer Stanhope, the fourth earl of Chesterfield, experienced in his later years deafness, political disappointment, and the death of his son. His friend and contemporary Lord Tyrawley was ignominiously dismissed from his post in 1763 on the grounds that he was too old. Near the end of his long life Chesterfield was asked by a mutual acquaintance how Lord Tyrawley was. He replied, "Tyrawley and I have been dead these two years, but we do not choose to make it known."[7]

At twenty-two, John Jones decided he wanted to become a physician. He married Mary after medical school, and together they raised three children and managed a thriving medical practice. Mary Jones was active in the church and volunteered for the Red Cross. Dr. Jones held a position with a local teaching hospital and trained interns. They supported the arts in their community and encouraged their children to work hard, be considerate of others, and live up to the family ideals.

At sixty-eight, Dr. Jones retired and handed his practice over to a younger doctor. Gone were the days of teaching and work. Gone were the young doctors that looked to him for guidance. Gone were the children—they had families of their own. There were no more phone calls in the middle of the night. No more desperate people begging for his advice: "What do I do, doctor?"

Was he still a physician? Was he still the man he once had been?

The losses of old age can make a person feel useless. Your parent may be depressed, and after your initial frustration, you may become depressed, too. This is not unusual. But there are ways to increase your parent's feeling of self-worth.

Our level of self-esteem depends on how well we like ourselves. According to researchers, most older people measure their personal worth by gauging how well they meet three particular goals: dependability, having close family ties, and self-sufficiency.[8] The emphasis is on personal qualities and personal relationships, not material things or personal positions. If we add to this the Christian's personal relationship to God, we begin to see the positive possibilities of a healthy self-esteem for the older person.

If older people can feel that they are dependable, close to their families, self-sufficient, and have a secure faith, they are likely to keep a positive view of themselves and overcome depression. It is important for the children of aging parents to know that these things will help their parents "bounce back" from a serious loss or setback. There is great hope here. Even through the inevitable losses that occur, if these areas can be maintained, an older person's positive self-esteem can be preserved.

ADDITIONAL WAYS TO COPE

In addition to the importance of preserving self-esteem, the following can be helpful to older persons and their adult children in coping with growing older and the various losses people face as they age.[9]

1. UNDERSTAND THE AGING PROCESS

It is important to understand the process of aging. We will discuss this more completely in following chapters, but older people and their children need to be aware of some of the major changes that occur in the body as age increases. This will enable them to accommodate and cope with these changes.

People also need to be aware of the opportunities available to them as they grow older. Growing older in America is not all bad. There are many positive benefits to aging: decreased pressure to perform in a job, more leisure time, less financial pressure to support children through college, recognition for past achievements, a sense of accomplishment for having done a job well, a sense of contribution to one's church and community, and knowing what is really important in life in the context of faith and maturity. Maturity brings its own rewards.

2. LOOK BACK OVER YOUR PARENT'S LIFE TO REVIEW SUCCESSES AND FAILURES

"Life review" or reminiscence is an important coping mechanism for most older people. Reviewing the joys and sorrows, successes and failures, and major and minor events of life gives most older people a better sense of who they are. This is particularly important for Christians because they can recount how God guided them through life's joys and trials. This is a wonderful opportunity for them to relate their faith to their children and grandchildren, and it is important for the children and grandchildren to listen to their stories even though they may have heard them many times before.

Ben Jonson once said, "It was near a miracle to see an old man silent, since talking is the disease of age."[10] Jonson apparently didn't understand that as people continue to grow older and become more dependent on others, including strangers, stories of what they did in the past become an important way to tell others who they are. This story telling is not a disease, as Jonson idly describes it, but a valuable way to help older people maintain a healthy view of themselves. In addition, many of the stories and experiences are interesting to the listener.

3. ENCOURAGE YOUR PARENT TO KEEP CLOSE FRIENDSHIPS
Recent studies among older persons have shown that satisfaction with life is more closely related to the quality of their friendships than the number of friends they have.[11] These same studies indicate that in many cases having a close friend may be more important than having a large family network. Friendship seems to help older people survive the losses they continue to experience as they age. But even though a good friend or confidant significantly adds to the life satisfaction of both men and women, it is more important for women.[12] This is largely due to the fact that more older men than older women are still married because women live longer than men. Old men who are married tend to list their wives as their best friend. As widows, women need friends.[13]

Sharing life's joys and problems with a similar-age friend makes facing losses easier for most older people. You can help your parents endure the losses that come with advancing age by making sure they have access to old friends. Even having one friend with whom they can feel comfortable and share memories can help your parents cope.

4. HELP YOUR PARENTS STAY INVOLVED
Another way you can help your parents face losses is to keep them involved in activities that gave them pleasure in earlier times. Older persons also have an opportunity to combine their associations and activities. When people are in their busiest years of working and having responsibilities for children, com-

munity activities, and church work, they often feel torn in several different directions. With the decrease of demands on people as they become older, your parents have an opportunity to combine their associations and activities and focus on the ones they really enjoy.

One of the best ways older people can feel good about themselves is to volunteer their services to meet a variety of needs. This is particularly appropriate for older Christians.

Opportunities for service are everywhere and open to people with a variety of interests and talents. Children need help learning to read. Latchkey kids need someone to be around until their parents get home from work. Other lonely older people would love to have a visitor, especially someone their own age. Homebound older people could use a friendly call on the telephone as part of a daily telephone contact program.

Many local newspapers list programs for older adults. These include RSVP, the Retired Senior Volunteer Program, which provides volunteer recruitment and placement; SCORE, the Service Corps of Retired Executives, which provides management counseling to small businesses and young entrepreneurs; Linking Lifetimes, a program that provides senior volunteer mentors to middle-school boys at risk of becoming delinquents or dropping out of school; and Adopt-A-Grandchild, which trains senior volunteers to meet weekly with children from single parent families. To find these types of programs for service in your community, you can contact your local Area Agency on Aging, the school system, the newspaper, the Red Cross, or other community agencies.

Opportunities for service for older people should abound in the church. Given the broad range of abilities of older adults, churches are shortsighted if they do not offer avenues of ministry and involvement by and for older adults. Just as churches organize programs and hire ministers to meet the needs of youth, churches can also organize to meet the needs of older persons, and to develop strategies to use the talents, resources, and energies of older persons in ministry. You can help your parents keep active by encouraging them to attend these types of activities and assisting with transportation if they no longer drive.

If your church doesn't offer programs for older adults, you can use your influence in your church to promote opportunities for service and activities by and for older persons. Your church should promote the biblical standard that older people are not to be discarded from an active life. Older people should be included in the decision-making processes of the church. Those who are active can participate in short-term missions projects or teach Sunday school. But they need to feel at home in the church. As the child of an older parent, you can have a real impact in getting the church to recognize and utilize the resources and talents of older people.

Vivian Greenberg, a social worker who specializes in geriatrics, urges older people to remain involved in life. "If you can get up, fix breakfast, read the newspaper, take a walk, maybe paint a picture, you have a lot to be thankful for and to look forward to," says Greenberg. "There is less we can do with our bodies as we get older, but if we had a rich life before in terms of activities and caring for others, we still can have a rich life. . . . As long as we have our minds, we always can learn."[14]

ROLE REVERSAL

In spite of all your efforts to help aging parents cope with role losses, the time may come when you feel pressured to assist your parents and assume a decision-making role for them. This is often called "role reversal." Role reversal is difficult because the people you are now guiding are the parents who gave you life, raised you, and guided you to maturity.

"This role reversal feels so unnatural that it threatens the very balance of our lives," writes Barbara Deane. "Enter the first line of defense against the unthinkable: *denial.* This is why many middle-aged people refuse to accept their parents' aging."[15]

"Many people come to me with the attitude, 'Aging is not supposed to exist; I'm not going to let it happen,'" says Richard P. Johnson, a psychologist in St. Louis. "The child within us screams for nurturance, and something dies within us when we can't get this from our parents anymore."[16]

Something within you also realizes that it really is not possible to change roles completely. Your parents will always be your parents and the parent-child relationship will never completely change. No matter how well-educated, talented, experienced, or mature you become, to your parents, you are still their child. "My mother still tells me how to wear my hair," one woman complained. "She still says I don't know how to dress myself properly."

A difficult situation will become tougher still when your parents are no longer able to make decisions that need to be made or to handle the daily skills necessary for living alone. Suddenly they are no longer independent, and it's a scary time for both parents and child. Your parent is faced with a new role in life—that of a dependent person.

This new dependency may come just as you were beginning to breathe a little easier because your own children are in college or married. You may feel "squeezed" in the sandwich of having responsibilities for the young and the old. But if you understand what your parents are feeling, you will be better able to cope with what the future holds.

EASING INTO DEPENDENCY

Your parents will naturally want to continue their parent-child relationship with you even though they may be dependent on you. It may be difficult for your parents to accept your advice, direction, help, or financial assistance. They may feel that they are totally losing control of their own life.

Your parents may react in frustration and anger. This does not mean they no longer love you; it's just that their independence and self-sufficiency has been threatened in a new and frightening way. They need time to adjust.

Suppose you visit your parents' house and notice for the first time how run-down the place looks. "Dad, just let me know and I'll come over and paint or do yard work for you," you volunteer.

"What—do you think I can't do it myself?" your father snaps. "It looks all right to me."

You retreat, thinking that Dad is getting grumpy in his old age. Your father feels inferior and unable to meet the simple physical demands of painting and pushing a mower. He can't afford what seems to him to be the outrageous cost of hiring someone to mow the lawn, and your simple offer of help reminds him that he doesn't have the money, strength, or patience that he used to delight in giving.

One way around this dilemma is to line up outside help so the parent is not dependent on you.[17] Encourage your parents to hire someone to cut the grass or bring in the mail on bad-weather days so your parents won't have to venture out. If they balk at the expense, ask what they're willing to pay, and you can privately subsidize the rest of the amount.[18] This will give your parents a sense of control. It won't solve every problem, but it will help keep your parents as independent as possible for as long as possible.

This is important because, as adult children are forced into the role of caregiver for aging parents, even the most loving and considerate children can experience resentment, anger, depression, and guilt.[19] Unlike child rearing, which seems to last forever but doesn't, caring for aging parents can go on until the death of the parents. As it progresses, caregiving becomes more intense and demanding.

OPEN WINDOWS OF OPPORTUNITY

One of the most important things an adult child can do to help an aging parent is to interpret modern culture and realities of life in modern America. This does not necessarily mean interpreting rock music or new fads to the older folks. Most of us would be hard-pressed to do that, and many of us wouldn't want to. But adult children can be of great help to their aging parents by learning about and helping parents receive services that are available to older people in community agencies and churches.

This is not a new role for children in America. The children of immigrant parents traditionally helped their folks understand the new world and tap into services and support systems that were available. Immigrant parents were not always willing to take advantage of all the opportunities in their new world, and similarly, the same is often true of elderly parents today. But at least you can make these opportunities known to your parents and help them get the benefits of programs, services, resources, and opportunities that have been developed.

> [Age Wave's] Goldstein asked for people's reaction to the temporary impairments, and these were the responses: frustration, confusion, anger, anxiety, panic, embarrassment, reduced confidence that led to fear, and even physical discomfort resulting from the disorientation.
>
> "Imagine how that might change your life," Goldstein said.
>
> The next time an elderly relative or friend asks that something be repeated, I doubt that any of us who were at the seminar will act impatient. The next time our aging parents seem out of sorts or don't want to join in on some outing, we won't browbeat them. No, those of us at the seminar got a good dose of consciousness-raising. And for no extra charge, a glimpse into our own futures.[20]

CHAPTER THREE

Physical Changes and the Aging Process

The aged actor John Barrymore was once interviewed by a young newspaper reporter who asked him whether he still found acting as much fun as it used to be. "Young man," replied Barrymore, "I am seventy-five. Nothing is as much fun as it used to be."[1]

Bernard de Fontenelle, the French writer and philosopher, was asked how he felt just a few weeks short of his 100th birthday. He replied, "I feel nothing, apart from a certain difficulty of being."[2]

The oldest documented living person was a Japanese man who turned 120 in 1985. He was in excellent physical condition when he appeared on American television with his children and great-great-grandchildren. Two months later, he contracted pneumonia and died.

"Most of the negative aspects of aging actually have nothing to do with the process of aging, but are connected with disease," says Dr. Michael Freedman, director of geriatrics for New York University Medical Center. "In other words, the enemy is disease, not growing old."

Dr. Freedman has done experiments with rats to study the human life span. He has found that by doing five simple things, the average life span of a rat is increased from eighteen months to six years. Those five steps to extend life are paying attention to the environment, proper diet, exercise, sociability, and sexuality. Dr. Freedman reports that with all disease eradicated and under optimum conditions, the human life span could be extended to one hundred and twenty years.[3]

But your parents don't live in a lab, and they probably haven't tried to address Dr. Freedman's five steps throughout their lives. They are aging, they may experience the ravages of disease, and they will feel changes in their bodies. Some of the negative effects of these changes can be reduced by improved health practices, including exercise. Others can be minimized by medications. Still other conditions can be improved by the use of corrective lenses, hearing aids, lotions, or vitamins.

Some physical changes are inevitable and some are not. It is important that Mom and Dad understand these changes so they can adjust to them. It is also important that you understand these changes. If your mother is complaining of pains in her joints, you have to know whether she really has severe pains, or if she is exaggerating the pain to get attention. Does Dad really not see well enough to drive, or is it that he's depressed and doesn't want to go out?

If you want to give your parents the kind of help they really need, you need to understand the physical changes that occur as a result of the aging process. Realize that your mom and dad are not going to look or feel at seventy-five the way they did at forty-five.

The Bible tells us that the body deteriorates as we grow older, but in its pages we also read that though we lose physical strength, we gain wisdom. As an adult child, you have the opportunity to enjoy the growth of wisdom in your aging parents and not focus on their physical deterioration.

PHYSICAL CHANGES
AND FEELINGS OF WELL-BEING
Physical well-being, self-esteem, contentment, and happi-

ness are a complex mixture of a person's physical condition and attitude. Some older people are so preoccupied with their bodies that they exaggerate every ache and pain. They describe in great detail every sign of physical change. They quickly become incapacitated and almost seem to enjoy their troubles.

Others rarely complain. Although in great pain and suffering as a result of some real physical problems, they tend to ignore their pain and continue on their way through life. By having an interest in others and the events around them, they function with a much better attitude than those who focus on themselves. Furthermore, keeping active increases their chances of maintaining their independence.

PHYSICAL CHANGES AND LIFESTYLE

Your parents can benefit from an appropriate exercise program. Exercise improves the cardiovascular system and posture. It reduces body fat and the risk of heart attack, high blood pressure, stress, and nervous tension. It improves the quality of sleep, the respiratory system, and joint mobility. Regular exercise increases blood volume and feelings of well-being.

The American Association for the Advancement of Science claims that exercise seems to reduce the probability of breast and uterine cancer for women. It also reduces the probability of diabetes. Physically active women produce a less potent form of estrogen and, as a result, tumors that depend on that hormone do not develop as frequently. Because physically active women have less body fat, they reduce their probability of diabetes caused by excess weight.[4]

Many apparent symptoms of aging are simply the result of a lack of exercise. People of all ages, including those in their nineties, can benefit from regular exercise. Evidence collected at Tufts University has indicated that regardless of age, people can increase their muscle size, stamina, and joint mobility by a regular program of physical training. The deterioration that is seen in some elderly people is really not the result of aging but of poor lifestyle.[5]

You probably know someone in his seventies who acts very "old." You also probably know someone else in his seventies who remains active, vibrant, and physically vigorous. We now know that lifestyle frequently is a major contributing factor to these differences. You will do yourself and your parents a great favor if you encourage them to exercise daily. Take a walk with your mother! Buy a stationary bike for your father. Encourage your parents to participate in an enjoyable exercise that will fit into their lifestyle.

Smoking is directly related to health and physical well-being. Smoking is one of the most destructive habits a person can have. It increases the probability of heart attack and emphysema. Smoking is the principal cause of lung cancer and the major contributor to heart disease. Smoking prematurely wrinkles the skin and is a contributing factor to various forms of cancer. Smoking is slow suicide. It destroys every organ in the body. If your parents smoke, you need to gently tell them that smoking may destroy their remaining years. You can help by not smoking yourself.

VISUAL PROBLEMS

For most people, changes occur in the eye after the age of forty. No amount of eye exercises will slow the almost inevitable changes that occur in the eyes as we grow older. A condition called presbyopia begins to take place, developing earlier for some and later for others. In this condition the eye begins to lose its ability to adjust for various distances. This usually can be helped by using bifocals or trifocals.

Presbyopia also makes it harder to adjust to darkness. It is much more difficult for a seventy-year-old to see adequately at night than a twelve-year-old. Any older person can test this by going out at night with a child and asking what the child sees in the distance. The child is aware of objects that the older person cannot see.

In addition, presbyopia makes it more difficult for older people to adjust to glare. With all these difficulties, you can understand why older people are at a real disadvantage driving at night with oncoming headlights. Your parents may be reluctant to drive at night, and they may be too embarrassed to admit why. It may be helpful if you offer to drive older folks after dark.

Presbyopia also makes it more difficult for the aging eye to adjust to what are termed "cool colors" such as blue, green, and violet in contrast to "warm colors" such as yellow, red, or orange.

People should not be upset about presbyopia because adjustments can be made. We are fortunate to be living at a time when medical science allows us to make up for physical deficiencies with glasses or contact lenses. Mom and Dad might need to have more frequent eye exams to get the right corrective lenses.

More serious than presbyopia in the aging eye is the development of cataracts. Medical evidence seems to indicate that, if they lived long enough, most persons would eventually develop cataracts. With cataracts, the lens of the eye becomes cloudy, like milk slowly added to water. The clouded lens can be replaced with a synthetic one through surgery. This surgery is routine these days, and the success rate is very high. What causes cataracts? One factor is too much exposure to the sun.

Some researchers also believe that there is a relationship between exposure to the sun and macular degeneration, another eye condition affecting older persons. In this condition, side vision is retained but vision in the macula, or central portion of the retina, is clouded by leaking blood vessels. The macula enables the eye to see the fine details involved in reading, sewing, and similar activities. It is important to note that macular degeneration does not result in blindness, but central vision is lost. Early detection is important because some cases of macular degeneration can be treated by laser therapy. The laser beam can stop the leakage of the blood vessels in the macula.

Another condition that can develop with aging is glaucoma, the result of increased pressure in the eye from a buildup of aqueous humor, a nutrient fluid that circulates in the anterior chamber of the eye. In glaucoma, fluid is produced faster than it can be eliminated, and the pressure in the eye builds up. This is a serious condition, and all persons who are older, as well as those who work with older persons, need to know the symptoms. People who have glaucoma tend to have a gradual loss of peripheral vision so they cannot adequately see objects to the side of the eye. Driving is dangerous for people who have this condition because they cannot see objects to the side of their car.

If it is not treated, glaucoma leads to tunnel vision, where the individual can only see straight ahead. Persons with developing glaucoma tend to see halos around objects, especially around lights. If your mom or dad mentions seeing halos, they should have an immediate eye exam. If untreated, glaucoma eventually results in blindness. It can be treated by medication, usually in the form of eye drops, but it will not be reversed beyond the point at which it was diagnosed and treated. That is why it is important for your parents to have regular eye exams.

Some people develop dry eyes as they grow older. In some cases this dryness can also cause redness in the eye. A person who has this condition should obtain professional diagnosis, assessment, and treatment. The treatment is simple and usually consists of regular use of eye drops.

In addition to eye surgery and the use of specific medications, older people with weak eyesight can be helped with large-print magazines and books. Most libraries have these available. If your library does not, you should request them through interlibrary loan. Churches can help older people by having large-print bulletins in addition to regular-print bulletins.

Many communities have something called "low vision" clinics, which are clinics designed to help people with minimal or low vision. You may find them in your phone book, or contact a local eye doctor to get information about these clinics.

Your aging parents need well-lit rooms because elderly people need more light to see adequately. Some older people can benefit by having the dials on their appliances color coded to help with reading numbers. For example, it might be helpful to use nail polish to paint an orange dot on the oven dial at 350 degrees, a black dot by 400, etc. This way Mom or Dad can select a temperature by color.

A magnifying glass will be of great assistance to some older people. Others will benefit from recorded books. Many libraries have books on cassettes. Furthermore, the Association for the Blind is available to give advice for the partially sighted.

The vast majority of eye problems related to aging can be helped with glasses, surgery, medications, or services and devices designed to help people with fading vision. We live in a time of virtually miraculous remedies.

THE EARS

As we age, we will all experience a gradual loss in hearing, a condition known as presbycusis. Most people first lose the ability to hear higher-frequency sounds. Hearing loss may be due to several factors, including a loss of tiny hair cells in the ear known as the organ of Corti, interrupted conduction of sound because of arthritis of the delicate bones in the inner ear, or simple wax buildup in the ear that blocks the sound from reaching the inner ear.

Older people who believe they are suffering hearing loss should have a hearing exam with an ear, nose, and throat specialist, or an audiologist. If the problem is due to a wax buildup, treatment is simple, and Mom and Dad can be taught how to adequately clean their ears of excess wax.

If there is a significant organic reason for hearing loss, there are many aids available to help. Modern hearing aids are marvels of technology—smaller than before, comfortable to wear, and hardly noticeable. It is important for the hard-of-hearing person to be diagnosed by a certified specialist and not by a salesperson.

If your parent does not hear well, it is helpful to talk slowly and enunciate clearly. Speak face to face. Let your parent see your lip movements. Try to eliminate background noise from fans, radiators, air conditioners, and other appliances.

One of the major problems of hearing-impaired people is isolation. Hearing loss is gradual for most people, so your parents may be unaware that they are not hearing entire conversations. Sometimes they may give inappropriate answers to questions because they did not hear correctly. Don't think your parent is mentally confused without considering that he simply didn't hear what was said. If people continue to draw away from your parent, he will feel rejected, isolated, and depressed. Be sure to recognize hearing loss for what it is. Have your parent's hearing evaluated by a doctor if you suspect hearing loss.

THE SKIN
Your skin probably began to wrinkle when you were in your mid-twenties. The process is aggravated by smoking and extended exposure to the sun. The wrinkling process is also related to a person's genetic heritage. Blond, fair-skinned people tend to wrinkle more quickly than those who are darker-skinned.

As a person ages, the skin becomes drier and more susceptible to cracking, a process accelerated by dry air and exposure to the sun. The sweat glands of older people do not function as well as they once did, and people do not perspire as they did when they were younger. (This also means that older people are more likely to experience heat stroke.)

Older people should take special precautions with exposure to the sun. The National Institute of Health has indicated that there is no such thing as a healthy tan. Direct exposure to the sun increases the probability of skin cancer and wrinkled skin. If you or your parent exposes your skin to the sun, you should have a sunscreen lotion with a rating of fifteen or higher for protection from ultraviolet solar radiation. Older people should avoid tanning parlors.

Because of a loss of blood flow to the toenails as one gets older, the toenails tend to thicken. It is especially important that your parents inspect their toenails and keep them cut. This problem with thickened toenails is one reason that visits to a podiatrist (foot specialist) become increasingly important as a person gets older.

Because of a loss of blood flow to the skin and limbs, older people are also at risk of hypothermia, a reduction of body temperature to the point where life is at risk. Recent research seems to indicate that the danger of hypothermia for older people is much greater than previously believed because it is difficult for pathologists to determine if death was caused by hypothermia.

If you care for an older person, you need to know the signs of hypothermia. These include a bloated face, pale and waxy skin, trembling on one side of the body or in one arm or leg, an irregular and slowed heartbeat, slurred speech, shallow slow breathing, low blood pressure, and drowsiness. Whenever an older parent has any of these symptoms, he should be taken immediately to a medical emergency service.

How can you help your parent cope with the dangers of hypothermia? All older people, especially those over seventy-five, should be able to keep their room temperature at seventy degrees or higher if they want to. This usually means that a room temperature that is comfortable for your folks probably will seem too hot for you. This is a special problem in nursing homes where a comfortable room temperature for the residents is too warm for the younger, active, working staff.

The rooms of older people should have sufficient moisture in the air so that their dry skin does not crack. If they cannot afford a humidifier, pans of water can be placed on a register to put moisture into the air. Mom and Dad should make liberal use of creams and ointments to soften their dry skin and prevent cracking. Your aging father may not exactly be thrilled by lotions and creams as a birthday present, but Dad's skin dries as well as Mom's, and he too may need lotion. If dry skin cracks, it becomes very susceptible to infection.

Your parents need to take special care in cold weather to make sure their heads are covered. Most body heat is lost through the top of the head.

HAIR

Your parents' hair eventually will turn gray or white if it hasn't already. No one knows why some hairs turn gray or white and others do not. It is known that cells within each hair follicle (tube-like structures in the skin) add color to the hair shaft. Each specific hair grows for about three years, then it rests for several months before it starts growing again. As one ages, the color-producing cells die, and hair then comes out gray or white. At the present time there is no known way to prevent this graying process. Genetics play an important role in the action of the color-producing cells. People whose parents or grandparents grayed early in life have a higher probability of developing gray hair at a relatively young age.

THE NOSE

About 25 percent of persons sixty-five to eighty lose some ability to smell; after eighty that may increase to 50 percent. Usually the sense of smell does not decrease until the forties or fifties. Apparently the sense receptors for odor in the upper nose lose their ability to function because of disease or injury. This creates some potentially serious problems for older persons because they may have difficulty smelling gas leaks, spoiled food, or smoke. They also lose the enjoyment of smelling flowers, perfumes, and well-cooked and seasoned foods.

THE URINARY SYSTEM

By the time they are seventy, your mom and dad will have lost 50 percent of their kidney and bladder capacity. This is not a symptom of disease, but simply a result of the aging process. Most elderly people suffer from a process called nocturia, the need to get up in the night to go to the bathroom. Your parents should know that if they have to get up during the night to go to the bathroom, this in itself is not an indication of any serious disease. But if they have to get up more often than once or twice, they should see their doctor.

In addition, something called the "micturition reflex" changes when a person ages. Micturition is the signal we receive when we have to urinate. For a young person, that signal is usually sent when the bladder is about half full. As a result, young people have some time left before they absolutely must go to the bathroom. This is not so for the elderly. The signal to urinate is given when the bladder is nearly full. That means that when they receive the signal to urinate, there is not much time for delay. The reduced capacity of the bladder, coupled with a delayed signal to urinate, can lead to problems of frequent urination and the need to urinate right away.

Some older people also have a problem with dribbling urine. This can be physiologically and psychologically damaging. If your mom or dad smells of urine, you should discuss the problem with them. Some older people are so embarrassed about this that they do not want to leave the house. Mom and Dad need to be reassured that this problem is not uncommon and should be discussed with their doctor.

With aging comes an increased chance of bladder infection, usually accompanied by a low-grade fever, a tired feeling, and a burning sensation during urination. Some bladder infections— an interstitial infection, for example—are difficult to eradicate, particularly in women. But most are effectively treated with antibiotics.

How can you help your aging parent in the sensitive area of bladder control? Older people should not drink much liquid before trips or before going to bed. If you travel with your parents, it is usually necessary to take frequent rest stops.

Older persons with a problem of urinary dribbling (incontinence) should consult with their doctor. Drinking juices such as cranberry juice can reduce the odor associated with this condition. Older persons with a continuing low-grade fever also need to consult with their doctor, as this is often a symptom of urinary infection.

The changes associated with the urinary system due to aging can be treated and dealt with effectively if your parents are aware of these changes and discuss them with their doctor.

CHANGES OF THE BONES AND MUSCLES
More than 25 million Americans, most of them older women, have brittle bones (osteoporosis), and this causes 1.3 million bone fractures each year. Among these are 500,000 fractures of the spine, 300,000 broken hips, 200,000 broken wrists, and 300,000 other broken bones. But most people are not even aware their bones are weak until they have broken a bone.

The National Osteoporosis Foundation says osteoporosis is characterized by "low bone mass and structural deterioration of bone tissue, leading to an increased susceptibility to fractures of the hip, spine, and wrist." The bones lose their density and mass. But loss of bone mass has no symptoms, and one quarter of the bone mass must be lost before an X ray can detect the disease.

Certain people are more at risk for osteoporosis than others. The factors that indicate increased risk are:

- menopause before age forty-five
- a family history of fractures in elderly people
- use of certain medications, particularly corticosteroids, which are used to treat arthritis and lung disease

- chronically low calcium intake
- thin and/or small bones
- Caucasian or Asian ancestry
- an inactive lifestyle
- cigarette smoking
- excessive use of alcohol
- advanced age[6]

One of the major reasons for osteoporosis is a loss of calcium. Without calcium, bones lose density and become brittle. This is especially true for postmenopausal women. After menopause, women have a significant reduction in the production of estrogen, which helps process calcium into the bones. With the loss of estrogen, the bones tend to lose their density. Many people do not get enough calcium in their diet. If your parents will not drink milk, it is important that they get calcium through other foods or calcium supplements.

Recently the National Research Council reported that the use of a calcium supplement is probably not as effective as estrogen in decreasing the probability of osteoporosis among postmenopausal women. In addition, many older women do not absorb calcium well from supplements. It is important for postmenopausal women to make sure that they have an adequate amount of vitamin D, which aids in the absorption of calcium.

Many postmenopausal women could benefit from taking estrogen therapy. Some experts have suggested that estrogen therapy increases the risk of cancer. However, although there is some risk, that risk seems to have been exaggerated and is often outweighed by the potential benefits of taking estrogen. Besides, today estrogen therapy is available in much smaller dosages than in the past. The risk of a broken hip is a greater danger than the risk of developing cancer from estrogen therapy, but it is important to discuss the potential risks and the potential advantages of estrogen therapy with your mom's doctor.[7] Doctors also stress the benefits of regular exercise, limiting alcohol intake, not smoking, and frequent medical checkups in preventing osteoporosis.

Older people with osteoporosis are at risk. The slightest fall can result in a broken hip or arm. Some older women fall because their hips break; their hips don't always break as a result of a fall. Bedridden elderly people need to be handled very carefully because a bone may be broken in moving them from one position to another.

You can help your parents by making sure they are careful on stairs. They should always use handrails. Their furniture should be sturdy so it will not move if they lean on it to help themselves in walking. Footstools should be available so they can elevate their legs. This decreases muscle spasms and increases blood circulation.

Bones retain their density better if people exercise. Many older women develop a "widow's hump," a curvature in the spine that makes them humpbacked and round-shouldered. This happens because osteoporosis causes their vertebrae to lose density, and the spine begins to bend, stooping the shoulders and spine.

As your parents grow older there is an increased probability that they will develop some form of arthritis, resulting in joint and muscle pains. The less mobile your parents are, the more pain they will experience when they attempt to move about.

Your aging parents will also lose some muscle coordination. Our aging reflexes tend to be slower. Eighty-year-olds cannot compete in the one hundred yard dash with eighteen-year-olds. Neither can seventy-year-olds high jump like kids. Older folks can be mobile, though, through regular and appropriate exercise.

CHOOSING A DOCTOR

Because elderly people have more chronic illnesses, your parents usually will see a doctor more often than they did when they were younger. It is important that the doctor not ignore their complaints just because they are old. Some doctors may see their older patients as bothersome and cranky.

The story is told of a ninety-two-year-old man who asked his doctor about a pain in his left leg. The physician shrugged and said the problem was just due to old age. "Is that so?" the older man replied. "Well, my right leg is just as old, but it isn't hurting."

It may not be easy for you to know who the competent doctors are or to judge a physician's training and preparation. However, for a physician to make an adequate diagnosis, your parents must be able to tell the doctor clearly and precisely what their complaints are. It might be best for your mom and dad to write out their symptoms, so they can remember them when they see their physicians. Any competent, caring doctor will be willing to take the time to listen to their complaints, but the doctor cannot make an adequate diagnosis if the complaints are vague and overly generalized.

The caring doctor will take the time for a thorough exam and state clearly what the problems are. A competent doctor will listen without unduly hurrying the patient. A competent doctor will also explain why specific medicines are prescribed and what the possible side effects are. If you are not sure what your parent's diagnosis is, the reason for the prescribed medicines, and the prognosis, you should call the doctor's office and ask for clarification.

If the physician orders tests or refers your mom or dad to a specialist, ask your parents for their permission to call the doctor's office for more information. The reason for tests or the referral should be explained to your parents in language they can understand.

Any elderly person who has more than one doctor because of multiple health problems should make certain that each doctor knows about the others and why they have prescribed certain medicines. It is a good idea for your parents either to list on paper what prescribed medicines they are taking or simply to take the medicines with them to show the physician. It is often dangerous to take certain drugs in combination with other drugs, and many drugs will not be prescribed if the doctor knows the other drugs are being taken.

Your mom and dad might feel too intimidated by their doctor to ask questions or indicate that they do not understand their condition. No caring physician is going to resent being asked to clarify the diagnosis or the reasons for prescribing certain drugs. Too many older patients do not understand their conditions, their treatment, or the possible side effects of drugs. You should kindly but assertively seek answers to these health questions.

Choosing an appropriate physician for older people is a personal matter and not often easy. Many people are fortunate to have a family doctor in whom they have confidence. But just as older people lose friends and contacts in the community, they also lose doctors. Some outlive their doctors' practices; others' doctors move away. How can your parents get a new doctor?

You can be very helpful. You can be a guide through the bureaucratic jungle of telephone inquiries and contacts with secretaries and receptionists. You can help fill out forms, determine who accepts Medicare or Medicaid payments as payments in full, and try to determine the doctor's competence. All of these things can be a real barrier for older people.

There are specific things you can look for as you help your aging parent choose a new doctor. Don't be afraid to ask questions. Generally a physician who will work well with your parents will be happy to answer your initial questions if and when you can get by the receptionists. Often you can get a pretty good idea of how a physician will interact with older people by a relatively short conversation. Recommendations from others are important in selecting a doctor.

The following factors can be helpful:

1. Does the doctor understand the aging process?

2. Does he or she attribute most health problems of older persons to "just getting old"?

3. Has the doctor had any geriatric training in medical school? Some doctors specialize in geriatric medicine. Some younger doctors have had at least some exposure to or course work in geriatric medicine. Some older physicians have had continuing education in treating older patients. Physicians with this training are becoming more available.

4. Does the doctor understand the importance of good nutrition for older people?

5. Is the doctor willing to have second opinions, or does this seem threatening?

6. Does the doctor understand and practice holistic health care, where the health of the total person is considered rather than only a specific complaint or problem?

7. Is the physician willing and equipped to work with other doctors on a specialty need basis?

8. Does the physician appear to have experience in dealing with older people?

9. Does the doctor have an adequate understanding of the community-based support networks that are usually available to assist older people in their special needs of daily living?

10. Is the doctor someone with whom you can work to provide care and assistance to your aging parent?

Clever marketers today have realized the scope of the elder market. According to Ken Dychtwald, author of *Age Wave: The Challenges and Opportunities of an Aging America,* the elders among us are smart shoppers. They want larger-size type in newspapers, magazines and books; they dislike small buttons and tiny snaps as fasteners; they're sensitive to changes in heat and cold and would like thermostats in every room. Their sense of taste has diminished, so they're interested in spices and sweeteners to make food as palatable as it once was. They're fearful of slipping and falling. They want bathtubs and kitchens with non-skid surfaces and chairs with arms to help them sit down as well as rise.[8]

HELPING YOUR PARENT BECOME PHYSICALLY FIT

Your parents may not know which of their physical changes take place because of aging and which are brought about by lifestyle. If your mom and dad believe that because they are a certain age they should not be active, involved, or energetic, they may be living a self-fulfilling prophecy of decline.

Some older people ski, play tennis, golf, travel, or jog regardless of their age. Many more walk for exercise. Their continued involvement in physical activity is not a matter of age but of their physical condition and mental outlook. At times it is difficult to know if Dad really needs help or if you think he needs help just because he is old. You do more harm than good if you help your parent become dependent.

Your parents should be encouraged to remain active. It is great to see people in their seventies play a vigorous game of tennis. It is not unusual for a seventy-six-year-old widow to drive from Michigan to Florida with friends.

It might be difficult for you to imagine your mom and dad lifting weights at seventy-five or eighty. But this might be very beneficial for them. With proper supervision by their physician, a regular program of exercise could make a significant improvement in your parents' physical and psychological condition. It is no longer unusual to see people in their seventies and eighties participating in twenty-six-mile marathons.

A parent who sits around all day is going to go downhill physically and mentally. Lifestyle is often the primary cause for loss of strength, excess weight, high blood pressure, depression, loss of sexual desire, and a loss of zest for life. Heredity and the aging process also have an impact on physical changes and general decline, but lifestyle can have a very significant impact on how a person's heredity is fulfilled in life.

Choices in lifestyle are real and lead to real results. Whether or not your parents exercise regularly, drink too much alcohol, smoke, and eat properly is going to make a tremendous difference in their health and mental outlook. Unfortunately, too many older people believe that they must restrict or alter their physical activities because they have reached a certain age.

Dr. James Jay, a cardiologist, ran the twenty-six-mile New York Marathon at age seventy-four. At seventy-six, Dr. Jonas Salk was hard at work trying to find a vaccine for AIDS. Hulda Crooks started climbing mountains at sixty-five. By the time she was ninety-one, she had reached her ninety-seventh summit. Arthur Rubenstein, at eighty-nine, gave one of the more exciting piano recitals in the long history of Carnegie Hall. Michelangelo, chief architect at St. Paul's in Rome, held that position until he was eighty-nine. At eighty-seven, Bob Hope toured the Persian Gulf with a Christmas show for U.S. service personnel. And while in his nineties, George Burns continued to play his hour-long comedy routines to standing-room-only audiences.

While some people in their forties think they are "over the hill," Nolan Ryan continues to pitch no-hitters. He also rides a bike up to four miles a day, and when traveling with his team, he will not leave his hotel room until he has done two hundred sit-ups. He believes his daily fitness routine is absolutely essential if he is to continue to pitch in the major leagues.

Lifestyle choices make a difference in life expectancy. In the general population, women can expect to live to seventy-eight and men to seventy-one. But for Mormons, life expectancy is now eighty-two years for women and seventy-nine for men. Experts in public health statistics have long been aware of the "Mormon Advantage."[9] Mormons do not use alcohol, tobacco, or caffeinated drinks. In addition, they have a strong religion that reduces stress, gives a purpose for existence, and a zest for life. These health experts estimate that a Mormon male who exercises will have an eleven-year life expectancy advantage over the average American male.

There is no miracle to prevent aging, but exercise can minimize its effects. A great gift for your parents would be a membership in a health club, a set of weights, a bicycle, a rowing machine, or a book on the benefits of exercising at any age.

All older people who have not been exercising should consult with their doctor before they begin to exercise. It is advisable to begin the process slowly, increasing the routines as the person gains strength.

Exercise does not have to be boring. A person can walk, bicycle, swim, play tennis, or stroll through shopping malls. The type of exercise should be appropriate to the condition of the person. The point is for Mom and Dad to get some kind of exercise on a regular basis, exercise that makes the heart beat a little faster and the lungs expand a little more.

Many parents who have not been exercising will make a lot of excuses. Some will say they are too old. You might point out that the older people are, the better exercise will be for them. One study of people from ages eighty-six to ninety-six found that even the very old benefit from exercise.[10]

Some older people may say that they get enough exercise around the house, but that is seldom true. While it is helpful, housework does not usually provide the kind of exercise that a person gets from a good brisk walk. Others may say that if they exercise, they will put on weight because they will eat more. This is really not true because if their appetite does increase as a result of exercise, they will usually "burn off" the added calories. In fact, most people who exercise lose weight.

Some older people will say that they have no place to exercise. Using weights, a stationary bicycle or a rowing machine doesn't take much space. You can even show your parents the benefits and joys of exercising by developing a program for yourself. Get into a habit of walking vigorously whenever you walk. Instead of driving around and around a shopping mall looking for a place to park near the entrance, park at the outer edge of the lot and walk vigorously to the mall. Walk up the stairs in a building instead of using the elevator. You and your parents will increase stamina, strength, and self-esteem by walking instead of always riding in a car.

In addition to developing healthy exercise habits and practices, we need to stop practices and habits that can hurt us. Excess body weight reduces life expectancy and quality of life. Extra weight can lead to high blood pressure, high cholesterol, fatigue, and joint strain. Excess weight is also a contributing factor in heart disease. A study of women by researchers at Brigham and Women's Hospital in Boston and by the Harvard Medical School indicated that even slightly overweight women who smoke are five times more likely to have heart attacks than overweight women who do not smoke.[11] Being overweight can lead to heart attacks because it increases the risk of diabetes, high blood pressure, and cholesterol.

Drinking too much alcohol can also shorten life and the quality of life. Physical changes brought about by the aging process slow liver and kidney functions and increase the sensitivity of nerve tissue to alcohol, increasing alcohol's effects. As many as 10 percent of the older population suffers from alcoholism.[12]

Alcohol use by the elderly is complicated because many older people use medications that are rendered useless or even dangerous when mixed with alcohol. For example, mixing tranquilizers and alcohol can be fatal. Alcohol mixed with antihistamines causes sleepiness, and alcohol combined with aspirin increases irritation in the stomach lining.

It is important to watch for warning signs of a drinking

problem among the elderly. Some signs of alcoholism that could be mistaken for the results of getting older are falling repeatedly, not paying bills, confusion, trembling, gaps in memory, aggressive or abusive behavior, depression, and poor eating habits. Some older people are early-onset alcoholics; they have been drinking excessively much of their lives. These people are very difficult to treat in old age. Others are later-onset alcoholics who have become excessive drinkers in their old age, usually as a result of loneliness, depression, or retirement. Both types need help to stop the misuse of alcohol. If you suspect that your parent has a drinking problem, you can get help from a pastor, a counselor, or one of the numerous alcohol treatment agencies that are available in communities across the nation.

Some older people are under a great deal of stress because of aging. Stress is the result of the body's response to external conditions, and it can produce physical changes in every organ of the body. Stress can cause nervous tics, back pain, rheumatoid arthritis, colitis, cardiovascular diseases, or cancer. It causes changes in body chemistry—under stress, the adrenal gland produces hormones that increase the heart rate, blood pressure, and insulin production.

Many therapists use relaxation, meditation, hypnosis, or medications to reduce stress. Each of these has been useful for some people. But what will probably benefit your parents the most is for them to know that their children love them, that they will not be abandoned, and that God never allows us to have more problems than his grace gives us the strength to handle. Prayer and trust are good antidotes to stress. For all of us, the question is not just what causes stress, but how we react to those stressors.

Scripture tells us that we can overcome stress: "Do not be anxious about anything, but in everything, by prayer and petition, with thanksgiving, present your requests to God. And the peace of God, which transcends all understanding, will guard your hearts and your minds in Christ Jesus" (Philippians 4:6-7, NIV).

CHAPTER FOUR

Mental Health and Aging

Tho' much is taken much abides; and tho'
We are not now that strength which in old days
Moved earth and heaven; that which we are, we are—
Made weak by time and fate, but strong in will
To strive, to seek, to find, and not to yield.
　　　　—Alfred, Lord Tennyson, *Ulysses*

Eleanore Kubus loved nothing more than cooking the traditional Thanksgiving dinner for her family. But in 1985, the tradition became a family nightmare. As all the ingredients were spread out in her kitchen, Eleanor's mind went blank. She couldn't remember how to cook. From her apartment in Michigan, Eleanor, then sixty-five, phoned her daughter and said helplessly, "Diane, I don't know what to do."

"She couldn't remember how to open a can of soup," says her daughter.[1]

No matter what our age, for all of us there is a balance between the stresses of life and our resources that enable us to handle those stresses. As people grow older, however, their stresses can increase while their ability to deal with them may decrease.

If your parent suddenly experiences a bizarre personality change, however, he or she needs to have a complete physical exam by a physician. If no physical causes for the personality change can be found, a mental health specialist should be consulted.

FACTORS RELATED TO THE
AGING PROCESS AND MENTAL HEALTH

CHRONIC ILLNESS
The physical health of an older person is important to his mental health. There are certain chronic illnesses that can adversely affect a person's mental well-being, including, but not limited to, Alzheimer's disease. Congestive heart failure can cause such a loss of oxygen to the brain that it ceases to function normally. Diabetes can lead to impotence in men resulting in damaged self-esteem, depression, or irritability. Severe diabetes in either men or women can result in significant mood swings. Kidney failure can lead to mood swings, depression, and suicidal feelings. Rheumatoid arthritis can lead to extreme exhaustion, and the constant pain of arthritis can result in irritability and depression.

INADEQUATE NUTRITION
Inadequate nutrition can also cause personality changes. People who eat too much starch and put on excessive weight may be tired, lethargic, and often depressed. People who drink an excessive amount of coffee may be tense, anxious, irritable, and unable to sleep.

People who live alone commonly do not eat balanced meals, so they do not get the vitamins, minerals, and protein their bodies need. Older persons should examine their eating habits. If you notice a personality change in your parents, you should try to find out if they are eating properly. Over a period of time, inadequate nutrition can have a profound impact on a person's personality.

DRUG MISUSE
The side effects of certain medications can cause personality changes and distortions. Elderly people are likely to misuse drugs for very simple reasons. Some elderly people with vision

problems do not read the instructions well. Others do not tell each of their physicians that they are seeing other physicians who have also prescribed medications for them. As a result, they often end up taking a dangerous combination of drugs. Others, trying to be economical, take only a few of their prescribed medicines, hoping to save money. Others get up in the middle of the night and in their half-awakened condition take the wrong drugs.

Some older people take drugs from well-meaning friends, not realizing the danger of taking someone else's medicine. Some have problems because they did not ask their physicians about possible side effects of their medications.

A bright, energetic, and helpful woman at a senior center demonstrated a striking personality change over three months. She became increasingly confused and irritable. The center director began to think she might need to be placed in a nursing home, but when he visited her home, he found twenty-one different prescriptions from five different physicians on the woman's dining room table.

The woman had not told any of her doctors that she was consulting others. The prescriptions she was taking included psychotropic drugs (major mood changers) such as Thorazine and tranquilizers such as Valium, along with a host of other drugs for numerous physical ailments. The woman had mentally deteriorated to the point where she was not only mixing the drugs in dangerous combinations but was taking them in quantities that would make anyone irrational. The woman was taken off most of the drugs, put under the supervision of one physician, and recovered her mental and emotional health.

If you observe mood or mental changes in your parents, it is important that you ask them what drugs they are taking and in what quantities. Physicians should always be informed about other physicians that might be involved in the treatment of the person, and physicians should make it perfectly clear to the elderly client what possible side effects drugs might have on their moods or mental condition. Patients need to know the instructions about taking the drugs as well as warnings. Older people need to thoroughly understand the impact prescribed drugs can have on them.

WORRY AND SELF-CENTEREDNESS: THE JOY THIEVES

As your parents grow older, worry can become their constant companion. They may worry over their future financial situation. They may worry that any stay in a hospital or nursing home will literally empty their life's savings account. They may worry about major surgery not covered adequately by insurance. They may worry over housing repairs that they will not be able to afford. Many worry that burial expenses will be a financial burden to their children.

Older people need to be able to talk to their friends or relatives about these fears. If these fears are constantly in their conversation and there seems to be an unrealistic amount of anxiety, it might be helpful to get professional assistance. It is unfair for older people to live in constant fear and anxiety.

As a result of anxiety, some older people engage in obsessive-compulsive behavior: repeated ritualized actions such as wringing their hands, pulling out their hair, constant rocking in a chair, or insistent moaning. Others become hypochondriacs and complain about every little physical ache and pain. Professional assistance for all these persons can be very helpful.

Some older people have a negative outlook because of their personal habits. A lack of exercise can lead older people to become lethargic. This process can begin a cycle of decline because the more sedentary a person is, the less he wants to get up. In the process he becomes irritable, isolated, and depressed. In their isolation, some older folks become alcoholics. Some cannot sleep well and believe they suffer from insomnia. In reality their lack of sleep may be caused by overeating, too many naps during the day, and a lack of exercise.

> Last to speak was Chris, whose father, a stroke victim at the young age of 57, has lost interest in life, Chris said. He watches TV all day, never moving from his recliner.
>   "I bet he has a remote, too," [family counselor Margaret] Longnecker said.
>   "Yes."
>   "Get rid of the remote," she advised. "Seriously, get rid of it." It only encourages sloth. An entire generation, she declared, is atrophying because of television, recliners, and remote controls.[2]

Some older people become self-centered as they age. They enjoy talking about all their problems, but in the process they drive others away. Even their children get tired of hearing about all their pains and anxieties.

Elderly people sometimes become argumentative and cranky when they feel they are losing the respect they had in the past. Some attempt to regain this respect by controlling, threatening, and demanding the impossible from others. Unfortunately, these behaviors cause others to turn away from them, increasing their isolation and anxiety. This in turn may result in complaints about things like aching joints, constipation, and chest pains.

If your parent has turned into a sourpuss and driven away all but immediate family members, it will be helpful if you can encourage him to talk through the anger. Ask insightful questions and help him unravel the tangled ball of emotions inside. Then he will be free to talk about more positive topics.

Some older people become depressed and begin to deteriorate emotionally because they feel they are no longer good for anything. They feel "over-the-hill," finished, "washed up." Some older people themselves have a negative view of old age. They develop "gerontological phobia," a fear and distaste of aging. These people who feel that life ended at sixty-five can be taught to become assertive, to speak up, to reject a negative view of aging, and to remain involved in life.

ISOLATION

Some older people appear to lose some reasoning abilities because they are isolated from others. This can be a special problem for widows or widowers who were dependent on their spouses. Among the very old there are many widows who cannot drive, so they are housebound. Some people become isolated because many of their friends are dead and their children live hundreds of miles away. Some folks lack the energy to go out and be with others; some are too sick to venture out; some are too insecure to reach out to others.

Whatever the cause, isolation can bring depression, resulting in a loss of clear thinking. Although there are some people who live in relative isolation all their lives without negative consequences, most people need regular interaction with others.

If your parents are becoming isolated, try to find out what local programs designed to meet the needs of the isolated elderly are available in community agencies and churches. Many churches offer such programs. If every church had regular weekly programs for older people in its community (and provided transportation for those who needed it), there would be far fewer lonely old people.

FAMILY FRICTION

Some older people experience emotional difficulties because of family friction. Usually the family is a source of tremendous support for aged parents, but if lingering family quarrels have never been resolved, these can become a source of anxiety and depression. Whether the friction comes from a relationship with a child, a sister or brother, or someone in the extended family, these problems should be discussed and dealt with in a positive way.

SUICIDE

Suicide is higher among the elderly than among persons of any other age group. About 25 percent of all suicides are among people sixty-five and older, and this group of people makes up 12.6 percent of the population.[3] When older people talk about suicide, they mean it. When they attempt suicide, they usually succeed.

Any older person talking about suicide must be taken seriously. Some older people use indirect means to end their lives by neglecting medical attention, not taking medicine as it was prescribed, refusing to eat, deliberately exposing themselves to harmful elements, overexercising to cause a heart attack, and wandering off during bad weather.

PHYSICAL CAUSES OF MENTAL DETERIORATION IN THE AGED

Aging by itself does not lead to a deterioration of mental abilities or emotional instability. Old age does not result in a loss of competence. There are physical diseases, however, that do.

ORGANIC BRAIN SYNDROME

One of the age-related mental disturbances of older people is chronic or Organic Brain Syndrome (OBS), sometimes referred to as Senile Dementia. There is a problem with the terms *Senile Dementia* or *senility* because they are used by some as "wastebasket" terms to refer to any condition of strange or irrational behavior. The terms lack precision. Children of aging parents need to carefully discuss with a physician, psychiatrist, or psychologist the specific reason for the strange behaviors of a parent.

Most older people will not develop any type of Organic Brain Syndrome; only about 40 percent of Americans over age eighty develop some type of OBS. But that 40 percent will burden our health care system in the future because the over-eighty category is the fastest growing age group in America. Money spent on research now could save billions of dollars and alleviate an enormous amount of human suffering.

PSEUDO-SENILITIES

Other mental disturbances in older people are called "pseudo-senilities." Pseudo-senilities are confused conditions that have the same symptoms as Organic Brain Syndrome, but pseudo-senilities are reversible. Patients may experience memory loss, lose track of time, be disoriented, change moods rapidly, and have difficulty with personal care. The big difference between pseudo-senilities and OBS is that pseudo-senilities can be treated and the patient's condition improved. Therefore, when older patients show the symptoms listed above, it is important that they are diagnosed correctly. If they are believed to be suffering from OBS, there is little hope for cure or significant improvement. If, on the other hand, they have a pseudo-senility, their condition can probably be greatly improved.

There are many causes of pseudo-senility, including thyroid malfunction, drug overdose, inadequate nutrition, and infection. In an elderly person, an infection can be devastating because her biological "defense" system is not as effective as a younger person's. The infection might be in the bladder, the kidneys, or the lungs.

Confusion might be the result of medications such as L-dopa, digitalis, Valium, barbiturates, or a host of other drugs. These drugs stay in the body longer as a person gets older because the kidneys and liver are not as efficient as they once were at processing medicines. Since drugs stay in the body of an older person longer, the danger of overdose is increased.

It is important that older persons have correct diagnoses of serious conditions so they can get proper treatment. Without an accurate diagnosis, adequate treatment cannot be given.

ALZHEIMER'S DISEASE

The leading cause of Organic Brain Syndrome is Alzheimer's disease. Alzheimer's disease was first described by German physician Alois Alzheimer in 1906. At the present time it is the fourth leading cause of death among adult Americans after heart disease, cancer, and stroke. It is a progressive, degenerative, irreversible brain disease. If your parent has Alzheimer's disease, he will usually experience emotional problems that spring from a physical condition.

Currently, the cause of Alzheimer's disease is unknown. It results in changes in the nerve cells of part of the brain. These changes in the hippocampus—the brain's center of thought, language, and memory—result in the devastating symptoms of Senile Dementia. In its early stages, there is no conclusive diagnostic test for the disease. Diagnosis is frequently done by eliminating stroke, tumors, other neurological diseases, and arteriosclerosis. After death, a microscopic examination of brain cells can determine the presence of Alzheimer's disease.

The effects of OBS diseases on the family can be devastating. As the disease progresses, the patient will need around-the-clock supervision and help with routine personal care. Usually it is only a matter of time before admission to a nursing home must be considered.

> For every one of the estimated four million people with Alzheimer's or another form of dementia, there is at least one person carrying the burden, a situation that several studies have shown may have a lasting, disruptive impact on a dozen or so other lives.[4]—Sandy Rovner, *Washington Post*

Alzheimer's has been described as a progressive disease that "relentlessly erodes the essence of what makes somebody uniquely him or herself. The anguish of the affected individual is understandable, but that anguish is soon gone, lost with everything else. It is the husband or wife or child who will bear the pain long after the illness has obliterated all memory, all personality, all sense of self."[5]

Barbara, forty-eight, was proud of her independent mother. Although she had been a widow for many years, she lived alone and was so healthy she never had to go to the doctor. But her memory began to fail and she couldn't recognize road signs and would forget where she parked her car.

One day at the mall, Barbara's mother forgot where she had parked. A stranger saw that she was confused and offered help. Her mother got into the stranger's car. "It was scary," says Barbara, who felt anguish and pain as she saw her mother, a pillar of strength, succumb to Alzheimer's disease.[6]

When dealing with a parent with Alzheimer's, most family members experience denial, anger, depression, frustration, and hopelessness. If the cause and a cure for this disease are not discovered, Alzheimer's has the potential to overwhelm the American health care system as our older population continues to increase. The percentage of the very old in America is growing at such a rapid rate there may not be enough money in the health care system to cover the escalating costs of care for Alzheimer's patients if we do not use more of our national resources to address the problem.

ENDOGENOUS DEPRESSION
Another major mental health problem related to aging is depression. "Endogenous depression" occurs when a biochemical imbalance causes a depressed condition. "Reactive depression" is brought about by some event in the life of the patient. Most of us have experienced reactive depression at one time or another,

and usually people get over this form of depression with the passage of time and the ability to focus on something else. If your parent doesn't get over reactive depression in a reasonable amount of time, professional help should be sought.

Some people suffer from Seasonal Affective Disorder (SAD). As winter approaches and the days get shorter, these people begin to feel depressed. Although there is continuing debate as to the exact symptoms and cause of SAD, it seems that a light-sensitive hormone called melatonin may be reduced by exposure to light. As daylight decreases, these people begin to feel depressed, irritable, and anxious. Exposing these people to light similar to outdoor light is effective in reducing their depression, but ordinary home lighting does not provide this effect. Persons who believe they suffer from SAD should see a qualified therapist.

Another type of depression is manic-depression, where a biochemical imbalance brings about emotional mood swings. The person may shift from mania, an overactive state, to depression.

Among the symptoms of depression are feelings of despair, a denial of one's self-worth, angry outbursts, and psychosomatic symptoms, such as loss of appetite, insomnia, constipation, and fatigue. There is real hope for depressed persons if they are diagnosed correctly and receive professional therapy.

PREVENTION AND TREATMENT
OF MENTAL PROBLEMS

Preventive programs are the best form of treatment for mental problems of the aged. If your parent isolates himself, doesn't eat properly, won't visit a doctor, can't snap out of a depression, or won't take care of himself, it is important to find a program that meets his needs. You can start with a senior center in your neighborhood or an older adult program in your church. There your parent can socialize, get a hot meal, and obtain referrals to other agencies for special problems. There are agencies that will observe and evaluate your parent's situation and prescribe the best course of action for help and treatment, if necessary.

Early therapeutic treatment is needed to keep mental health problems from becoming more serious. Although the elderly comprise 12.6 percent of the population, they constitute only about 3 percent of outpatients in our mental health clinics. Too many older persons have negative attitudes toward the mental health field and are reluctant to seek help from mental health professionals. They think mental health care is only for "crazy" people.

For some elderly depressed persons, the treatment of choice is electroconvulsive therapy (ECT) or "electroshock" therapy. The movie *One Flew Over the Cuckoo's Nest* probably has done more to confuse people about ECT than anything else. Modern ECT treatment can be effective with many older patients.

It is not clear why ECT works, but it is very effective with a certain type of patient. For many severely depressed persons, parts of the brain are overactive. ECT treatments tend to return the brain to a more normal level of functioning. The entire procedure takes only about five minutes and is done under the supervision of a psychiatrist and an anesthesiologist. Very light electric pulses are given to the patient, lasting only one or two seconds. These pulses induce a very brief seizure that lasts about a minute. Some researchers claim that ECT causes memory loss, but for patients who do not respond to other types of treatment, it can be effective in treating severe depression. The American Psychiatric Association has guidelines for its use.

Drug therapy will be part of the treatment process for many elderly persons with mental health problems. Many prescription drugs, if prescribed and taken properly, can have miraculous results in assisting people with psychiatric conditions. Unfortunately these medications can be misused or abused. That is why it is important to understand that these medicines need to be taken *exactly* as prescribed. More of something is not necessarily better.

When people lose rational thinking, two current treatment approaches are used in conjunction with medical treatment. For a person suffering from reversible mental conditions (pseudo-dementias), Reality Therapy is often used. This involves reminding them of the reality of their situation such as the right time of day, the right day of the month, where they are, who they are, etc. Since they can regain their mental faculties, this therapy can be extremely beneficial.

For others who are suffering from true dementia, which is irreversible, the treatment is different. They may receive Fantasy Therapy in which they are allowed to continue in their fantasies since they will not be able to return to reality. For example, if an elderly widow with true memory loss is unaware that her husband has died, she should not be told every day that he is dead. To do so is to put her through the grieving process over and over. It is better for her to live in the happy memories of the past when she enjoyed a relationship with her husband.

If your parent is undergoing either Reality or Fantasy Therapy, it is important that you understand how to encourage the treatment during the time you spend with your parent. Obviously, if your parent is being encouraged to continue a fantasy, you should not interject stark reminders of reality. Likewise, if your parent is engaged in Reality Therapy, you should not encourage a useless fantasy.

It is possible that your parent does not need professional help as much as she needs the friendship and willingness of others to spend time with her. She needs someone who is a good listener. She needs someone with whom she can recall the good times of the past. A fondness for nostalgia is not a sign of senility. Most people like to recall the past with someone who loves them enough to listen. Family members, church friends, and neighbors can help older persons by taking time to listen. They will learn about the past, demonstrate their love by taking time to relate to an older person, and strengthen the older person's self-esteem.

Your parents may be struggling to adapt to changes occurring in the world around them. It often makes a great deal of sense for older people to return in conversation and thought to former times when they were more secure. They turn back to periods of the past when they had vital roles in the community, the security of family and friends around them, and strong feelings of acceptance.

Whatever your situation, the worst thing you can do is believe that it is hopeless. Children of the elderly have many opportunities to help their parents get the help they need.

PART TWO

Part Two

CHAPTER FIVE

Planning Ahead
for the Golden Years

Frances Schloss, a vice president of Shearson Lehman
Hutton, Inc., was asked to speak at the Freda Mohr Multi-
purpose Senior Services Program in Los Angeles. Schloss
chose to speak about long-term health insurance, a relatively new product on the market. For a monthly pre-
mium, people between the ages of fifty and seventy-nine
can get insurance to cover the costs of living in a nursing
home, should chronic illness or disability require long-
term care.

The men and women in the audience wouldn't listen.
After several interruptions, Schloss was abruptly told to
end her talk. "This is something I simply do not want to
think about," muttered one elderly woman. "I suspect a
lot of people feel that way."[1]

One of the most important things children can do to help
aging parents is to plan with them for the days and years ahead.
It is never too late to plan. Without planning ahead, families are
left to make rushed decisions when emergencies arise. And
planning *with* your parents is usually much better than planning
for your parents.

"A lot of adult children are very anxious, worrying about
what's going to be required of them as their parents become more

dependent on them," says Raeann Hamon, a professor of behavioral science at Messiah College. "A lot of the anxiety is undue. Parents and adult children need to talk about what they expect."[2]

"Don't wait for the crisis," says Barbara Feinstein, director of a geriatric planning and referral service. She tells seniors, "Do you have a durable power of attorney for finances and health care? Who knows your wishes? Do you have them written down?"[3]

No matter how old we are, most of us do not plan well for the future. Some of us are just lazy. Some of us do not want to face the future. Some of us do not want to think about or face changes; we are often afraid of them because they force us to face new realities. Some of us think that long-range planning is contrary to Jesus' teaching in Matthew 6:25-34 about the birds and the lilies of the field and how they don't worry because God provides for their needs. "Don't be anxious about tomorrow," Jesus said. "Live one day at a time" (verse 34).

Jesus gave very sound advice for many of us who are caught up in the fast-paced American life with its quest for status and material riches. But one of the best ways to avoid being anxious about tomorrow is to begin some long-range planning today. We can use the resources God has given us to develop at least tentative plans for the future, taking into account the changes that will occur and the needs most older people will have if they live a long life. Ignoring these realities is to ignore the means God has given us to live together happily as Christian children and aging parents.

As Christians, we have prepared for eternity, so why shouldn't we prepare for the next twenty or thirty years?

WHY OLDER PEOPLE DON'T PLAN AHEAD

"I'VE ALWAYS BEEN ABLE TO TAKE CARE OF MYSELF."
There are many reasons why older people don't plan ahead for the changing circumstances most will experience.

Many of today's elderly had to cope with life on a daily, weekly, or monthly basis. Our current generation of older people includes all those folks who lived through World War I, the Great Depression, World War II, the Korean War, and many other catastrophic world events and conditions. The business of daily survival was something that occupied most of their time and energies. Not many of our older generation had the luxury of planning ahead if planning involved money. It was a major accomplishment to keep a roof over their heads and provide the basic necessities of life for their families. Providing for one's family, supporting the church, and being a good citizen were the important things in the lives of so many of our elderly people.

"WHY, I NEVER THOUGHT I'D LIVE THIS LONG!"
Another reason many older people have not planned ahead is that they simply didn't believe they would live as long as they have. Many older people, having reached eighty or eighty-five years of age, still don't plan ahead to any degree because they don't think they will live much longer.

When many of the present-day elderly were born and grew into their teens, the average life expectancy wasn't nearly as long as it is today. Sure, there was the old man or woman down the street, but the percentages and numbers of older persons who lived to old, old ages were relatively low.

The life expectancy for males born in 1900 was forty-six years; for females it was forty-nine years. By 1983 this had increased to seventy-one years for males and seventy-eight years for females. By 1990 the projections were seventy-two years for men and seventy-nine years for women. We now expect about four out of five people in America to reach the age of sixty-five.[4]

Equally important, in previous years most people didn't live long after retirement. Many people in the early part of this century averaged one or two years of retirement before death. So a person focused on his working life.

Things have changed drastically. Since 1900, the trend has been longer life expectancies and earlier retirements. Many of the nation's retirement and pension plans have encouraged early retirement. In the United States, statistics currently indicate that between one-fourth and one-third of a person's life is spent in retirement. This is a dramatic shift from the early part of the twentieth century. The increase of "golden years" will have a great impact on older people and on the nation.

Many people are unaware that once they reach old age, their chances of reaching an even older age are really pretty good. One study indicates that once a person reaches sixty-five, their chances of living past eighty are greater than 50 percent.[5] The older a person gets, the greater the likelihood of his living longer. For example, life expectancy at age sixty-five is seventeen more years.[6] Those who reach eighty-five are expected to live more than five additional years.[7]

Since 1950, the year the Korean War began, the number of people sixty-five and over has more than doubled, the number of those eighty-five and older has increased about five times, and the number of people reaching one hundred has increased ten times.[8] No wonder so many of our older people did not plan to live so long! These tremendous changes occurred in the last forty years of their lives. They are the pioneers of old age on a mass scale.

"I DON'T WANT TO THINK ABOUT GETTING SICK."
"My parents are eighty-one and did not expect to feel bad until they were at least ninety," one woman said. "They have been surprised by their difficulties."

Many older people do not plan for the future because they do not want to face the possibility of declining health. They have not realized that very old people experience high rates of chronic health conditions that affect their daily lives. Of all people sixty-five and over, 86 percent have one or more chronic health conditions that limit their daily activities, according to Dr. Trilok Monga in a publication of Northwestern University.[9] In addition, 50 percent of the physically disabled elderly also experience mental problems.

> *Newsweek* reports that increased life expectancy "will only prolong the problems of aging for many families, while dramatically increasing health care costs. Medical advances are extending life faster than they are slowing the onset of chronic disabling conditions such as arthritis, stroke and senile dementia. Today some six million Americans require help in dressing, eating, bathing and going to the bathroom."[10]

Alzheimer's disease is estimated to affect 10 percent of our population sixty-five and older and 47 percent of those persons eighty-five and older.[11] The implications of these realities for the families of these victims and for our health care systems are staggering. How does a person plan for this? The Alzheimer's Association today estimates that it costs a family between eighteen and twenty thousand dollars a year to care for an Alzheimer's patient at home.[12] Nursing home care for this type of patient may cost as much as thirty-five thousand dollars a year, with the average about twenty-five to thirty thousand dollars, depending on the region of the nation.

Given the growth of the older population and the high incidence of Alzheimer's disease among this group, the deputy director of the National Institute on Aging says the disease is creating "one of the biggest public-health dilemmas we've ever encountered."[13]

It is difficult for the elderly or their children to plan for these types of chronic health conditions. Fortunately, a majority of older people will not have conditions this severe. But even though the majority of older people will not be stricken by something as severe as Alzheimer's disease, chronic health conditions need to be included in long-range planning that includes supportive living arrangements and possible care providers.

"I DON'T WANT TO BE A BURDEN TO ANYONE."

Many older people don't want to face the possibility of becoming increasingly dependent on others, including their children. Because independence is so important, most people don't want to think about the day when they might lose it.

Planning for dependency goes beyond planning for poor health. It involves planning for medical and nonmedical support systems, including public, private, family, and nonfamily resources. Together, a family can begin to line up the kinds of resources that are available to older people through community and governmental agencies, churches, private sector services that can be purchased, and, of course, family caregivers.

This type of planning can help us recognize the help older people may need with some of the basic tasks of daily living and where these types of services can be obtained. Even though some services may be free of charge for older people in some communities, there is usually a fee for them. It also takes some effort to find out what these services are and how to qualify for them.

"I DON'T WANT TO LEAVE MY HOME!"

For many older folks, it is unthinkable to plan to leave their home. It's like walking away from their life. Leaving their old home means leaving neighbors, friends, familiar surroundings, stores, restaurants, service centers, and the neighborhood church. Most older people are firmly tied to their community. They are not eager to plan to leave these familiar ties and the home that shelters their happiest memories.

There are exceptions. Some older people, particularly recent retirees, are happy to follow the sun. Some are eager to travel after a lifetime of work. But even these folks tend to come back to the old home territory as they continue to get older. Even these folks need to plan for a time when the old home and the old neighborhood are no longer suitable for their changing needs.

HOW TO PLAN FOR THE FUTURE

How can you encourage your parents to make plans for the future? You need to recognize that your parents may not be open to any discussion of this type. Some may become defensive and even hostile if these topics are raised. The best way around this problem is to work through a friend, a pastor, or a business contact. Facing tough issues about the future can put a real strain on some older parent/adult child relationships. Working with or through a third party can be very helpful in these situations.

Assuming you can talk to your parents about the future, for what should you and your parents plan?

CHRONIC HEALTH CONDITIONS

Older people and their children need to be aware that chronic health conditions after sixty-five can limit the activities of daily living. Some of these conditions will be minor, at least in the beginning. Some of them can be handled rather easily if they are recognized and dealt with early. Some chronic health conditions can develop at any age.

If an older person has a physical or mental condition that appears to be new and doesn't go away in a relatively short period of time, it is important to get proper evaluation and diagnosis of the condition. Not all doctors are experts in all areas.

If the condition appears to be serious, or if it is treated by the family doctor and doesn't go away, diagnosis and treatment should be sought by a specialist. Not all illnesses or conditions require a specialist, but if, for instance, your mother is suspected of having the beginning stages of Alzheimer's disease, she should be evaluated by a neurologist, not just the family doctor.

If a condition is serious or potentially serious, a second opinion by another doctor is not only advisable but often necessary. No doctor who is secure in her profession is threatened by second opinions. In fact, many physicians who value mutual support in medical decision making prefer this approach. This is where group practices or teaching hospitals can be helpful.

If a patient has the opportunity to seek evaluation or treatment from a university medical center, this can be a wonderful opportunity to get the latest and best in diagnosis and care. This is another instance where you can make a tremendous difference. Most older people will not make the effort to seek out a university medical center for evaluation and treatment, thinking that it is too complicated or threatening. The distance to such centers can be a real problem, particularly if the patient isn't feeling well or has a physical limitation.

University medical clinics offer some of the finest approaches to evaluation and treatment by specialists who usually function as a team. Most of these doctors are involved in research in their specialty areas, which generally means they have the most up-to-date treatments. Most of these medical centers are open to the public. Some require a referral from a local doctor, but that should not be a problem. In addition, many of these centers have housing assistance referral programs that help out-of-town patients and their families find relatively low-cost housing in the university town. Some even have arrangements for half-price rooms in first-class hotels and motels.

LEARN ABOUT YOUR PARENT'S CHRONIC ILLNESS
Once a diagnosis has been made, it is important for children and their aging parent to learn as much as they can about the condition. Doctors usually have pamphlets about chronic con-

ditions. Other literature is available in libraries and bookstores. Learning is the first step to coping with a condition with which the older person must live, probably for the rest of his or her life.

Talking to other people with the same or a similar condition can help your parents cope with a chronic illness. Ask your doctor for a referral. Make an appointment to see the person he suggests and ask questions about the chronic condition. Find out if there is an organization in your area that focuses on that chronic condition.

There are national organizations for most of the chronic conditions from which older people suffer. It is helpful to write to them and request any literature they have. Many are listed in the appendix to this book. Your doctor may be able to give you the addresses of additional organizations or support groups. If your doctor cannot help you, visit your public library and ask the librarian to help you.

As you help your older parent cope with a chronic or disabling condition, it is also important to learn about treatment possibilities. This does not mean there are treatments for all conditions. You have to be careful not to get involved in medical quackery, which is widespread. But you can search for legitimate treatment possibilities from highly respected sources.

For example, years ago little research and few treatment possibilities were available for macular degeneration, a serious eye disease. Although the progress of this disease does not result in total blindness, it often leads to such limited vision that the patient has difficulty with the most basic activities of daily living. More extensive research is now underway to understand this condition and help doctors develop treatment possibilities. Most of these experimental treatment approaches are limited to clinical research projects in university settings. Not everyone with difficult chronic health conditions needs to go to a university medical center, but it is helpful to be aware that these opportunities are available.

In addition to finding out about treatment possibilities for chronic conditions, you can help your folks if you find out what treatments might be coming in the future. Rays of hope are always encouraging, even if these approaches are not available now. We live in rapidly changing times, and medical discoveries occur every day. The dedication of medical researchers and their discoveries are ongoing blessings of God.

BE ADAPTABLE

It is important for children of aging parents to help their parents adapt to the conditions that limit daily activities. In the early stages of a condition, adapting may be easy. Just a little help here and there, just a little modification to daily routines or in some living condition, may do the trick for a while.

In the early stages of some limiting eye conditions, for example, added reading light may be all that is needed to help your mom. But as her condition progresses, especially if it is not treated or treatable, more difficult lifestyle changes may be necessary. If Dad develops a heart condition that limits his ability to drive in heavy traffic, it is going to be hard for him to drive on the freeways to a doctor's appointment. This means he will need a ride to his appointments and meetings, which can put a strain on both him and you.

Not all adaptations to chronic health conditions are as traumatic as giving up driving. Other adaptations that may be necessary include making the living environment friendly and safe by providing plenty of light, large numbers on dials, and handrails for bathtubs and stairs.

FIND STRENGTH IN NUMBERS

If there is a support group for children of aging parents in your community, you might find it helpful. A support group will reassure you that you are not alone. You will be able to share your frustrations and feelings of anger, guilt, and fear with others who have felt the same way.

Children of Aging Parents (CAPS) is a national organization founded in 1977 by Mirca Liberti and Louise Fradkin. "We touched on a sore spot," Fradkin says. "Caregiving wasn't considered an issue at that time."[14]

In 1982 CAPS was mentioned in the "Dear Abby" advice column and received four thousand letters from across North America. In 1989 CAPS was mentioned in the Ann Landers column, and eighty-five hundred letters flooded into the organization.

CAPS specializes in information. A call to their office from anywhere in the United States can bring answers to questions about any local, state, or federal aid that may be available, as well as advice on products, services, or anything else you might need.[15] The address and telephone number are listed in the appendix.

June Van found it necessary to place her father with Alzheimer's disease in a nursing home. Torn by guilt, she attended a CAPS meeting. "When we came to CAPS we found that a lot of people were going through the exact same thing," she said. "We found out that what we were doing was not wrong, that we were not mean, nasty people. Our situation is still not ideal. But talking to people is what helps you out with the hard times."[16]

FIND THE SECRET OF CONTENTMENT
In Philippians 4:12-13 Paul says, "I have learned the secret of contentment in every situation . . . for I can do everything God asks me to with the help of Christ who gives me the strength and power." We live in a fallen world where sin abounds, where sickness, weakness, and death are part of our mortal life. But God's grace gets us through all situations and conditions, even the pangs of death.

We can overcome anything. We can cope with any condition, even death, because the Holy Spirit aids those who trust in him.

This is the witness we have been given by other Christians who have experienced these things. It does not mean that these situations are easy. They are not. It does mean that God's grace is sufficient for all—elderly parents as well as their adult children. Families and caregivers can benefit greatly from the support of their church, their pastor, their friends, and an appropriate support group.

PLAN FOR POSSIBLE LONG-TERM CARE

"Long-term health care is an uncomfortable topic. . . . The common image is that of a nursing home and that connotes a loss of dignity and control," says Pam Keely, director of therapeutic recreation at a hospital in Philadelphia.[17]

Most people think the last thing they will do is plan for their parents' admission to a nursing home or total care institution. "It's a concept that none of us even want to think about—that one day we may not be able to care for ourselves," says Cynthia Isles, a hospital social worker. "Many think it means a one-way ticket to a nursing home, but less than 5 percent of elderly are in a nursing home at any given time."[18]

It is true that at any one time the percentage of older persons (sixty-five and older) living in institutions is only about 5 percent. But with people eighty-five and older, the percentage rises to 23 percent, a dramatic increase.[19]

As you plan for a time when a total care setting might be necessary for your parent, it might be wise to talk with friends about their experiences and observations with different nursing homes. It also may be helpful to talk with your pastor well before you may need such an arrangement. Many pastors have had considerable experience visiting their church members in nursing homes. Even though you do not want to think much about this reality, it will be helpful if you make notes for future reference.

You may not need a nursing home for your parents, at least

not in the near future, but you would do well to plan how you can help your parents when maintaining their own home becomes too much to handle. The time to see what is available in housing options is while your parents are still able to get around on their own and care for themselves. Keep in mind that 86 percent of people develop some form of chronic health conditions by age sixty-five. It is estimated that persons eighty-five and older spend up to eight hours each day just taking care of their personal needs, not to mention all the tasks necessary to maintain a home.

Irene Hendren Rex planned for her retirement after her husband died. She knew she didn't want to go into a nursing home, so she sold her home and moved to a smaller, more manageable place. "I thought I better make this decision while I was still able," she says.[20]

Irene moved into Springfield Residence, sort of a college dormitory for seniors who don't have to go to school. "Most seniors are perfectly able to take care of themselves, but maybe they can't cook anymore or drive," says Jefferson Kaighn, marketing coordinator at Springfield. "And they should not live in the same five-bedroom and three-bath house. Mostly we get people who are looking for security and safety. Up to a few years ago, where would these people end up? Around people with feeding tubes."[21]

"This is a good option," says Helen VanVoorhees, eighty-three, who has been at Springfield ten years. "It's small and you can get to know people real well. They recognize me as a landmark here. My theory is: come early enough. Come when you're active enough to enjoy it."[22]

If possible, planning for future living arrangements should take place when older folks still have options. Waiting until a parent is no longer capable of caring for himself drastically limits the options you have in choosing alternate living arrangements.

WHEN YOUR PARENT LOSES A SPOUSE

One of the toughest losses any married person faces is the loss of a spouse. It is devastating to lose a husband or wife. Certainly most of us do not want to think about such a possibility, much less plan for it. But realistically, unless they die together in an accident, one of your parents will become widowed at some point. Statistics tell us this is particularly true for women. As a rule, they simply outlive men.

Older women outnumber older men three to two, 18 million to 12 million. And because women tend to marry older men, women can expect to spend many years as a widow. To illustrate this on a local level, compare the number of widows to widowers in any church. We don't really know for sure why women usually live longer than men. Experts in aging have cited some explanations, which include females having an additional X chromosome, a better immunization system, superior vitality over the long term, and different social roles, attitudes, and lifestyles. Whatever the reason, women generally outlive men by quite a few years.

With this in mind, what can women do so they will be prepared when widowhood comes? It would be helpful for them to enrich their present lives. They should cultivate and keep old friends, develop new friends, maintain their interests and hobbies in life. They should understand the household finances, investments, and credit. And they should become active in organizations they find interesting.

Involvement in outside activities can give meaning and purpose to life. Helping disadvantaged children learn to read, for instance, gives a person purpose and perspective and builds self-esteem. Helping disabled patients in a local hospital often does more for the volunteer than it does for the patient. This type of community service can give older people a sense of well-being, purpose, and importance.

For many of today's older women, the loss of their spouse

means the loss of their transportation. Many older women never learned to drive, or they gave it up and let their husbands take over. If your mother doesn't drive, consider teaching her if it is physically possible. What freedom and independence this will bring!

This could be helpful even while both your parents are alive. Your mother might be younger than your father and in better physical condition for the demands of driving.

Both of your parents should know how to run the household. Your mother should know which mechanic is trustworthy. She should know how to light the pilot light on the furnace if it goes out on a cold morning in January. Your father should know how to cook simple meals and do a load of laundry. The more your parents know about household maintenance and repair, the less likely they are to be ripped off by a con artist.

Planning for widowhood is not a pleasant prospect. But doing things that promote independence and self reliance not only helps to prepare for being alone, but also enhances the quality of a person's life while they still have their mate.

If your parent loses her spouse, the church can be a place of belonging and tremendous comfort. It can reinforce her Christian perspective on the meaning of life in the face of difficulties. She can be involved with other people and feel needed. Her spiritual journey can serve as a guide to younger people who are trying to find their way. Being involved and active can give her life real meaning.

LIVE YOUR LIFE NOW!

As you plan with and for your aging parents, you have the opportunity to look ahead to your own later years. You can plan your own retirement. Review your options, thinking about these options in terms of your personal preferences and lifestyle, and make some tentative or general choices to plan for the future.

By doing your own planning early, you will have the luxury

of time to refine, change, and act on your plans. This is one of the benefits of helping older folks.

Another benefit of helping older folks plan for changing life circumstances is the realization that you cannot pin all your hopes for enjoyment on your future retirement years. Helping elderly parents cope with physical or mental limitations can help you realize that you should enjoy the blessings of life each day.

You need to enjoy your middle-aged physical vitality. Working closely with elderly parents will enable you to appreciate all the things you can still do, many of which the elderly can no longer do. It will give you a better appreciation of how short life really is, or more accurately, how quickly it goes by.

So don't put off that trip you promised your wife or husband. Don't let all the roses wilt without taking time to stop and smell their fragrance. Don't put off telling your spouse and children how much they mean to you and how important they are to your life. Don't put off doing things with and for your own children. And don't be so overcome by working with your aging parents that you see them as "the problem" instead of as the parents they are. Take time to enjoy them while you can.

> "Every man desires to live long, but no man would be old."
> —Jonathan Swift, *Thoughts on Various Subjects*

CHAPTER SIX

Why Does Money Grow Short as People Get Older?

I hang up the telephone after talking with my paternal grandmother and continue to feel the pain I heard in her voice. This Sunday, like so many other days, was long and lonely for her. And she sounded worried about money again.

"Would it be so terrible if they charged us $100 less for rent?" she asks as she worries aloud about trying to stretch her Social Security check to meet her expenses. "I've just been so tense about the check this year."

When my grandmother hesitated to get her teeth fixed "because it might cost another $1,000," I knew she was really worried. The dentist was unable to fix her problem for a two-month period, and every visit prompted more anxiety in my grandmother about money.[1]

John and Mae thought they had earned a pretty good living in their business. John was a painter, and Mae worked in an office where she supervised fifty other workers. After they were married in 1928, Mae continued to work in the office for a while until her first child was born. Mae never went back to work, and in the next six years the family added two more children.

John continued to paint homes and commercial properties. It was rough raising a family during the Great Depression, but John managed to keep going. With some financial help from their parents and the friendship and goodwill of their neighbors and friends, most of whom were in the same situation, John and Mae managed to get by. Money was never plentiful, but the family had plenty of faith, love, and hope for the future.

During World War II, painting jobs were easy to get. With the end of the war and the building boom that followed, John expanded his business and hired other painters to work for him. The children were growing up, and Mae was eager to do some work outside the home, so she and John decided to open a paint store.

It was a smart move. Millions of returning servicemen and women were eager to settle down and establish their own homes and families. Because John and Mae were hard workers, knew their business, and had timed their expansion well, their business prospered. They did not get rich, but they sent all three of their children to college and generously supported their church. They had nice clothes, a good car, and took a vacation every year.

Life was good beyond their dreams. Although becoming wealthy had never been their highest goal, a sense of financial security was nice. In 1963, John and Mae began to think about retirement. Their children were grown, and John felt it was time to slow down and get out from under the pressure of the business. He and Mae wanted to enjoy life while they were still young enough to travel and do the things they had been too busy to do while running their own business.

In 1963, John and Mae sold their paint store and invested the proceeds for retirement income. They thought they had enough money to last them the rest of their lives. In addition to their Social Security income, they were sure their investments would allow them to live the comfortable, modest life they had enjoyed.

But they didn't plan to live as long as they did. John and Mae had no way of knowing how much inflation would affect the economy. Like your parents, John and Mae never dreamed the cost of living would rise so dramatically.

THE RISING COST OF LIVING

John and Mae have now been retired for close to thirty years. During that time the cost of living has doubled every fifteen years. Even though Social Security benefits have been tied to rising inflation rates since 1975, the benefits to which the increases are applied are based on incomes earned in years when incomes were lower. For example, if a 4 percent raise is mandated, the person receiving four hundred dollars a month receives an extra sixteen dollars, but the recently retired person who receives one thousand dollars a month will receive an increase of forty dollars per month.

Inflation can be devastating for people in the very old sector of our population. As Harold Cox points out in his book, *Later Life: The Realities of Aging,* "Rising prices versus relatively fixed incomes means either a reduction in the standard of living or the selling of assets accumulated over the working years in order to maintain a given lifestyle. Liquidation of accumulated assets is an especially difficult choice because of the specter of outliving one's income."[2]

Cox points out that the cost of living in the United States is measured by the Consumer Price Index (CPI). "Recently the inflation rate as measured by the CPI has been led by (1) rising food prices, (2) sharply increasing prices for energy, and (3) a continuing escalation of prices for medical care. These three components of CPI work a much greater hardship on the over-65 nonwage-earning population than on the general population."[3]

A Harris and Associates survey revealed that older persons who are retired worry more over money than over crime or poor health. What many of these elderly persons fear is not their present financial situation, but running out of adequate funds to meet their basic needs as they continue to grow older and prices continue to rise, year after year.[4]

SELLING THE FAMILY HOME
MAY NOT BE ENOUGH

The constraints of retirement incomes and benefits based on work and earnings that stopped twenty to thirty years ago not only make many older persons afraid of not being able to maintain their basic standard of living, but they often make it difficult or impossible for them to move to different living arrangements. It costs money to move to a retirement home with a supportive living situation: money for the move, money to get in, and money to remain there. Many of these life-care facilities are relatively new or newly remodeled structures and are simply too expensive for too many of our older citizens.

The only way most older people can consider moving to a retirement community is to liquidate many or most of their assets. Usually this means selling the old family home or other real estate. This is a possibility for many older persons, but the proceeds of the sale of the old home may not be enough to cover the entrance costs of a new retirement home and its ongoing monthly fees. The more care elderly people need, the more quickly their assets will be depleted.

Even though John and Mae do not need a nursing home yet, they are facing lean times as they continue to grow older in an economy with ever higher prices. Any illness they face may require large sums of money in spite of Medicare, and they may have to sell their home to move into a housing arrangement that provides supportive services.

MANY OF THE OLDEST PEOPLE ARE POOR

Retirement brings financial devastation to many old people. The poverty level for all persons sixty-five and older is lower than that of the general population (12 percent versus 13 percent),[5] but poverty rises among older persons as they get older. For the group of older people seventy-five to eighty-four, the poverty rate was 15 percent in 1986, and for those eighty-five and older, the rate rose to nearly 19 percent.[6] If we add the "near poor," those persons who are just above the official poverty line (125 percent of the poverty standard), the percentage of the poor and "near poor" combined increases to 32 percent.[7]

These figures represent the financial status of the fastest-growing population group in America. These are the people who raised us; built our churches, schools, and colleges; paid taxes; fought our wars; and sacrificed to give us the heritage we enjoy in America today.

As George Haskel's father, Ron, neared retirement, George noticed that Ron became downright stingy. He pinched pennies, complained about money, and even sold several family heirlooms that George had hoped to someday give to *his* children. George couldn't understand what Ron was going through, but Ron was simply afraid that what he had wouldn't last through the years ahead.

If your parents have been retired for several years and seem to be financially pinched, don't blame them for poor money management. Their lack of financial capital does not reflect on how hard they worked. Most aging parents are simply caught in the "longevity-inflation squeeze" that has developed in the past twenty years. More people are living longer while the economy continues to inflate prices. Simply put, the money your parents saved ten or twenty or thirty years ago may not pay for their needs today. And as prices continue to inflate, even at a relatively slow rate, their money will buy less in the years ahead. The house they may own is undoubtedly worth more than they paid for it, but unless it's in an area where land values are increasing rapidly, the house may be depreciating with each passing year.

You and your parents aren't alone in this financial crunch, and you'll be glad to know there are special programs, services, and policies to help older people cope financially. Once you inform your parents of these programs and services, be prepared for possible resistance. Your parents may not want to take advantage of them because they feel they are some kind of welfare or "giveaway" programs. You may have to convince your folks that these programs are made possible through the tax dollars they have paid through the years and the efforts of elected officials who represent them.

THE SPECIAL FINANCIAL PROBLEMS OF AGING WOMEN

Unfortunately, the majority of our older population—women—experience the most problems with financial insecurity and worry. Traditionally, women have had four roles in our society: wives and homemakers, nurturers of children, caregivers for the sick and infirm of the family, and volunteers in the church, school, and community. Society has placed high values on these roles for women, particularly in years past when your mother was actively fulfilling these roles.

As valuable as these roles are to our family and society, these are not roles for which women are paid. They are fulfilled out of love, and they do not add financial capital to a woman's retirement income. As a result, because women typically outlive men by quite a few years, many elderly women are finding it hard to pay for the basic necessities of life.

> Life has been difficult for my grandmother, who is in her early 80s, since her husband died 25 years ago. Because of her fierce independence, I know that she has suffered quietly and kept much of her pain to herself.
>
> While she has, for example, managed to lead a largely independent life, she still has not grasped the mechanics of her checkbook. As a single woman who lives alone, I

identify with her trials of managing everything for her-self. I know the fear of being alone and sick and still hav-ing to tend to chores like laundry and food shopping. If you do not have the energy for these tasks, you just go without clean clothes and food.[8]

—Andrea K. Hammer, *Philadelphia Inquirer*

According to Hooyman and Kiyak in their book, *Social Gerontology*, women sixty-five and older accounted for nearly 71 percent of the older poor population in 1985, with 16 percent living in poverty.[9] Even if your mother worked for many years, her working years were not likely to be consistent. Many women interrupted their careers to have children, care for sick family members, or to be full-time homemakers. Even if your mother worked consistently, she probably worked in a job that paid women considerably less than men. It is also likely that she did not receive a full share of retirement benefits.

If your mother is a widow, she has probably lost her primary source of income: her husband's pension or retirement plan. That is why some scholars have described many older women as being "only one man away from poverty." Hooyman and Kiyak point out that only about 2 percent of widows receive survivor's benefits from a husband's pension.[10] This is because, in order to get the maximum income in their pension, many men in years past chose pension options that did not continue to pay the wife after her husband's death. Of those eligible for benefits, only 25 percent of widows receive them in full, primarily because of misinformation about how to access those funds."

The key to survival for older women is to have income in addition to basic Social Security benefits. Social Security was not designed to provide *all* the resources an older person needs in retirement. Also, most older women today did not have the opportunity to develop their own work record with the Social Security system that enables them to draw maximum benefits.

Because of this, most older women draw upon their husband's work record with the Social Security system, but once he dies, the amount of money they receive usually decreases by 50 percent. As a result, a person who depends solely on Social Security income in retirement is seven times more likely to be poor than a person who has wage and salary income.[11]

In their book, *Eighty-Five Plus*, Bould, Sanborn, and Reif cite U.S. Bureau of the Census data showing that, in 1987, 58 percent of women aged seventy-two and over living alone and relying only on Social Security checks were poor.[12] They go on to point out that older women aged seventy-two and older living alone who were actually receiving Supplemental Security Income (SSI, a program to supplement the income of the poorest old) had a poverty rate in 1985 of 78 percent. What makes this statistic even worse is the fact that some 35 to 50 percent of these older persons who are eligible for SSI do not participate in the programs because of stringent individual state guidelines, not being aware of the program, or thinking that it is demeaning to ask for this type of assistance.

Even older women who were able to work outside the home are not worry-free. Hooyman and Kiyak point out that only 20 percent are eligible for pensions, compared to 44 percent of men. In addition, those who do receive pensions collect about half the benefits men receive because of the differences in salaries and the number of years worked. So unless your father was one of the few who set aside large financial reserves or a store of inherited wealth, your widowed mother may be in a vulnerable financial position.

LONG-TERM HEALTH CARE: THE MONEY-HUNGRY MONSTER

The financial picture becomes extremely bleak when older people find themselves paying costs associated with long-term health care. Even with Medicare, there are large numbers of older people faced with medical bills they simply cannot pay. And if long-term care in a nursing home becomes necessary, few people can afford the required twenty-five to thirty-five thousand dollars per person per year. This can bring a tremendous load of stress upon a family.

> "Medicare will pay for the cost of care at home *only* when an individual requires part-time skilled care requiring a doctor, nurse, or physical therapist, etc."[13]

Our nation's health care delivery system is in turmoil. Even some of our more conservative publications carry articles such as the one in *U.S. News and World Report,* "America's Scandalous Health Care." Whether the care is needed for a premature baby or an aging parent, very few people are financially prepared for the spiraling costs of catastrophic health care.[14] *Modern Maturity* described the American delivery system of medical care in an article entitled "Bordering on Collapse."[15] It covered the case of Rose Williams:

> She is 70 years old and lives on a fixed income, but because of a rental property she inherited, her assets are too high to permit qualification for Medicaid. Like many seniors, Williams is finding that health care costs can decimate a small budget.
>
> "Today I went to my doctor, and it hurt," says Williams. The doctor charged her $40 for a visit and gave her three prescriptions to have filled. Williams couldn't afford to pay for both, though, so she didn't buy the medicines. Yet, "If I don't take the pills, my blood pressure goes up and I end up back at the doctor's."
>
> Medicare coverage doesn't cover routine checkups, part of other medical bills, or her medications. So Williams juggles her expenses and counts her change—-

buying pills when she can, skipping when she can't, choosing which she needs more: medication or food on the table.

Many other older persons choose between buying prescription medicine and paying the bills for heat or rent. The financial consequences of long-term care for the elderly are frightening to both old people and their children.

What many families don't realize until too late is that government programs currently don't cover the cost of long-term care. Medicare generally doesn't pay for nursing homes or custodial services at home. Many private insurance plans don't either. Medicaid will pay for nursing-home stays, but only after an elderly person has depleted their assets to the poverty level. As a result, many disabled elderly are forced into nursing homes, and poverty; alternatively, family members often have to quit their jobs—and spend their life savings—providing care at home.
　　—Melinda Beck, *Newsweek*[16]

We hope we've helped you understand why your parents may be worried about their financial future. If your parents are not concerned, perhaps they should be. Many older people who were once relatively well-off face poverty or difficult times for the first time in their lives as they grow old because they outlive their financial nest egg or retirement income, they become chronically ill, or they become widows with limited incomes. If a relatively well-off person can find himself in financial difficulties, imagine the plight of an older person who was unemployed, a member of a minority group, handicapped, or poor in his younger years. The economic vulnerability of older people is not due to laziness or lack of effort or planning. These conditions are the result of circumstances beyond their control.

> The burden of [caring for aging parents] must not fall solely on families. Support networks outside of families are also critical. Volunteers who provide relief for caretakers would provide essential emotional and physical support. And a more dependable financial program to support our elderly population, and comprehensive health care, would make the prospect of aging less frightening.
>
> If we ignore the financial worries, depression, and loneliness of our older relatives, the meaning of family will totally disintegrate. The aging problem is not about some remote difficulty that catches our attention on the evening news. It's about real people who are suffering—my grandmother and yours. If we continue to anesthetize ourselves to the problems, who will care for us when we are old and alone?[17]
> —Andrea K. Hammer, *Philadelphia Inquirer*

CHAPTER SEVEN
How to Help Aging Parents Cope with Finances

Children of aging parents recently wrote to *USA Today* for answers to troubling questions:

- How can I get help for financial planning?
- Will Medicare cover the costs of full-time custodial health care at home?
- What is a relative's financial liability for the care of their infirm?
- How much will I be able to count on Social Security?
- Will my father lose everything because he is incapacitated and physically unable to take care of his financial affairs?[1]

In order to help your parents handle their financial responsibilities and manage their investments, it is important to first understand the basic elements of the changing American economy as it applies to older people. Your understanding won't give your parents more money, nor will it reduce their expenses or pay for the nursing care you may need, but it will help you understand what can be done to help them.

Your parents need to be willing to share financial information with you. This may be difficult for them. After all, when you were growing up, they kept their money worries away from you. You were the child, and they were responsible for you. They may continue to feel that you shouldn't be bothered with their financial affairs. But it will be helpful for you to know what your parents have in terms of savings, investments, annuities, and real estate holdings. Before your parents will share this information, they need to feel they can trust you completely. It may take some time and effort before they will talk openly with you about money matters.

LEARN ABOUT ENTITLEMENTS AND BENEFITS

Once you have a good grasp of the resources available from your parents' income and investments, you can learn about the governmental benefits to which your parents may be entitled. It is helpful to learn about Medicare, what it covers and what it does not cover. You can find out which doctors in your area accept Medicare as payment in full and which do not. You need to know that Medicare has two parts: part A for hospital services and part B for physician services.

Medicare is a federal health insurance plan for people sixty-five and older who are eligible for Social Security. Medicare will pay for the cost of care at home only when the patient requires part-time skilled care. Medicare will pay for hospice care if the physician's prognosis is that the patient has six months or less to live. But when Medicare does cover a bill, it pays only 80 percent of reasonable physician services. The patient pays the other 20 percent.

Free publications describing Medicare benefits are often available from Area Agencies on Aging and other agencies that serve older people. The American Association of Retired Persons (AARP) has a free publication, *Medicare: What It Covers, What It Doesn't,* which can be obtained by writing: AARP Fulfillment, 601 E Street, Washington, DC 20049.

What Medicare Won't Cover

- items or services not reasonable or necessary for the diagnosis or treatment of an illness or injury

- items or services for which the Department of Veterans Affairs or another government agency pays
- health care outside the United States, unless it is emergency care in the nearest Canadian or Mexican hospital or while traveling in Canada en route to Alaska
- items or services required as a result of war
- items for personal comfort or convenience such as television, telephone, or air conditioning
- routine physical checkups, except for Pap smears and mammographies
- eyeglasses or eye exams for fitting glasses or contacts, except those dealing with cataract surgery
- hearing aids or examinations for hearing aids
- immunizations, except when directly related to an injury or when there is an immediate risk of infection
- routine foot care, including treatment of flat feet and dislocations or displacements of the feet, as well as foot supportive devices
- cosmetic surgery, except when required for prompt repair of accidental injury or for improved functioning of a malformed body part
- charges imposed by physicians or others who are Medicare recipients, relatives, or household members
- dental services, including care, treatment, filling, removal, or replacement of teeth or structures directly supporting teeth
- custodial care to assist you in daily needs such as dressing, bathing, feeding, and medications that you can self-administer
- meals delivered to your home
- domestic or housekeeping services unrelated to patient care
- transportation services except for covered ambulance service

- items or services for which an automobile or liability insurance policy or no-fault insurance plan has paid or can reasonably be expected to pay
- items or services for which an older worker's employer group health insurance will pay[2]

Medicaid is a combined federal-state program to help poor people with their financial needs. Medicaid covers many health care items that Medicare does not, including inpatient and outpatient hospital services, physician services, and long-term nursing home costs. To qualify for Medicaid, persons need to qualify for Supplemental Security Income or spend down to an asset and income level that puts them in or near poverty. When your parent is at the poverty level, Medicaid begins to cover expenses. Adult children are not held financially responsible for the health care of their parents unless they choose to be. Medicaid does not calculate the income or assets of the children of persons applying for assistance.

Almost every adult in America is familiar with the Social Security Act of 1935, generally referred to as Social Security. Although it does a number of things, its primary goal is to provide a basic income for older people. The developers of the Social Security program were careful not to make it a welfare program. It is based on a person's work record. Even millionaires can collect Social Security if they meet the age and work record guidelines. Most people support the program and feel good about collecting from it.

Supplemental Security Income (SSI) is a program intended to supplement the income of very low-income older persons with limited assets. Its roots go back to 1935 and the establishment of the Social Security Act. At that time, as part of the newly established Social Security programs, funds mostly from the federal government were distributed by the states to the needy older persons as old-age assistance. Programs similar to this were set up for the blind and disabled. In 1972, as an amendment to the Social Security Act, SSI was established as a new program. SSI included provisions for the elderly poor, the blind, and the disabled. These provisions replaced some of the state-operated welfare programs.

Because SSI is an assistance program and not an entitlement program, a person must prove need by meeting income and asset "tests." In 1989, an individual's assets could not exceed $2,000; a couple's could not exceed $3,000.[3] Excluded from assets were the value of one's home (up to a certain level), household goods, personal effects, a car worth under $4,500, a life insurance policy worth less than $1,500 at face value, and $1,500 set aside for funeral and burial expenses.[4] Not excluded was money saved to purchase something.

In his book *The Realities of Aging,* Cary Kart cites the story of a widow in Iowa who lost her SSI income entirely because the rent she didn't pay was more than the rent she did pay. She lived in a trailer her son owned. It was determined that the amount of rent she paid to live in the trailer was far below fair rental value, or what her son could have gotten by renting to strangers in the open marketplace. So the difference between what she paid and fair rental value was determined to be income which, added to her Social Security checks, made her ineligible for SSI even though she was really in the SSI qualification range.[5]

Horror stories like these make some governmental programs unacceptable to some people. This is one reason why some people are reluctant to participate in assistance programs. For example, the Social Security Administration estimates that about one-third of eligible older persons do not participate in the SSI program.[6] Other studies have indicated that up to one half of eligible persons actually get benefits they are entitled to from SSI.[7] Another study found that some 45 percent of those not participating had never heard of the program.[8] If your parents have spent nearly all their assets, they may be eligible for the SSI program, but you must know about this opportunity in order to take advantage of it.

Another program that supports a range of services to older people is the Older Americans Act (OAA) of 1965. This act and its amendments represent a major effort to help older persons throughout the U.S. The act has broad goals:

- to help older Americans have an adequate income in retirement in accordance with the American standard of living
- to make available the best physical and mental health programs without regard to economic status
- to design, locate, and make available suitable and affordable housing for older Americans
- to provide full restorative services for those who require institutional care
- to provide efficient community services, including access to low-cost transportation, a choice in supported living arrangements, and readily available social assistance
- to provide immediate benefits from proven research knowledge that can sustain and improve health and happiness
- to allow older Americans freedom, independence, and the free exercise of individual initiative in planning and managing their own lives[9]

The overall goal of the OAA is to provide authority to combine and organize a range of public resources for older people. The OAA led to the establishment of the Administration on Aging on the national level, state Agencies on Aging in each of the fifty states, and Area Agencies on Aging in every region of each state. Everyone in America lives in a region covered by an Area Agency on Aging. In the large cities, the Area Agency on Aging may cover part of a metropolitan area. In sparsely settled regions, an Area

Agency on Aging may cover many counties. You can find your local Area Agency on Aging by checking your telephone directory, calling your local United Way, calling a senior center, or visiting the reference desk at your public library.

The broad objectives of the OAA are translated into specific programs and services that can be very useful to your older parents and make your life easier as well.

One of the most important features of most OAA programs is that eligibility is not based on income or assets. They are the results of collective efforts of persons in both major political parties to help older persons survive in an ever-changing economy and world. The provisions of the OAA are intended to preserve the dignity and self-esteem of older persons.

OAA programs include information and referral services, outreach services, protective services, protection in nursing-home settings, specific programs to help older people remain in their own homes, nutrition information and services including serving and delivering hot meals, adult day-care and respite centers, recreation, transportation, and case management services.

All of these are vital resources to meet the most pressing needs of people as they grow old. Older persons and their children should become familiar with the range of resources coordinated, sponsored, and offered by their local Area Agency on Aging. The OAA may offer you more help than you dreamed possible.

If you encounter any opposition from your parents because they feel they may be on some form of welfare by participating in a government-sponsored program, remind them that government has been developing programs for various groups of people in America for many years. The government aided students when it established and supported state colleges, universities, and community colleges. Thousands of businesses across the country have been encouraged through tax abatement, investment, or depreciation allowance programs. Home owners can buy homes through special low-cost government mortgage loans. Special programs for the aged are something to which your parents are entitled. Their tax dollars have provided for these services.

You should also be aware of special programs in your community. For example, if your mother hasn't been taking her pills because she can't afford to fill her prescription regularly, there may be a special program for drug rebates in your state. A few years ago Michigan began to offer such rebates for eligible older residents, subject to specific income requirements. Eligible rebates may range up to six hundred dollars, but a majority of older persons in Michigan are not aware of the program, according to the Michigan Office of Services to the Aging.

HELP IS OFTEN A PHONE CALL AWAY

There are special programs and financial provisions in many areas of the nation for older people, including:

- home heating assistance
- property tax rebates
- various services designed to allow people to maintain their homes, including help with heavy cleaning chores, the installation of smoke alarms, etc.
- discounts for seniors from private businesses
- discounts for members of the American Association of Retired Persons (AARP)
- neighborly meal sites or "dining centers" that provide inexpensive, hot, nutritious noon meals for older people who cannot afford to eat adequately, as well as for those who no longer prepare meals because of loneliness and isolation (an elderly person doesn't have to be poor to participate)
- geriatric research programs and dental units that provide general health screening and dental care for older people with low incomes

- geriatric mental health support teams providing psychiatric services for people in private homes, foster homes, or adult congregate living facilities (services can include caregiver training, assessment, day treatment, and respite care)
- legal hot lines that provide free legal advice for older residents
- transportation services run by American Red Cross volunteers for older people who need help to reach physician appointments
- help and information from the community bus service to teach new bus passengers how to read passenger schedules, transfer to other busses, and reach convenient bus stops
- employment programs that train people fifty-five and older for jobs and place them in jobs throughout the community
- special recreation classes for senior adults that stress weight training and good health

Not all of these services may be offered in your community or state. To get a complete list of services offered in your area, call your local Area Agency on Aging, a senior center, or a United Way office.

KEEP TRACK OF PENSION
AND RETIREMENT FUNDS

If your parent has retired and is dependent upon a pension or retirement fund, you should be aware of the provisions of these funds. Many of these benefits are now protected by law, but the laws are complex, and your parent's pension plan could be lost in the shuffle when two large companies merge or a company declares bankruptcy. Horror stories abound of people who worked thirty or forty years for a company only to be let go just before they secured their pension. Some people have lost their pensions when their former employer declared bankruptcy.

It is important to be aware of the status of your parents' particular pension or health-benefit provisions as well as having a general understanding of the law as it applies to that plan. It might be helpful to get in contact with a lawyer familiar with pension protection laws as well as your parents' pension and benefit plans.

Pensions were first protected by the federal government in 1974 when Congress passed the Employee Retirement Income Security Act (ERISA). This legislation was designed to establish minimum standards for pension programs and provide for their regulation and supervision.[10] As good as the ERISA was, it left many women unprotected because many women have interrupted work records due to the responsibilities of their roles of mothers and homemakers. As a result, they are less likely to accumulate private pension benefits. This need was addressed to some extent in the Retirement Equity Act of 1984 and the 1986 Tax Reform Act. Still, women participate less in private pension programs than do men.[11]

PERSUADING YOUR PARENTS

One of the most important things you can do to assist your parents financially is to encourage them to take advantage of programs, discounts, and entitlements that are set up for older people. This may sound simple, but often it isn't.

Henry and Jan, both in their eighties, live in a small Midwestern city. In the Great Depression they were forced to seek public assistance—welfare—when Henry lost his job. It was the most humiliating thing they had ever done. There were no food stamps back then, and going to pick up surplus food was painful for Henry and Jan even though many of their friends were forced into the same circumstances.

As soon as Henry found a job in 1935, he and Jan wanted

nothing to do with any kind of program that hinted of govern-ment support except Social Security and Veterans benefits, which they felt they had earned. As they got older and tried to maintain their old home, they really needed help with shopping, getting to the doctor's office, and nursing when one of them was ill.

Their daughter heard about some in-home services coordi-nated by a local agency with support from the Older Americans Act. She suggested to her folks that she might look into it, but the mere mention of a government-related program was enough to put an immediate halt to the conversation. Henry and Jan didn't want anything to do with help from a public agency. They had been on welfare once, and they promised themselves they would never do it again. Attitudes like Henry's and Jan's stop thousands of older Americans from getting the help they need.

You might encounter the same difficulty with your parents. If you will make the effort to find out what programs are available for your parents, you will be doing a worthwhile service for them. Some of these programs could mean the difference be-tween your parents being able to remain independent in their own home or being forced either to move in with you or into a supportive-care institution, such as a nursing home. Being able to remain independent, with the help of services, is a far more conservative economic approach than moving into an expensive nursing home. Even more important, it is clear that most older people welcome the chance to remain as independent as possible for as long as possible.

GUARD AGAINST SCHEMES AND FRAUDS

Consumer fraud cheats millions of older people out of billions of dollars each year. As sad and disgusting as it is, there are unscrupulous people who intentionally defraud older people through schemes, scams, and worthless products. This happens in all parts of the nation. Older people are not the only targets of con artists, but they are among the most vulnerable.

Why are older people so vulnerable? They read or hear of many technological breakthroughs, and when someone presents something to them that sounds really innovative, they may fall for it. Also, many older people have diminished vision or hearing, which makes it more difficult for them to check on products or services. Many older people find it difficult to shop around for goods or services and are more likely to buy from a door-to-door salesperson selling goods or services. In addition, many older people are lonely, which may make them more vulnerable to a salesperson who is talkative and friendly.

Even if the service or product is not fraudulent, too many older people buy products and services they don't need, or they buy too much of a good thing. For example, in their fear of economic catastrophe, many older people buy duplicate or multiple insurance policies they don't need and can't afford.

Frauds fall into various categories, and many relate to maintaining a home. Con artists talk older people into roofing schemes, sealing driveways (often done with motor oil!), and phony furnace cleaning schemes. Many older folks prepay for work that is never done.

Some home repair/home maintenance situations may not be outright fraud. Too often older people are simply overcharged. Unless you or your parents know the reputation of the repairperson or contractor, it might be wise to advise your parents to either include you in their discussions with a contractor or businessperson or to get at least three bids on the same job. Remind them never to rush into a major financial decision for home repairs. If a roofer offers a special "for today only," it's usually too good to be true. Your parents may not like the idea of including you in their decisions, but getting at least three bids on a job is always a good idea.

Another area of consumer fraud is health care. In a four-year investigation, a U.S. House of Representatives subcommittee uncovered hundreds of unproven, worthless, and sometimes harmful health products. The late Rep. Claude Pepper, chairman of the subcommittee, stated, "We found the inventiveness of the quacks to be as unlimited as their callousness and greed. We found promoters who advised arthritics to bury themselves in the earth, sit in an abandoned mine, or stand naked under a 1,000-watt bulb during a full moon. These suffering souls have been wrapped in manure, soaked in mud, injected with snake venom. . . ."[12]

"Moon dust," sold in three-ounce bags for a hundred dollars and guaranteed to cure arthritis, turned out to be plain old sand. The "miracle spike," to be worn around the neck as a cure for cancer, was nothing but a penny's worth of the chemical used in rat poison. Cruel hoaxes like these prey upon the illness of older persons.[13]

Other fraudulent schemes revolve around the bank accounts of older people. In the classic "bank examiner" scheme, an older person is called by a person posing as a bank official. They ask the older person to draw out and hand over their savings in a plan to trap a crooked bank employee. People who fall for this scam find out too late that the "bank examiner" was the crook who disappeared with their savings.

There are variations on all these schemes. As the child of an aging parent, it is important for you to be aware of these schemes and help protect your parents' financial resources. And in the case of medical quackery, it is important that you protect not only your parents' money, but also their health. Don't let your parents rely on a fraudulent medical scheme that could prevent them from seeking proper diagnosis and treatment.

ACT AS A GO-BETWEEN WITH AGENCIES, ORGANIZATIONS, AND BUSINESSES

"I don't understand this form."

"I called the office and they said I had to pay the whole amount."

"They are not a participating office."

"Could you get me an appointment? They always put me on hold. They never seem to have any openings for six months, and I need to see the doctor soon."

"I don't know how to do that. Years ago I could handle this, but I just can't anymore."

"They talk about things I never heard about. Would you call them and get it straightened out for me?"

Sound familiar? If not, just wait a few years. Being an intermediary between your aging parents and an array of offices, agencies, and businesses may become a major function for you in the months and years ahead. You may have to get a doctor's appointment for an immediate or ongoing problem, call a plumber to fix a leak in your folks' shower, and help your parents fill out insurance forms and pay medical bills.

This type of help is time-consuming, but very important. Your parents may not be able to see or hear well enough to handle these things on their own. One man was called by his doctor and told to report the next morning at eleven-thirty for tests. The man, who lived an hour away, got up at six o'clock, drove the hour to the doctor's office, and pulled into the parking lot even before the receptionist arrived at seven-thirty! He had not heard correctly.

Your parents may feel insecure about filling out forms or become too easily intimidated by receptionists, nurses, and secretaries. They may feel overwhelmed by pushy salespeople or tired clerks. They will need an intermediary to help.

Being a go-between for your parents can be stressful because you are acting on behalf of someone else. Even though your parents need you, your actions and decisions must be approved by them. It is not easy to help them manage their money and make decisions.

There will be times when you don't have a good understanding of what you are dealing with. In the beginning, you may feel as intimidated by doctors' offices, businesses, and governmental agencies as your parents do. You may question whether you can be expected to know what is best for your parents. You may wonder if your parents secretly question your motives or your intentions.

If you do what you can for your parents, that's all you can do. You cannot be too hard on yourself when you make a wrong decision. You cannot wallow in self-pity when they do not seem to appreciate all you are attempting to do for them. There are no perfect solutions. Just remember that if it weren't for you, your parents might not have anyone else to help them.

When you have to guide your parents in a financial decision, first explain the situation to them as best you can. Give them the options they may have, and explain the consequences of each option. Recommend your choice and explain your recommendation. If the options are not pleasant, don't sugarcoat them, and don't feel responsible for them. You did not create the situation, make the policies, or set the rates or fees.

Your task is to help where you can. This is not an easy job. If your parents' financial resources are not adequate for a certain situation, explain to them that maybe this is the time to take a new approach, even if that approach includes an assistance program such as Supplemental Security Income or Medicaid. Help them to understand that it is no disgrace to take advantage of these programs. These programs have been designed to help.

TRY TO BE A FINANCIAL PARTICIPANT

Jill's dad had always been very private about his financial matters. Even Jill's mother didn't know what Dad's income was, the amount in his savings accounts, or how much he paid for their house. He managed all the family's finances. At ninety-two he suffered a heart attack and was hospitalized for the first time in his life.

Who would manage the bills, the checking account, and all the rest? Jill offered to help her dad, and he accepted, with the provision that he would still be in charge. Jill agreed. What else could she do? After Jill's dad got home and regained some strength, she and her dad went over the bills together.

One of the bills was a hospital bill for nine hundred dollars. Jill's dad thought it was too much considering he had Medicare and his private supplemental insurance. Jill said she would check into it. She called the hospital billing department and wrote a letter to the insurance company where Dad had his supplemental policy. The amount due was correct. Everybody had an answer to justify the amount. Jill's dad still said it was too much. He didn't want to pay it.

What could Jill do? The bill had to be paid. She knew the amount was right, but nothing she said would change her father's mind. Finally, she simply got the courage to tell her dad that he was being unreasonable, the amount was justified, and the bill had to be paid. This took a lot of effort because Jill was torn between being a good daughter and being responsible for her father's bills.

This type of situation occurs every day in America. There was no easy solution for Jill's situation. Jill could only do her best and go on from there. To prevent, or at least to temper, such situations, it might be helpful for you to set up financial strategies that will make it easier to act on behalf of your parents in financial matters *before* they become ill. This may be done by setting up a joint checking account, establishing a power of attorney by a written document, or by setting up a durable power of attorney.

In a *joint checking account,* there are two names on the account, and either party may write checks. This arrangement might not have helped Jill because she agreed, at her dad's insistence, that she would help him in financial matters, but he would be in charge. But with a joint checking account she could have at least paid the bills if she had to. Her father might have disputed it later, but the bill would be paid. And if her dad became incapacitated, she would have had access to the account.

With a *power of attorney,* a parent voluntarily gives another person, often their adult child, the power to handle all their affairs. The powers granted in this arrangement may be as narrow or as broad as the person who gives this power chooses. If the person granting the power of attorney becomes incompetent, the power of attorney ends.

The way to overcome this is to grant something called a *durable power of attorney,* which is not affected if the person who grants it becomes incompetent. In setting up a power of attorney or durable power of attorney, it is helpful to have the assistance of a lawyer.

Children can also help aging parents by investigating and purchasing a supplemental health insurance policy to cover the gaps in Medicare. Ask the insurance company to send you duplicates of the bills so you can be sure the bills are paid. Also make sure your parent files for benefits. Millions of dollars are lost each year because older people don't file medical claims.

If your parent cannot handle his finances, it is important for you to have a list of all his income and assets. You may be able to help your parent earn more by moving money out of a savings account and into a certificate of deposit or some other sound investment, or by taking a loan against an insurance policy. Certain income, such as Social Security benefits, can be deposited directly into your parent's bank account. Bills can also be paid automatically, reducing the risk that your parent will forget to make a deposit or pay a bill.[14]

IF YOUR PARENTS BECOME HOSTILE

Sometimes as the result of a psychiatric condition, Alzheimer's disease, or something else, many people become hostile and distrustful. Some of these patients are not willing to grant powers of attorney. In some cases, older people even think their kids are out to steal their money.

Sometimes the aging parent's personality changes completely.

This is a heart-wrenching time for everyone, but what can the children do? This is a complex legal situation and a reality that many children of aging parents face at some point.

First, adult children in these situations need to reach out for support from family members, friends, and the Christian community. It is a great comfort to know that others are thinking of and praying for them and their parents.

The next step for adult children whose parent has become incompetent but is opposed to granting decision-making powers to their adult child is to contact an attorney who can help set up a *guardianship* through the probate court. This is a very difficult step for most children, but it is sometimes necessary when a person is clearly no longer capable of managing his own affairs.

As difficult as this situation is, a guardianship cannot be avoided too long. If your parent is mentally or physically ill to the point of incompetency, he needs supervision, and his affairs need to be managed.

Finally, a person caught up in this complex and difficult situation needs to understand the consequences of a court-appointed arrangement to manage a parent's affairs. Resources are available that will help you to better understand the complex legal issues dealing with money and the management of personal affairs. Pamphlets are available from senior citizens organizations. The American Association of Retired Persons developed a book, *Your Legal Rights in Later Life,* that covers legal issues pertinent to older people: Social Security, Veteran's benefits, pensions, health and medical care, private insurance, landlord/tenant disputes, probate, estates, and other important legal issues.

PARTICIPATE IN UPDATING WILLS
AND EVALUATING ESTATES

It is helpful to sit down with your elderly parents to review their wills, trusts, and other estate arrangements before they are incapable of participating in such a review. This can avoid big problems later on. Circumstances and situations affecting your parents' money and estate frequently change.

You can be very helpful if, in a loving and cooperative way, you discuss with your parents changes that might need to be made in their wills and trusts. Very often, parents will initiate these discussions for their own peace of mind. They want to know that they are doing the right thing to help their children when they die. With the assistance of a trusted attorney or financial planner, this can be a productive, cooperative effort for you and your parents. The American Association of Retired Persons offers a book, *Essential Guide to Wills, Estates, Trusts, and Death Taxes*, that deals with these issues.

ASSIST WITH INSURANCE

One of the most practical things you can do is to help your folks with insurance. You can help your parents choose whether or not to buy insurance or supplemental insurance policies, understand the benefits of policies they already have, and assist in filing or refiling claims.

You've probably heard of a couple like Mr. and Mrs. Jones. They were friendly and somewhat lonely, so one afternoon they stepped out on their porch and heard an insurance salesperson forecast that one day they would be a burden to their children unless they bought the product he was selling. Mr. and Mrs. Jones bought a policy they didn't need. It was a duplicate Medicare supplemental policy that would never pay because the Joneses were already covered by another policy. Yet another policy in the salesperson's briefcase had so many restrictions in the fine print that it would have been meaningless for Mr. and Mrs. Jones, but he would have gladly sold them that one, too.

There was nothing illegal about the salesperson's work, but all Mr. and Mrs. Jones got from the deal was a smaller balance in their checking account. Older people need to be aware of insurance situations and wait to buy supplemental health insurance until after they have discussed the matter with their adult children or a trusted friend.

You will find it helpful to make a list of your parents' benefits under each policy they own. This way you won't overlook important benefits for which your parents have already paid. It also will avoid the stress of trying to find out what might be covered during a medical emergency. Making a list of benefits will require an afternoon of reading fine print, but one day you will be glad you know exactly what is covered by your parents' health insurance.

Filing insurance claims has to be one of the more frustrating experiences of modern life. And to do it for others, even your parents, is even more difficult. The forms are often confusing and tricky, and many older people (as well as younger people) have difficulty with detailed forms. This is particularly true when claims are initially rejected or modified.

It is important to understand refiling and appeals processes. In many cases, initial decisions to deny claims can be reversed if you refile the claim with additional information from the hospital or doctor. Sometimes just restating the case to another level of the bureaucracy will turn a negative response into a positive one. Refiling is usually worth a try. It is also important to know that each state has a commissioner (or similar title) of insurance you can contact if you think you are being unjustly denied after an appeal.

Prior to September 1, 1990, many physicians required their patients to complete and file their own Medicare claims. Others would file the claim for a fee. This is no longer the case, and now doctors are required to file the claims anywhere in America. This is a great benefit for older persons; a 1989 government survey found that Medicare beneficiaries were losing between $90 million and $130 million a year on Medicare claims that were never filed. Kathleen Vallee, the regional coordinator of the Los

Angeles Medicare Advocacy Project, said they had hundreds of frustrated people coming in with paper bags filled with bills and Medicare forms asking for help.[15] Now older persons will get the benefits of Medicare coverage they are entitled to without the confusing paperwork.

TRY TO ANTICIPATE COSTS OF LONG-TERM CARE

Very few older people can afford extended long-term institutionalized placement, which costs about twenty-five hundred dollars a month or more. Unless they are rich, there is no way for your parents to have prepared for these kinds of costs. Nursing-home insurance is not available to the very old at any cost. And most elderly people simply were not able to save the kind of money that is needed for long-term care. Those who are eighty-five and older are particularly vulnerable because their financial situation is based on the lower incomes of earlier times, and because they are the biggest users of medical services and long-term care. As a result, 65 percent of America's elderly end up "spending themselves into poverty" to qualify for Medicaid.

As distasteful as this is, you need to be aware of new guidelines that apply to Medicaid for long-term care. This information can be obtained from local departments of social service and Area Agencies on Aging. These rules went into place following the repeal of Medicare provisions of the Medicare Catastrophic Coverage Act in November 1989.

SHOULD I PAY MY PARENTS' BILLS?

What are our obligations to nearly poor aging parents? What can we do for people who fear becoming poor and burdening their children? How can your family help support your parents when you may be struggling financially to send your own children to college and pay off the mortgage?

These days are difficult for many families. Perhaps you have recently lost your job. Perhaps you had to help your kids pay college tuition and living costs. Perhaps a grown daughter has moved back home as the result of a rocky marriage. Or maybe you have had to tell your husband or wife you'll have to postpone that dream vacation for a while. Maybe you want to help your recently married son or daughter scrape together a down payment for a home. With all this upon you, how can you find an appropriate solution to the pressing financial needs of your parents? Are you expected to somehow do it all? Too often we expect more of ourselves than we are logically capable of. We are not expected to sacrifice our own health, our own family, or our own stability in caring for our parents. We can only do what we can within the framework of our own family, our own health, and our own needs.

As our old moms and dads make up the fastest-growing sector of our population, we begin to realize that their problems are the problems so many older people face in our churches, our cities, and our states. Their problems have become the subject of national debate. How can we as Christians respond to all these concerns? Do we throw up our hands and say, "It's beyond me. I can't do anything about it." Or do we only look to our own parents or the old folks in our church. But even here we can quickly run out of solutions and ideas when faced with long-term nursing home costs, old people who have outlived their savings, or older women living alone who find themselves among the poorest people in America. Certainly we want to help our own folks—that's what this book is all about. We want to help them in ways that don't overwhelm or destroy our own life and relationships. But how can we help them? What is the best way? And how can we help other old people who also need help as they face economic problems that threaten to overwhelm them? The answers to these tough issues are rooted in the Scriptures and are addressed in the next chapter.

CHAPTER EIGHT
How Can Christians Help Older People?

In *Growing Old in the Country of the Young,* former senator Charles H. Percy told the story of Jean Rosenstein of Los Angeles. She wrote the following letter to the *Los Angeles Times:*

"I see no human beings. My phone never rings. I feel sure the world has ended. I'm the only one on earth. How else can I feel? All alone. The people here won't talk to you. They say, 'Pay your rent and go back to your room.' I'm so lonely, very, very much. I don't know what to do."

Mrs. Rosenstein enclosed a dollar and six stamps with her letter. The dollar was to pay for a phone call; the stamps were to be used if anyone would write to her. In a city of nearly three million people, Mrs. Rosenstein, age eighty-four, had no one to talk to.[1]

A Christian's journey through life does not consist of just looking out for himself or for those in his faith community. We are directed to use our personal and collective resources to help those around us who are in need. This includes the elderly among us who can no longer work, have minimal resources, and are experiencing the infirmities and physical limitations that come from illness and chronic health conditions.

We need to develop an approach to social help that reflects the totality of the gospel. Back in the sixteenth century, John Calvin wrote and spoke about two aspects of redemption: the redemption of the person, which we commonly refer to as salvation, and the redemption of society, because a Christian is a social being who should be involved in the problems of society.

Calvin refers to the sovereignty of God: God is the ruler of all life. Until Calvin's conversion in 1533, he saw the religious world and the secular world as two separate worlds. Once converted, Calvin no longer separated faith and the world. He pointed out that concern for the secular world is a direct expression of a person's Christian faithfulness. He went on to say that through Christ, a person becomes a new creature, one that has new relationships and responsibilities to God and to the total society.

Christians, according to Calvin, are to be aware of and act on the responsibilities that flow from their faith. They are to do so by involvement and participation in a Christian community within one's culture, contributing to this religious community's faithfulness to the gospel and engaging in action to better the social life of the society through institutional means.[2]

In 1955, Billy Graham wrote in his best-seller *Peace with God:*

> Jesus taught that we are to take regeneration in one hand and a cup of cold water in the other. Christians, above all others, should be concerned with social problems and social injustices.[3]

More than a decade later Graham wrote:

> I lay a great deal of emphasis on the social applications of the Gospel. For a Christian to ignore the social problems around him is a tragedy. . . . My first responsibility is to win men to Christ, and then and only then, can and will they live as Christians in the world. There have been

Christians who have neglected their social responsibilities, but let us remember that almost all of the great social reforms have come through the application of Christian principles.[4]

Another noted evangelical spokesperson, founder of *Christianity Today,* Carl F. H. Henry, pointed out "that the gospel was once a world-changing message, but that it had been narrowed to a world-resisting message by an embarrassing divorce between individual salvation and community responsibility." He called for "a 'new reformation' that would make clear the implications of divinely given personal regeneration for individual and social problems."[5]

In his book *Saints and Society,* Earle E. Cairns notes that evangelical Christianity was a major influence on many social reforms in industrial societies during the eighteenth and nineteenth centuries.[6] It greatly influenced the abolition movement, prison reform, the treatment of the mentally ill, and the working conditions of the industrial laborers in England. We only need to look at the work of John Wesley and his brother to catch the spirit of bringing the totality of the gospel to the factory towns of England. In our own nation we can look about us today and see the results of all kinds of Christians actively working in society to improve the lives of the hurting: Baptist hospitals throughout the South; Presbyterian, Roman Catholic, and Methodist hospitals throughout sections of the North and West; Catholic orphanages in cities across America; mental health hospitals and clinics by various denominations across the nation; emergency shelters and food pantries in churches of all types in nearly every city and hamlet in America; youth centers, family shelters, and alcohol detox centers, to list only a few of the services offered by organizations such as the Salvation Army.

The history of foreign missions on behalf of many of our denominations is replete with illustrations of medical assistance, agricultural assistance, and educational assistance, to name only a few. The first medical facility in India to train Indian doctors was established by a relatively small American denomination, the Reformed Church of America. The goal in all these missionary efforts was to bring the Good News of the gospel through winning people for Christ and putting in place institutions and systems that would improve the lives of the people.

In his book *Insomuch: Christian Responsibility in the Twentieth Century,* David Moberg addresses the question of Cain, "Am I my brother's keeper?" (Genesis 4:9, NIV) by stating: "Sometimes in the case of Cain, it is asked with a note of defiance or to justify or excuse sinful deeds. Sometimes it is asked in frustration as men look at the complex network of social institutions and the inescapable snare of human problems, wondering how they can even do anything effective to alleviate suffering and promote good. Sometimes it is asked in humility by people with a genuine desire to do God's will in their relationship to their fellow men."

Moberg goes on to say: "Answers to this question are found in the Bible from Genesis to Revelation. The Old Testament Law and Prophets repeatedly refer to man's obligation to his fellow men. The teachings of Jesus Christ by moral and example, experiences of the early Christians and instructions in the New Testament Epistles, all affirm that man is indeed his brother's keeper."[7]

In Matthew 25:31-46 Jesus describes the judgment when he says:

> But when I, the Messiah, shall come in my glory, and all the angels with me, then I shall sit upon my throne of glory. And all the nations shall be gathered before me. And I will separate the people as a shepherd separates the sheep from the goats, and place the sheep at my right hand, and the goats at my left.
>
> Then I, the King, shall say to those at my right,

"Come, blessed of my Father, into the Kingdom prepared for you from the founding of the world. For I was hungry and you fed me; I was thirsty and you gave me water; I was a stranger and you invited me into your homes; naked and you clothed me; sick and in prison, and you visited me."

Then these righteous ones will reply, "Sir, when did we ever see you hungry and feed you? Or thirsty and give you anything to drink? Or a stranger, and help you? Or naked, and clothe you? When did we ever see you sick or in prison, and visit you?"

And I, the King, will tell them, "When you did it to these my brothers you were doing it to me!" Then I will turn to those on my left and say, "Away with you, you cursed ones, into the eternal fire prepared for the devil and his demons. For I was hungry and you wouldn't feed me; thirsty, and you wouldn't give me anything to drink; a stranger, and you refused me hospitality; naked, and you wouldn't clothe me; sick, and in prison, and you didn't visit me."

Then they will reply, "Lord, when did we ever see you hungry or thirsty or a stranger or naked or sick or in prison, and not help you?"

And I will answer, "When you refused to help the least of these my brothers, you were refusing help to me."

And they shall go away into eternal punishment; but the righteous into everlasting life.

As mature Christians, then, it seems clear that we need to recognize and effectively address the problems of the needy and vulnerable throughout our nation and the world. But how can you do this? If you are struggling with your parents, how can you be expected to tend to the needs of thousands, indeed millions, of hurting older people?

You start by helping one person at a time. In your situation, it is doing the best you can do for your parents.

If your parents are not in need of a great deal of care, you can seek out a needy older person in your neighborhood or church who could use some help in the tasks of daily living. This is especially important for older people who are trying to maintain their own homes.

Most older people could use help with transportation for doctor's appointments, church services, and shopping. As it is difficult for poorer, older people to pay for these services, your help can be invaluable. You could also volunteer for organized community or church programs to assist needy older people.

But as Christians we need to go beyond helping our own parents, our own church members, people in our own communities. How can we do all this? We are grateful for the blessing of freedom and independence we enjoy in the United States. We are thankful that we have an open society where we can work together to solve, or at least work toward solving, some of the real problems that we face. We are thankful for the opportunity we have as Christians living in a free land where we can do things together to improve the lives of the most vulnerable among us. We are thankful that as Christians we have the freedom to do things individually and cooperatively through our churches as well as social institutions to meet the needs of needy people.

HELPING CAREGIVERS

Christians need to take a strong role in undergirding and supporting caregiving children of aging parents. A caregiver faces enormous tasks, and the caregiver's spouse, family, friends, pastor, and fellow church members should understand this role and offer to help when practical.

Religious education directors can also help by offering training programs for caregivers. Many caregivers want to know about the conditions and diseases with which they deal in caring for aging parents. They want to understand how the drugs and treatments of older people work. Many want to know what to expect as a disease or condition lingers or progresses. They want to know how to cope with all the complex health-care reimbursement forms and regulations.

Christians can assist caregivers when possible. Care teams can be organized to relieve a caregiver. Often even one person can be a great help to a primary caregiver who needs help with chores and shopping.

Christians can provide emotional support for the caregiver. Much of this can come from support groups, but individuals can provide emotional support, too. We need to let caregivers know that we care. Too often caregivers who are isolated in their own home feel they are all alone with unending tasks and worries. Often they are. We need to let caregivers know that we appreciate them as individuals involved in tough situations. You could send a card every week, or telephone and talk for a few minutes. Just let the caregiver know that you are thinking of and praying for her.

Christians, individually or collectively, have the opportunity to promote and provide relief from the financial strain of caregiving. Perhaps through a benevolent fund or another project, money can be raised to help support elderly people cared for in their children's homes.

Christians need to organize special recognition for caregivers. More people need to become aware of the needs of caregivers and the real possibility that more and more adults will be caregivers over the next few decades.

BECOMING INVOLVED IN HOUSING

Many churches, denominations, and ecumenical organizations have developed homes for the aged in years past, but many of these facilities are now old. There is a tremendous shortage of appropriate housing units for low-income older people in almost every section of America.

We need to promote and develop housing arrangements where older persons can retain as much independence and control over their own lives as possible and where they will be taken care of as they continue to grow older and need more and more assistance. Working together, Christians have the opportunity to mobilize and pool their resources to sponsor housing developments that would restore dignity, provide security, and improve the quality of life for countless older persons.

TAKING TIME FOR THE OLD

As people grow older they usually suffer significant losses in their lives. Christians can help older people and their caregiving families by taking the time to visit, listen, and encourage the parent to socialize with others. They need to know that God's promises still hold and people still care about them.

Depression caused by loss is not healed at all by religious clichés spouted by hurried persons who read brief biblical passages, mutter a prayer, and leave. A supportive friend, neighbor, pastor, or church member can provide significant help if they take time to visit and listen.

DEVELOPING CHURCH PROGRAMS FOR THE AGED

We can encourage our churches to develop specific programs for older people. There are outstanding examples of church ministry for and by the old. Some churches have realized the desperate need for supplemental food among some older persons who live almost entirely on modest Social Security or Supplemental Security Income checks. Old people should not go hungry in the richest nation in the world, a nation where millions of people worship God and proclaim the gospel to others. Ministry to the elderly among us can be most rewarding. Those who have been involved in it tell of the blessings they have received from being part of such ministries.

A number of interesting and rewarding programs in ministries for and by older people have been developed. The Huntington Reformed Church of Belle Meade, New Jersey, has developed a ministry in adult day care. "Our experience with adult day care has taught us that growing old also means growing lonely," says Casey Santye, a member of the church. "When a person is no longer able to leave the house and visit with friends and neighbors—whether because they are disabled or because they are the primary caregiver for another—isolation and loneliness are heavy burdens," Mr. Santye writes in *The Church Herald*. He goes on to say, "Adult day care provides a safe, protective, respective environment for older adults. It is a place where individuals can feel like a contributing part of a larger group."[8]

Mr. Santye points out that the center welcomes all sorts of people, including old relatives who are no longer safe at home alone, single people who are old and lonely, and the physically disabled who need mental stimulation or a place they can feel at home in. "Anyone well enough not to need twenty-four-hour care but not well enough to go to a local senior center is welcome. Our goal is that all clients who come to our program know that they are loved and liked, and that someone cares about them."

Another effective church program is a shared housing project operated by the North Branch Reformed Church of North Branch, New Jersey. The congregation voted to purchase an old home next to the church and develop it into a shared housing unit. They named it Kirkside, which means a house next to the church. Kirkside's stated purpose is "to provide a shared living arrangement in a Christian setting for seniors capable of self-care, and to fill the gap between private homes and health care facilities." In doing this, "Kirkside has also positively affected the lives of many of the church's members," according to the Rev.

Peter Nordstrom, pastor of the church. A part-time social worker oversees the needs of the residents, and a cook-housekeeper provides one hot meal a day for them Monday through Friday. According to the Rev. Nordstorm, many of the residents have been active worshipers with the congregation, although this is not a requirement to live in the house.[9]

Another church, the New Hackensak Reformed Church of Wappingers Falls, New York, operates two homes for elderly people who do not require nursing care. "Our residents have taught the staff what life is really about," says Janet Boehm, a member of the church. "We see our residents helping each other daily. When a resident is sick, the roommate helps to comfort, to support, or to stand by to hold a hand." One of the residents stated, "Time, patience, basic needs, and the kindness of the management and staff have brought me through five years of associations with great and caring people."[10]

The Addisville Reformed Church in Richboro, Pennsylvania, has effectively developed a ministry of caring and visitation. According to the Rev. Herbert S. Van Wyk, a retired pastor and member of the church, "The Sixty Plus Senior Citizens fellowship and ministry of the church is to ensure that every senior citizen in our church has a convoy of caring people who are able, ready, and willing to provide a supporting relationship for members of our church in their golden years of life."[11]

He goes on to say, "We have a great variety of programs which are planned by a steering committee. At each Sixty Plus meeting we give our members an update concerning the well-being of members of the church who have special needs. Because we all have a need to be needed, we try to provide opportunities for older adults to perform meaningful services to the church and community."

Another church ministry for and by older persons has been developed in the First Reformed Church of Sioux Center, Iowa. A core of volunteers visits lonely older people and transports them to hospitals for treatment. "It only takes a little research to find them," says the Rev. Harold Lenters, minister of visitation at the church.[12] "While many older adults enjoy frequent visits by their families, some older adults do not have families around. And just as younger people seek the company of peers and others outside of their families, older adults need other people to talk to. This is the best therapy for older adults. It reaffirms the value of their lives." Rev. Lenters continues, "Ministering to older adults takes a concerned heart and some organization. A wealth of people in our congregations have both the time and health to join together in a continuing program of visitation."

Perhaps one of the most unique church programs for and by older adults is the development of a church specifically for older people. This has been the ministry of the Classis of New Brunswick of the Reformed Church in America. According to the Rev. Paul Kranendonk, associate pastor at the Community Reformed Church in Whiting, New Jersey, the Classis of New Brunswick has organized three new churches since 1975 in Ocean County, New Jersey. One is the Community Reformed Church, composed entirely of older adults. It was designed to minister to the "steady influx of retired people from the north and west into Ocean County. The church serves a retirement community and was designed to be a senior adult congregation.

"We have but one evening gathering per year—Christmas Eve. Consistory meetings, choir rehearsals, and guild meetings are all scheduled during the daytime. We have no youth group, no nursery, no Sunday School. What we do have is a happy, friendly, and active congregation of older adults," says Rev. Kranendonk. "Older adult Christians bring a depth of experience to their worship and witness. Bible study finds growing numbers of highly motivated participants. For a significant number of members, this is the richest time of their spiritual lives." But the pastor goes on to say, "Their vision goes beyond personal goals. It embraces the local church, the denomination, the church universal, and all of God's creation. Peace, Justice and the Integrity of Creation was the theme of last year's summer Bible school." Rev. Kranendonk concludes, "Ministry with older adults is a joyous privilege, and old age is a very special gift from God to be treasured and lived to his glory."[13]

Northside Baptist Church, in St. Petersburg, Florida, had a senior adult ministry headed by an associate pastor. When the pastor retired, seventy-year-old Chet Vanscoy volunteered to step into the vacancy. The Golden Heirs program was officially inaugurated, and for more than seven years, on every Thursday morning of the year, Chet has been holding meetings for senior adults in the St. Petersburg vicinity.

The weekly meetings are held in a large, open room at the church, and people gather early to share coffee, doughnuts, and fellowship. At the back of the busy room, ladies sell greeting cards and craft items made by fellow Golden Heirs. The money raised is put into a missions fund.

At ten o'clock, Chet calls the meeting to order. First-time visitors are recognized, anniversaries and birthdays are celebrated in song, and announcements are given. Everyone is made to feel at home. Every hand is shaken, and hugs are exchanged frequently.

Chet then introduces the morning's program, which could feature a singer, an attorney, a magician, or a doctor. The Salvation Army band has proven to be the most popular program, but when doctors come to speak, the question-and-answer session that follows can easily last an hour.

Northside Baptist Church provides the building and designates approximately four thousand dollars per year for the Golden Heirs ministry, but Chet and his fellow volunteers provide everything else. The *Golden Heirs Gazette,* a quarterly newsletter, is sent to five hundred homes in the area with news of upcoming programs, encouraging information, poignant poetry, and Chet's Column, "Reflections While Shaving." For older persons who may be homebound, the *Gazette* is a vital link to friends.

What is required to implement a program similar to Golden Heirs? "First, you need to find someone willing to devote time to it. Next, you need to realize that people who are sixty-five and over, or even fifty-five and over, may not want to come because they don't want to admit their age. When we first offered our yearly retreat, only 24 people signed up, but last year we took 135. It starts small, then begins to grow and build up. You have to promote it, offer interesting programs, and play by ear. People are different, churches are different, and pastors are different. You have to sit down with the sponsoring church staff and see what they want to accomplish with the program."

Not only are the Golden Heirs ministered *to,* they also minister to others. In addition to their mission fund, the group occasionally gets together to make crafts for nursing home residents. "We go out and sing carols at Christmas and give small gifts," Chet says.

Chet knows that perhaps the greatest need of seniors is to be wanted, and he tries to make his people feel needed. "Many of the group are widows and widowers, and there is a special ministry to this group. Many do not drive, so someone else volunteers to provide transportation to and from meetings. Others are particularly lonely, and they really need a friend or something to do to keep busy. They appreciate all you do, and they let you know it. They're glad to have a group to come to."[14]

YOU CAN BECOME POLITICALLY ACTIVE

As individuals, groups of individuals clustered in churches, and churches working together, Christians in America have unique opportunities to improve the lives of poor and near-poor older people across America. We can do this by supporting and strengthening national programs that have become the economic lifeline of so many of our older citizens. In a society that began primarily as a collection of farmers and frontier people, we have developed into a complex nation that is primarily urban and suburban, industrial, technological, and economically interdependent. When an economic slowdown hits one industry, others feel the consequences.

As a nation we are slowly and sometimes painfully beginning to realize that we are all economically interdependent. And hopefully we will begin to realize that as Americans of all ages, we should be concerned about the basic economic survival of everyone. We need to recognize and meet the needs of people of all ages so that the conflicts between the generations over Social Security and other benefits that some predict will occur as the number of older persons continues to increase will not happen. We are blessed to be Christians in America, where the very preamble to our U.S. Constitution includes the phrase "promote the general welfare." It is a cooperative goal for the whole of society, for the welfare and well-being of all.

What an opportunity for Christians to put into practice Christ's teachings about how the nations will be judged in regard to Matthew 25:31-46. We actually live in a nation that is designed from its foundation to allow anyone to work for the betterment of all. For vulnerable older Americans this means: (1) strengthening and supporting Social Security, SSI, and Medicare; (2) developing real catastrophic health coverage so that persons who worked all their lives and saved what they could will not have to spend themselves down into poverty for the first time in their lives in order to be supported by a welfare program called Medicaid to stay in a nursing home; (3) supporting job retraining programs for older people who are able and want to work to supplement their incomes and give themselves a feeling of being a part of productive America, but whose skills no longer match an ever-changing workplace; (4) developing adequate housing for low- to moderate-income older people through creative and cooperative financing plans; (5) initiating policies that give dignity to the words *senior citizens, older persons, third-agers,* or whatever term is used to describe older people in America; (6) developing ways to recognize the years women spend in child rearing, homemaking, volunteering, and caring for the sick and elderly in family settings that are the foundations of our families, but earn no credits toward Social Security or any other retirement plans; (7) developing policies and practices that result in treating women as equals in the workplace, especially in equal or comparable wages, promotions (which affect retirement benefits), and equal retirement benefit opportunities; (8) recognizing other areas of life where individual Christians and Christian communities can exercise their prophetic roles.

Too often we are caught up in the values and orientation of our materialistic society. It is important for us to heed the gospel and recognize our role in doing Christ's work in the world. It is our mandate. In this free land we have the opportunity as Christians to develop and support policies that will improve the lives of the vulnerable elderly among us through a variety of means.

Older Christians and their adult children have the opportunity to influence the ongoing development and administration of the Older Americans Act and other public programs so they can more efficiently and effectively meet the needs of the vulnerable older people who have given us the freedoms and opportunities we all enjoy. What you do as one person can make a real difference in your parents' lives. What we do collectively to promote policies and programs to assist older people can make a real difference in the lives of millions of vulnerable older Americans.

PART THREE

PART THREE

CHAPTER · NINE

Should Mom and Dad Leave Their Home?

Several years ago, my 76-year-old mother's life collapsed around her.

She was evicted from her home of 23 years because she hadn't been opening mail, and though she was certain she had made arrangements for the mortgage to be paid, she hadn't. Her blood pressure was out of control, she could barely walk even with assistance, in part because her legs were swollen and infected with sores from a fall she'd taken at the shopping center a month or two before. She had intended to see her doctor about her legs, but it had just seemed too hard. She wasn't eating or bathing regularly, and she was more or less incontinent. Up to that point, she had refused formal help, insisting she wanted no strangers in her house and could manage her own affairs.

How I, as her only daughter and at 39 the elder of her two children, could have let her situation deteriorate to this point is probably something only an adult child who has taken charge of a feisty, elderly parent clinging to their last shred of independence will understand.[1]— Amanda Spake, *Washington Post*

IMPORTANCE OF HOME

Even if you have not faced a situation as dramatic as Amanda Spake's, you may have to consider the possibility that someday your parents will have to leave their home. Before you think about the details of such a move, consider first the full meaning of the word *home* and all that it signifies.

We are taught to love our homes. You may even have one of the following common adages framed and hanging on a wall of your home:

Home Is Where the Heart Is.

Love Makes a House a Home.

Having somewhere to go is home; having someone to share is love; having both is a blessing.

God Bless Our Home.

At the most basic level, home is a shelter from the elements as well as the storms of life, a place to go after a hard day's work, and the center of the family. At its best, it represents a place of retreat, renewal, love, and sharing. It is the center of our human existence.

Throughout the Old and New Testaments, the Bible is filled with references to *home* and *house.* In Deuteronomy 24:5 we read, "A newly married man is not to be drafted into the army nor given any other special responsibilities; for a year he shall be free to be at home, happy with his wife." Here God considers the establishment of a home a top priority for newlyweds.

In 2 Corinthians 5:6, the concept of home is used to give Christians assurance of our destination for eternity. "Now we look forward with confidence to our heavenly bodies, realizing that every moment we spend in these earthly bodies is time spent away from our eternal home in heaven with Jesus."

The word *house* is also used in many ways in the Bible. It means a place to live; the family living in a house; kin, lineage, or relation; a place in which we worship God. Jesus visited people in their houses, their homes. In John 14:2-3, Jesus referred to the concept of home when he said: "There are many homes up there where my Father lives, and I am going to prepare them for your coming. When everything is ready, then I will come and get you, so that you can always be with me where I am."

For the Christian, then, home is not only the center of family and earthly life, but a place that is promised and prepared for in heaven for eternity.

IMPORTANCE AND TIES OF HOME
TO OLDER PEOPLE

Unlike our ultimate heavenly home, our earthly home can develop problems. For our old parents, these can become so severe that it might be better for them to move from the old homestead to a different type of residence.

About 75 percent of older people live in their own single-family houses. This should not be surprising. Home ownership is a goal for most Americans. Because of a strong work ethic, generally rising incomes for most Americans in this century, and the availability of mortgage money in the past (VA loans, FHA loans, bank and savings-and-loan mortgages), millions of working Americans were able to purchase and pay for their homes over twenty to thirty years.

Home ownership has been a blessing that has been part of the American lifestyle during our parents' lives. The home your parents own gives them ties to past memories. Unless they become dissatisfied with their house or neighborhood, your parents are probably strongly attached to their home.

Doris and Harry Oakes are in their early 60s and responsible for Harry's 88-year-old mother, who lives alone in her home. They worry constantly about her safety, while she staunchly wishes to remain where she has been for 60 years.

"It's hard to leave a house where all the memories are," Harry Oakes said wistfully.[2]

Your parents may have lived in their home for thirty years or more. Perhaps they have been in the same house since they were first able to get enough money for a down payment. The house they live in may be where they first established their identity as a family unit. Their home is where they raised their children. Your mother prayed for you in her bedroom, she cooked your meals in the kitchen, and your father repaired the family car and spent Saturdays mowing the lawn. Your parents' home has been their shelter from the storms of life.

Their home is also the place of gathering for the children after they have left and established their own homes. It is where they bring grandchildren to visit. For widows and widowers, home is a constant reminder of their life's companion.

Home is the center of life for older people because they spend most of their time there. They no longer go off to work each day or off to many meetings or shopping trips. When they do go out, it is usually to familiar shops, stores, or church activities.

As your parents age, their world contracts and begins to revolve more and more around their home and neighborhood because their lives are more restricted. Because younger Americans live fast-paced, mobile lives, they find it hard to understand the reality of a restricted life. But restrictions are well understood by many aging parents.

If you are attempting to help your parents remain in their home, you should first analyze the home itself. The homes in which most older people live are typically more than forty years old, too large for the couple or remaining spouse, energy inefficient, and located in an older, often deteriorating part of the community. Your parents' home is probably not equipped for older people. It may have too many stairs, steps that are too steep, laundry facilities in the basement, and no safety rails on the stairs or in the bathrooms.

In short, too many people live in houses designed for younger families in an earlier time. Too many older parents are overhoused and living in facilities not designed to accommodate their needs as they continue to age. This does not mean that all people should move as they grow old. It does mean that we need to look at the condition of their homes to see if they meet the changing needs older people have.

The housing needs of older people differ from person to person. There is no typical older person. Although we can notice percentages and trends, older people react differently to the circumstances of life. Some older people love to travel and move about. In recent times, with retirement lasting up to a third of a person's life, we have seen dramatic changes in the way many older people have been able to enjoy their later years. Many of even modest means were able to purchase second homes or mobile homes or travel trailers. As a result, they were able to follow their dreams throughout the year, spending months in a second home.

Some older people, after seeing their children grow and leave home, looked for alternative living arrangements in their local communities that were more suitable to their changing circumstances. Some bought efficient and secure condominiums. Some bought mobile homes or rented efficiency apartments. Some, in their early retirement years, bought into life-care agreements in retirement villages, where they are looked after regardless of their condition.

Most older people, however, have remained in their old homes in their old neighborhoods. Even the adventurous elderly who bought a second home, mobile home, or condo in Florida or some other southern state held on to their home in their old neighborhood for the sake of family, friends, church ties, and to keep a feeling of rootedness.

Many of the snowbirds who spend several winter months in Florida or other warmer climates come back to their old neighborhoods and homes when they grow too old to travel back and forth. Rather than retiring permanently in sunnier climes, they choose to live the rest of their days in old familiar surroundings back home.

So how can you help your elderly parents who want to stay in their home? Can you make it easier for them? How long can they manage independently?

STAYING IN THEIR OWN HOME

Older people should be free to stay in their own homes as long as possible. Most older people prefer to be in their own homes. It gives them a feeling of independence and self-direction. It enhances their self-worth and self-esteem. Most of the homes of the elderly are paid for. Helping them stay in their own homes, therefore, is the most economical way to house older people in America.

What does this mean for you? If your parents are in the age group between sixty-five and seventy-five and have no pressing medical conditions that severely limit their activities, it should not be difficult for them to stay at home. It is helpful if one of your parents is able to drive in daylight. It is also helpful if they are able to cook, clean, visit friends, get out when they want to, and do all the things people normally do. But as the aging process continues, the ability to do all these things and maintain independent living begins to decrease. Sooner or later, someone will have to be called to help with one or more of the tasks necessary to maintain their home. Most often, you will be the person called.

At first the demands may be few: a call every day or so to see how the folks are and see if they need anything, or maybe a little help with shopping for something they can't find. Perhaps your parents will ask for help in finding a specialist for a stubborn skin problem or will need a ride to see that specialist. No big deal, just a little help now and then.

But as the years go on, your parents may become less able to manage on their own, and their demands, subtle or not so subtle, may increase. Studies indicate that about 80 percent of the help given to aged parents so they can remain in their own home is provided by the family, primarily by children who themselves may be approaching retirement age.[3]

As an adult caregiving child, you may find yourself needing help. As the stress of caring for your parents grows, you may wonder if the work of keeping your parents in their own home is worth the hassle.

In order to prevent the stress from overwhelming you, you need to know that you are not alone. There are many others like you in the "sandwich generation," and, like you, they have found themselves reaching out for help. Fortunately, that help is often available in your community, sometimes in your church. You do not have to carry the burden of caring for your parents alone. No one benefits if children get so involved in providing for the needs of their aging parents that they ignore their own lives and families. It is important to know what resources are available in your community and to use the assistance that can make your caregiving easier.

MAKING THE OLD HOUSE LIVABLE

If you want to make your parents' home more livable for them, the first place to start is with the house itself. Have someone take your folks out for the day, or involve them directly in a "spruce up" project. Try to see the house from your parents' perspective. You don't want to move your mother's treasured knickknacks, but you want to make the house safer and more pleasant.

You might want to begin with a call to your electric or gas utility. Many electric companies, for a nominal fee or no charge at all, will tour a home and make suggestions about how to improve energy efficiency. One of the most important conditions for the comfort and health of older people is to have the house warm enough. Older people are susceptible to hypothermia, a lowering of body temperature that can lead to death. Unlike you, older people are not comfortable at sixty-eight or seventy degrees. They will probably want the house to be seventy-five degrees or warmer. This may require the addition of insulation, particularly in the ceiling where most of the heat escapes. It may mean adding storm windows and doors if there are none. It may mean replacing an old furnace that is inefficient and possibly unsafe.

Older people require brighter lighting without glare. This is important for reading, moving about, identifying dials on the stove, using the bathroom, and all the activities of daily living.[4] It may mean adding light fixtures and lamps as well as using larger wattage "soft light" bulbs while trying to avoid or reduce glare at all times.[5]

Numbers on appliances, telephones, and thermostats need to be large. Contrasting colors are useful. It helps to have the dials on the stove in the front of the burners. Reaching over a hot burner to turn a dial has caught too many sleeves on fire.

Slippery floors should be avoided. This applies to overpolished wood or tile floors. Throw rugs should not be used. It is often too hard to see the edges of throw rugs, and they are easy to trip over. Also, they slide easily and can cause a fall. The house should be made as "fall-proof" as possible. Adequate electrical outlets are needed to eliminate the use of extension cords or long cords that can be tripped over.

Steps are to be avoided if at all possible. Ideally, the laundry room should be on the first floor. This is also true of a bathroom. Steps are barriers for many elderly people. If it is absolutely necessary to use the stairs, install a sturdy handrail.

Handles on faucets need to turn easily. Doors should open and shut smoothly. Windows should work easily enough to be opened by older people with arthritis and decreased strength.[6]

Special attention should be given to the bathroom. The bathroom is one of the most dangerous areas in the house for falls. Special attention needs to be given to make it bright and as slip-proof as possible.

Raised toilets can be installed to help old people get up from the toilet. If this is not feasible, raised toilet seats can be added to compensate for loss of strength in older peoples' legs. The bathtub needs to be made safe by adding solid grab bars and applying nonslip material to the bottom of the tub.

Various things can be done in the home to compensate for hearing loss. Devices can be added to increase the sound of the telephone's ring and voices over the phone. Extra-loud doorbells can be installed. Wall-to-wall carpeting reduces background noise in the house, noise that contributes to the confusion of the hearing impaired. Most older people welcome these types of alterations to the home to make it more livable if they don't cost too much money.

Many older people stay in their old homestead because they can't afford anything better. Many don't fix up their houses to meet their changing needs because they don't think they can afford renovations. In some instances, children of aging parents are able to help their parents afford better housing. Sometimes they are able to help them fix up their old home to meet the types of needs we have outlined.

Often, however, the children are not able or willing to spend the amount of money necessary to move their parents to new housing or help them fix up their old house. Many are helping their own children with gifts or loans. Others are trying to save enough for their own retirement, which is either at hand or coming soon. What can be done to help the folks without exhausting a person's own resources?

REAL ESTATE BREAKS FOR OLDER PEOPLE

It is important for children and their aging parents to be aware of and use the real estate tax breaks that are available in some form in every state in the nation. They have different names in different states. Some are called "circuit breaker" programs, which give total or partial relief from property taxes that exceed a certain percentage of a person's income. Others are called "homestead exemption" programs and exclude a dollar amount or share from the valuation of property against which taxes are levied.

Home ownership can be a financial plus in older age. Older people usually do not have a monthly house payment. About 80 percent of the houses occupied by the elderly are owned free and clear. A new tool, the "equity conversion mortgage" or "reverse mortgage" can help older people convert their equity in their home to a monthly cash payment. Although the values of the homes older people own are generally less than those of younger people, most have risen in value since they were purchased. Reverse mortgages are offered by some banks or lending institutions to help older people who are "house-rich but cash-poor."

"It is the exact opposite of a mortgage," says David Zalles, a Philadelphia accountant. "Instead of paying money in, you take money out on a monthly basis."[7] Under a reverse mortgage, the lending bank agrees to pay a fixed monthly annuity to the homeowners for the duration of their lives, based upon their ages and the equity in the home. At the time of the last homeowner's death, the bank takes title to the house, sells it, compensates itself for the interest already paid in the annuity, and the balance goes to the heirs. At any time, however, the homeowners can change their mind about living at home and terminate the agreement.[8] The house can be sold, the bank repaid, and the homeowners free to move.

The disadvantage of this arrangement is that usually there is little money from the sale of the home passed on to the heirs. The advantage is that the older people are able to stay in the house as long as they live and get a monthly check to live on to supplement their income.

Many gas and electrical utilities will help low-income elderly people. Older people can apply for special rates and for assurance against cutoffs, which is vital to their health and life because older people do not tolerate cold or hot temperatures well. In addition, many gas and electric utility companies make low-cost loans available to the elderly to insulate their homes, making them more energy efficient. This is important to keep a house warm and free of drafts.

COMMUNITY RESOURCES AND SERVICES

Many of the provisions of the Older Americans Act focus on providing services to help older people remain in their own homes as long as possible. Some of these services of the OAA include information and referral; transportation; nutrition services; meals on wheels; in-home care, including home health aids; homemaker chore services; and case management.[9] Not all of these services are funded and available in every community.

MEALS PROGRAMS

Many OAA funds are spent on meals programs. Proper nutrition is vital to life, but many older people lose the ability or interest to prepare balanced meals, especially if they live alone. Poor nutrition has been found to be the cause of a range of physical and mental problems in older people. Therefore, one of the basic goals of the nutrition programs of the OAA is to get people to come out of their homes, if possible, to eat nutritious meals together. No charge is made for these meals, but those who can afford it are asked to contribute to the cost of the meal.

Meals on Wheels provides one good meal a day for older

people who can't get to a senior meals program. It is a great help to the older person who is not able to prepare a balanced, nutritious meal as well as to their children who know that Mom and Dad will have a balanced meal delivered to their home.

CASE MANAGEMENT

Mr. and Mrs. Smith live in a semirural area. Everything was fine for them until Mr. Smith had a heart attack at age eighty-five. Mrs. Smith doesn't drive, and she had always depended on Mr. Smith driving her to the store every week to do their shopping.

Mrs. Smith also has severe arthritis and has paid a helper to come in and help with cleaning and cooking. The Smiths' daughter and her family live fifty miles away and usually visit on Sundays, but they are busy the rest of the week.

When Mr. Smith was scheduled to come home from the hospital, his daughter was worried. What should be done? He couldn't drive anymore, so who would do their shopping? Should they be put in a nursing home? What if they had to be separated?

A case management team—a social worker and a nurse—was invited into the Smiths' home. Their help was offered free of charge under provisions of the OAA. The case workers talked to Mr. and Mrs. Smith and found out exactly what kinds of help they needed. Then the case workers decided what services could realistically be offered by family, friends, or neighbors, and which needs could best be met by private and public agencies whose business is serving older people.

Working together with family and community-based services, the Smiths were able to stay in their own home. The woman who helped with cleaning was retained. A home health nurse was brought in to provide Mr. Smith with nursing services as he recovered from his heart attack. A Red Cross volunteer drove Mr. Smith to his doctor appointments. Someone else was found to take Mrs. Smith shopping. Although this arrangement resulted in some additional costs for the Smiths, staying in their own home with help was much less expensive than going to an institution, and they much preferred to stay together at home. And even though Mrs. Smith had people coming in to help her, she was still in charge in her own home.

This approach is very reassuring for the daughter and son-in-law of the Smiths, who know that the needs of their parents have been professionally evaluated and provided for without taxing their strength, resources, or endurance. It is a great way to lower their stress and frustration levels in caring for their aging parents. It is important for you to become aware of and use the services available in most communities across the nation for older people.

Laura DeHope is a social worker with a service for aging adults. She spends most of her workday visiting seniors in their homes and helping them come up with ways to care for themselves. "People of this age are hesitant to let a social worker come into their home, but we tell them that their tax dollars are paying for this," DeHope says. "Sometimes they see us as taking their decision making away from them. They've lost so much already, they want to hold on to what little they have control over."[10]

OTHER SUPPORT SYSTEMS
Other services that allow older people to remain in their own homes include "ring-a-day" or "chat-a-day" programs, which are usually organized by the Red Cross, community agencies, or churches. These programs check on elderly people who live alone by calling them every day to see if they are all right, or by having a conversation with them each day to provide some companionship as well as to check on their welfare.

Another high-tech resource that provides peace of mind to older people living alone is an electronic device that transmits a signal to a participating hospital or service agency. If the older person wears the device around his neck, he can simply push a button if medical help is needed. While these devices can be quite expensive to purchase or lease and usually have high ongoing maintenance fees, some local hospitals and community agencies offer these services at much more reasonable rates. It is a good idea to check around for the best service at the best price.

> According to Janet Nassif [author of *The Home Health Care Solution: A Complete Consumer Guide*[11]], using a for-profit care-finding or case management firm can be convenient "for persons who must arrange for care at long distance." It might also be convenient for those who can readily afford these services. But the best home health agencies make their own in-home assessments and help find other needed services. If you hire a case-management firm, Nassif says, "Check credentials. . . . Deal only with services staffed by professional licensed or certified social workers. Ask for customer references. Discuss all fees in advance."
>
> A national home care association says: "How an agency treats you when you call can be very revealing. . . . You don't have to tolerate insensitivity. . . . After your talk with the agency nurse or coordinator, answer these questions yourself: Did the agency representative put you at ease? Was he/she knowledgeable and did he/she instill a sense of confidence? . . . Were your questions answered completely? Were you rushed? Do you feel you could discuss any problem with this agency's personnel? Do you feel the agency will respond promptly to correct any problems?"[12]

If you want your parents to stay in their own home, you should investigate what services are available in your community. Some services will be available free of charge, and others may charge a fee. You should investigate the nature of these services and encourage your parents to use them when they are needed and can be afforded.

WHEN IT'S TIME TO MOVE

Question: I am writing to seek advice for my mother, who is in her 70s and living alone in her home of 45 years. The house is paid for and taxes on it are about $2,300 a year.

Answer: You're going through the same wrenching decision that hundreds of thousands of middle-aged Americans are going through every day in trying to do the best possible thing for their aging parents.

The piece of the equation that is missing here, however, is just how does your mother feel about this? Is she relatively comfortably fixed financially? Is her health robust enough to handle the hassle of maintaining a single-family residence?

From a tax standpoint, selling should be no problem for her—up to $125,000 of gain that she has in her house is sheltered. Investing this at, say 8 percent, would give her an annual income of about $10,000 or roughly $833 a month and, of course, she would also escape the $2,300-a-year property tax bite.—Don Campbell, *Los Angeles Times*[13]

Sometimes, in spite of planning, effort, the coordination of services, and a strong desire by older people to stay in their home, the time may come for elderly parents to move to some other living arrangement. Your parent may plan to move or be forced to move because of illness or chronic health conditions.

Few people plan to move from their own home. Perhaps your

parents will be among the few people who realize that someday the demands of keeping a big house will be too much. Perhaps your mother will realize that a four-bedroom house is too big for her to live in alone. Your parents may want to take advantage of the IRS provision that after age fifty-five they can sell their home without having to pay any tax on as much as $125,000 profit. This money can go toward paying for living arrangements more appropriate to older people. Many older people sell their principal residence and move to apartments, condominiums, or mobile homes in two sections of the country so they can enjoy relatively good weather year around.

Other older people buy into a life-care agreement with a retirement home or village that will offer them a place to live as long as they live, from independent living to a nursing home setting.[14]

Planned moves are best made after discussions between the older folks and their children. If your parents see the benefits of making a move while they are still active and healthy, their lives may be made much easier in the long run.

Most moves for older people, however, occur after a sudden and severe illness or injury. This is particularly true for older people who live alone, or for those very old people whose spouse is too weak or frail to care for them. Some old people suffer illnesses or injuries that require such a high level of personal care that they are not able to return home after their stay in an acute-care hospital. They may have suffered a stroke that requires around-the-clock nursing care, or they may be in the later stage of Alzheimer's disease, where the spouse just can't cope any longer.

Many of these situations strike quite suddenly, and an alternate living situation needs to be found quickly. This is a time of great stress for the children of aging parents who feel they must make these decisions. If this situation arises, you need to know whom to call about options and alternatives.

A hospital's discharge planner usually can give valuable help in finding an extended-care facility. Your pastor may have had experience visiting long-term care facilities and may be able to make suggestions in addition to offering support and comfort. Among your friends or within your church there may be others who have been in the same situation. They can be a real source of help, support, and guidance. Being able to talk and share your feelings and concerns with another person who has gone through the experience can be very helpful.

John and Mary sold their home when they were in their sixties. It was a nice home in the suburbs, and they earned a pretty good profit on their original investment. They bought a new cottage on a northern lake for a reasonable price in 1969. The same year they bought a mobile home in a nice park in Florida. For twenty-five years they traveled back and forth between their lake home in the North and their mobile home in Florida. When John was eighty-seven, they decided they could no longer make the trip to Florida each year. Both John and Mary had developed health conditions that worsened gradually as they got older. Also, most of their friends in Florida, who were mainly from their church in the North, either died or were not able to go to Florida any longer. Although they made new friends over the years in Florida, they became more and more isolated when John could no longer drive on the busy roads. Like so many of her generation, Mary did not drive.

Back home up North, they decided to spend the winter in their home on the lake. Although they were happy on the lake and had help with some services from close neighbors, they had forgotten how long the winter could be. John had no indoor place to walk for exercise. Their adult children, who had their own families, lived fifty miles away, and became busier in the fall and winter and were not able to visit as much.

In the spring John's heart condition got worse, requiring a two-week hospital stay in the city. Separated and vulnerable,

147

John and Mary began to think that maybe it was time to consider a move to a retirement home or village close to their children, where they could enjoy walking in indoor corridors, eating balanced meals with new friends, and feeling the security of knowing they were not alone if a medical crisis occurred.

Even when an older person's home is compact, efficient, and surrounded by caring neighbors, he or she may be forced to move because of an ongoing decline in his or her mental or physical condition. Some may want to be closer to their children. Their level of dependence may have increased to the point where outside services provided in the home for daily living are inadequate, unrealistic, or too expensive. Sometimes these services simply are not available.

Some older people must move because the physical condition of their old house has deteriorated to the point where it no longer meets their needs. Or their neighborhood may have deteriorated so that it is no longer safe. Some old neighborhoods have lost basic services such as grocery stores. When the old person is no longer able to drive, or does not want to, it may be time to look for a living arrangement that does not depend on transportation for basic daily living.

In their lake home, John and Mary missed daily contact with other people. Isolation may cause older people to look for alternative housing arrangements. Being confined because of severe weather for long periods of time may lead to lack of exercise, which can contribute to health problems for older persons.

Finally, some older folks must move because the caregivers who have helped them remain in their home finally give out. If you have spent several years caring for your aging parents in their home, you may come to realize that a move would be best for all of you.

The demands and stresses on the adult caregiver can be great. If outside services for your parents are not adequate or available, you need to realize there is only so much you can do. Most of us want to help keep our parents in their own home as long as possible, but we need to recognize that there are practical limitations to this goal. The key to success in this is to do your best in trying to help your aging parents stay in their home for as long as possible by using the support systems in the community that can help them with the tasks of daily living. But you must realize when certain limitations are reached. When you and your parents can no longer cope, it is time to move.

> Katheryn Swalm, 92, was widowed in 1924 and supported herself by teaching. She still manages the three-flight hike to her apartment and, despite her failing eyesight, is determined to stay in her own home. But after hearing so many options [at a meeting of retirement and health-care facilities operators], she acknowledged that her mind might be changed.
>
> "This has given me food for thought," she said.
>
> Catherine McCall, a spokeswoman from the Burlington County Office on Aging, said that winning the older person's trust when making a change is a battle not easily won. She said that a forum such as this could make a decision to get outside help less traumatizing.
>
> —Barbara E. Sorid, *Philadelphia Inquirer*[15]

CHAPTER TEN

Should Mom and Dad Move In with Me?

When Patricia Anderson's eighty-year-old father came to live with her family a year ago, it was a major adjustment for both of them. "My dad just followed me around," Anderson said. "No matter where I go, he wants to go because he's bored."

He couldn't go anywhere by himself because of recent cataract surgery, she said. And Anderson found it difficult to get out of the house because she was afraid to leave him alone.

"It was very hard because I am busy, believe me," said Anderson, who has children at home and helps with her husband's business. "It gets pretty hard to be on call 24 hours."[1]

Remember Jennie and Jim from the introduction to this book? Well, after Jennie's mom died, Jennie had her hands full helping her dad keep up his house while she kept up hers. She cooked some of her dad's meals, did his grocery shopping, and helped with his cleaning. She and her husband, Jim, wondered if it would be easier and cheaper for all of them if Dad sold the old family home and moved in with them. Even though they lived in a three-bedroom house with only one bathroom, her sons were growing up and were away at college nine months of the year.

Dad was lonely in the old house, and Jennie felt guilty thinking of her father in some living arrangement other than the family setting. She felt it was her responsibility as a loving daughter to have him move in with them. Wasn't this what families were supposed to do? Jennie thought so. Besides, she thought having Dad in her home would give her some free time so she could go back to work.

After much discussion, she and Jim asked Dad to move in with them. They'd sell his home and take over one of the boys' rooms for Dad. The boys had shared a room when they were small, and they could do so again.

Suddenly their three-bedroom home got much smaller. With only one television in the living room, recreation time became tense. Dad liked a whole different set of TV programs than did Jennie and Jim. The boys' music, while tolerated by Jennie and Jim, was absolutely intolerable for Dad. Even though it was contemporary Christian rock, Dad thought it was of the devil. He'd never heard anything like it before.

The boys began hanging out in the small, damp rec room in the basement. Jennie found she couldn't even retreat to a private corner to take a telephone call. Dad took too long in the bathroom, and Jennie began to wonder what would happen when she and Jim invited friends over. Did she automatically have to include her father? Or could she tactfully ask him to find somewhere else to go for the evening?

While trying to be a dutiful daughter, Jennie didn't think through the possibility for conflict and everyone's basic need for privacy, fellowship, and relaxation. She simply overlooked planning.

Planning for what a person might do in the future gives both the aging parents and their children the opportunity to examine options before life-changing events take place. These events will occur at some time in most everyone's life, so it is wise to look at possibilities that could make particular situations better. For example, did Jennie's dad have any close friends or relatives his own age with whom he might be able to share a house or an apartment? Were there any retirement homes or villages that would be affordable and acceptable? Did Jennie's dad have any friends in any of these living arrangements? Why hadn't Jennie's dad looked around at these options during the extended illness of his wife? Couldn't he see that asking Jennie to keep up two homes and drive him to stores, doctor's appointments, church services and meetings, and meals three or four times a week was too much to ask of a loving daughter?

SHOULD YOU INVITE YOUR PARENTS INTO YOUR HOME?

Should a loving daughter throw open the doors of her own home to an aged parent? Consider these basic questions before making a decision:

CAN YOU TOLERATE EACH OTHERS' LIFESTYLES?

Have you and your parents recognized that different generations have different tastes in food, music, conversation, and clothing? One generation will like one set of television shows; another will prefer movies on the VCR. One generation will like going to bed early in peace and quiet, another will enjoy staying up late and sleeping with the radio or television on.

CAN YOU RELATE TO EACH OTHER AS MATURE ADULTS?

Two generations can usually tolerate each other fairly well, particularly in a parent-child relationship where the children are in some way still dependent upon their parents. But when a third generation comes into the household, family dynamics change. Although they may love each other dearly, the aged parent and the middle-aged child usually have lived apart for ten, twenty, or thirty years. The middle-aged child is a child no longer. Not only has she become used to her independence, but she is

153

literally not the same person she was when she last lived with her parents.

"All of a sudden, I was an eight-year-old girl again, trying to please my parents," says Cindy, a thirty-two-year-old woman whose elderly parents moved in with her eight months ago. "You slip right back into the pattern of 'mommy and daddy and kid'—and it's a shock."[2]

"In an argument, you revert back to the person you used to be as a kid instead of the person you've learned to be as an adult," explains Susan Scott, a psychotherapist who leads a support group for adult children of aging parents.[3]

It is not fair or logical for the old folks to expect their middle-aged children to react in a child's role. Those expectations are unrealistic. In a close living situation, differences become evident and tensions can easily arise. Change is difficult for older folks to deal with, and the different lifestyles of dissimilar generations usually surface as problems. It is important to recognize these possible differences in lifestyles before Mom or Dad moves into your home.

DOES YOUR HOME HAVE ADEQUATE SPACE?
Adequate physical space and privacy can simplify problems. If one or both of your parents are going to live successfully and happily with you, they need to feel that they have their own space. Both Jennie and Jim felt they had given up their privacy and independence when Dad moved in with them, because they had only one bathroom and one sitting room. At the same time, Dad felt out of place when Jennie and Jim's friends came to visit. The boys loved Grandpa, but they resented the fact they no longer had their own rooms.

Space is very important to successful intergenerational living. A family doesn't have to be rich and live in a mansion to make this arrangement work, but they do have to be open and willing to see if their home is adequate or appropriate for this type of living arrangement.

Ed, Jane, their children, and Ed's parents were a close-knit, loving family. Ed's father died unexpectedly of a heart attack at age sixty-two, and Ed's mother carried on in the old homestead, even though she missed her husband and frequently got lonely. The old house was too big for her and too costly to heat. Ed's mother came over two to four times a week to eat dinner with Ed and his family, and she continued to drive, stay in contact with her friends, and attend her church meetings and other activities.

When Ed's twenty-four-year-old daughter planned to get married, Ed and Jane asked Ed's mother if she'd like to move in with them. Ed and Jane's house wasn't a mansion, but an older two-story home with four large bedrooms, one with its own small bath, a large living room, a den, and a recreation room in the basement. Their home was close to schools, shopping, and their church.

After much discussion, Ed, Jane, and Ed's mother decided the move would benefit everyone. Ed knew his mother's house would sell easily, and with the additional spare bedroom, Ed's mother would have her own private space. She could entertain her friends in the living room while Ed and Jane had guests in the den. Their teenage son could listen to his music in the rec room, and no one got in anyone else's way. Best of all, Ed's mother could keep her car and her independence, since she didn't have to drive far to maintain her usual schedule of meetings and activities.

Ed's mother kept her home for a year, just to make sure things worked out, and she also investigated other living options. But Ed and Jane's situation has worked well, primarily because they talked about possible problems before they surfaced, and each generation had space for privacy and conversation with friends.

Remember Jennie? She asked her father to live with her out

of a sense of duty. Ed and Jane invited his mother to live with them because they knew it would be practical and workable.

MYTHS AND REALITIES OF EARLY FAMILY LIFE IN AMERICA

Most people in America believe that today's families are radically different from the families of yesteryear. Obviously, much has changed. Modern divorce rates have soared from earlier periods. Fast-paced and materialistic lifestyles surround us. We have become a disposable society, using and wasting the earth's resources at a breakneck pace. Most of us take too little time for the really important aspects of life and too much time on trivial things that bombard us every day.

Contrary to common belief, what hasn't changed in American family life is our living arrangements. Most people like Jennie and Jim believe that they should automatically ask their aging parents to move in with them. Jennie thought of "The Waltons," where three generations lived together in a rambling house and everybody pitched in to keep the family together. Problems were always solved in a television hour. Why couldn't they be solved in her home? When their situation did not work out, Jennie and Jim were knee-deep in guilt.

The Waltons did not reflect the average American family. Clark Tibbitts, an expert on the study of aging, wrote: "It is now clear that the nuclear parent-child family has always been the modal family type in the United States and three-generation families have always been relatively rare."[4]

Even in American colonial families, the three generation family was an exception, not the rule. Some of the evidence for this conclusion comes from the examination of family wills in Plymouth Colony.[5] Another study of Massachusetts family life in the seventeenth century distinguished between the family of residence, which was nuclear, and the family of interaction or obligation, which was termed "modified extended family."[6] This was a kinship group of two or more generations living in a single community (not a single house), who were dependent on each other.

Additional studies in New England indicate that "married adults lived with their own children and apart from all other relatives."[7] The concept of three generations living together was not the ideal, normal, or preferred way of life in the American colonies. When it did occur, it was necessary because of some tragedy. The desire for independence, privacy, and control over one's own life is not a modern family development.

Whether we live in separate homes, apartments, condominiums, mobile homes, or retirement villages, the concept of being independent and yet depending on extended family members is alive and well. We want to be as independent as possible in managing and living our own life on a day-to-day basis, but we want to know that we can call on our extended family members if they are needed.

This can be called the independent-dependent family, close but not living together.[8] This independence-dependence works in both directions for older and younger family members. In fact, this whole process works best when each generation has something to offer to the other, whether it is financial help, assistance with personal needs, psychological support in tough situations, or baby-sitting. The ability of each generation to contribute to the needs of other family members in the independent-dependent process enables each person to develop a sense of self-esteem.

In our culture there has never been an emphasis on older people moving in with a grown child's family unless it was necessary. You might feel obligated to offer your home to your parents, but if you are honest, you and your parents might be better off considering an alternative living arrangement. There are two instances in which you might not have a choice: if there is not enough money to pay for any other living arrangement, or if your parent has become so ill that he cannot provide for his own personal day-to-day living.

If you have debated moving your parent into your home, make sure you are not doing it out of misguided notions of tradition or duty. Don't automatically assume that your mom or dad would prefer to move in with you. It is very likely that your parents would prefer to live away from you, not because they don't love you, but because they value their independence.

If you investigate an alternate living arrangement, you are not abandoning your parents or being disloyal. Most adult children in America are committed to their parents. If you do find an alternative living arrangement for your parents, it is very likely that you will continue to visit, call, and care for them.

WHEN MOM OR DAD MUST MOVE IN

A temporary crisis may require you to move your parents in with you, but as soon as the crisis is over, it may be in your best interests to help your parents reevaluate their living arrangements. Don't let your sense of obligation and duty blind you to the daily realities and changes in lifestyle your entire family will have to make if your parents move into your home.

Peter and Diane have a close-knit family. Peter's mother, who lived two miles away, has been widowed for ten years and managed to maintain her home. Everything was fine until she fell and broke her hip.

Peter's mother was hospitalized for a time, but being immobile and on medication made her chronic conditions worse. Her general health failed rather quickly, and Peter and Diane felt they should do something to help her until she was able to regain her strength. Peter's sister, Jane, lived on the other side of the state and spent most of her time caring for her sick husband. So where should Peter's mother go to recuperate? She couldn't go to Jane's, so were Diane and Peter expected to take her in?

Diane wasn't ready to become a total caregiver. She wanted to help, but she didn't want to give up her job to stay home and care for Peter's mother. Peter and Diane needed to find another solution.

Diane's story is not an isolated one. Stories like hers are repeated over and over every day across America. What should we do with Mom and Dad when they can no longer take care of themselves in their own home? Who is responsible? Who will do the work? Who will sit with them through the night when they are in pain, confused, or lonely?

The answers to these types of questions in modern America are often difficult to find for many people. They don't know where to look. Among all the free industrialized nations of the world, we are the only one without an overall national policy to take care of these situations. We are the only one without systematic policies and programs to help families provide for the care of sick elderly parents. Some people think that if a lot of help were provided for families in this type of situation, the families would not accept their responsibilities toward their parents. This may be true in some instances. But research data from many sources do not bear this out.[9] Most Americans want to help their parents. This is particularly true where the elderly parents have become too ill or too feeble to care for themselves.

When an ill or frail parent moves into an adult child's home, that child becomes the total caregiver. Most of the burden for around-the-clock care falls on the middle-aged women in the family—the daughter or daughter-in-law. It is important to recognize that this person can quickly become one of the most vulnerable persons in the whole family. It is particularly tough for the person who is caring for an ill parent in their own home. What can be done to help these in-home caregivers? What can they do to help themselves? Realizing that most people in America feel obligated to help their sick and frail elderly parents, sometimes even caring for them around the clock in their own homes, what can caregivers do to help them? Where can they turn for help?

In Diane's case, she first called the local Area Agency on Aging and found out what programs were available for her mother-in-law. She found out that Meals on Wheels would deliver a nutritious hot lunch while she was at work. Better yet, once Peter's mother could be transported, she could attend the adult day-care center in town.

ADULT DAY-CARE CENTERS

In addition to home health care services available through community organizations and some other for-profit agencies, there are other services available to people like Diane who cannot stay at home day and night to give an older person around-the-clock care. Other programs exist to give full-time caregivers much-needed breaks.

Gerry D'Arcy runs The Tender, Incorporated, a social adult day-care center in Moorestown, New Jersey. This care center is for senior adults with health problems that don't require extensive medical attention. The cost is about twenty-eight dollars per day, but some families might be eligible for reduced fees under Medicaid programs.[10]

"This population is very much at risk of being prematurely placed in institutions simply because caretakers have no respite from their duties," D'Arcy says. "They just can't take any more. What do you do with an aged parent when you have to work but can't leave him or her alone?"[11]

Adult day-care centers provide a range of services including screening for physical conditions; medical care that is generally arranged with an outside physician; nursing care; occupational, physical, and recreational therapy; social work; transportation; meals; personal care that includes such things as help with going to the toilet; educational programs; crafts; and counseling. Not all adult day-care centers offer all of these programs. It is important to check to see what is offered at each center that might be helpful for your parent.

Unlike senior centers, adult day-care programs and centers are usually not "drop-in" situations. They are generally offered on a five-day-a-week basis with folks going a regular number of days each week (up to five) on an eight-hour basis. Adult day-care centers offer the caregiving adult child a wonderful opportunity to continue to work or get back to a job to earn income and/or participate in an activity outside the home that gives the adult child real satisfaction. It provides them with the opportunity to get away from the ongoing responsibilities of caring for a frail, dependent, aged parent.

Funding for this type of program comes from a variety of sources including Medicaid, Social Services Block Grants, Title III of the Older Americans Act, and fees paid by the recipients and their families. These centers may be located in an independent facility, a senior center, a neighborhood center, a hospital, or a church.

Some churches have recognized the burden that caring around the clock for elderly parents can be for caregivers. Some of these churches have established adult day-care programs as part of their outreach ministries to help their members and community residents in these tough situations. This is a marvelous way to involve Christians in recognizing and helping those in need in the church and in the community.

RESPITE CARE

Another form of help for the caregiver is something called respite care. The elderly person requiring care on an ongoing basis is placed in a nursing home, group home, or hospital, or is looked after in their own residence by a trained caregiver for a relatively short time so that the primary caregiver can have some time off from their ongoing responsibilities. The length of the assistance ranges from a few hours to a weekend.

This type of service is relatively new and generally underfunded by our social support systems. Some are being developed on a fee basis. Although this is still the least available type of community service to help caregivers, a recent study indicated that it ranked at the top when caregivers asked what help they needed most.[12] This type of service could be an excellent project for a church that wants to address some of the most pressing needs middle-aged adult children have in today's world.

CASE MANAGEMENT

Case management is available not only to help older people remain in their own homes, but also to help people who have an aged family member living with them. Outside professionals, usually a nurse and a social worker, are invited into the home to help the caregiver determine what type of services the older person needs, who can help with these services, and who can help pay for these services.

It is difficult for many of us to call someone into our home to help us with this kind of assessment. Most of us think we know what needs to be done, and most of us want to do what needs to be done by ourselves. We think it is our duty and our responsibility. But deep down we also know that we can't do everything. We can't continue to give around-the-clock care and continually worry about our parents without paying the consequences in terms of our personal health, family unity, and emotional well-being.

With case management, there is no obligation after the initial assessment. Suggestions are made to be followed, rejected, or modified. Using one of these services and following some of their suggestions for help does not mean that we are abandoning our responsibilities to our parents. It really means that we are wise enough to know that we can't do everything by ourselves all the time. Using a case management approach, we can plug in the types of assistance that we need so that we can continue to be effective caregivers. It means that we are using our own resources in more effective ways.

In some areas of the nation, case management services are offered on a nonprofit or low-cost basis to help keep elderly people out of institutions as long as possible. In other instances the service is on a fee basis, which should be discussed ahead of time. In many instances, case management services provide adult children living distances from their aging parents the opportunity to help directly in the care of their elderly parents without moving near them. But this generally applies only when the elderly parents are able, through an array of supportive services, to stay in their own home.

INFORMATION AND RESOURCES

Information becomes a key to matching the needs of your elderly parent and the resources your community might have to help you meet these needs. How can you learn about the resources and services in your community and in other communities? Area Agencies on Aging, listed in nearly every phone book, have all kinds of information including names, addresses, and telephone numbers where a person can get information. Senior centers and their staff usually know a lot about community services. Local branches of the United Way often have an Information and Referral Service. A more complete list of agencies and organizations to call for additional information and assistance is in the appendix.

SUPPORT GROUPS

Another valuable resource you can explore is an appropriate support group. Professionals who work with these groups, and the caregivers who participate in them, overwhelmingly report the benefits of these groups. This type of support enables overburdened caregivers to express their feelings in a supportive setting. They come to realize that they are not alone in the kinds of situations they face and the kinds of reactions they feel. In an article entitled "Family Caregivers: America's Primary Long-Term Care Resource,"[13] Dr. Osterkamp lists the very important things a support group for caregivers can provide. These include (1) help in setting limits in caring for an elderly parent on an ongoing basis, (2) help in considering the effects of taking on or continuing caregiving responsibilities, and (3) help in making difficult decisions—decisions that directly affect the ability and resources of the caregivers to care for their elderly parent.

EMPLOYERS AND ELDERCARE

The Travelers Insurance Company conducted a survey of its employees several years ago and found that 28 percent of workers over the age of thirty were providing some form of care for an older person. Nearly 8 percent of the surveyed employees reported spending thirty-five hours or more a week caring for an elderly person—"nearly the equivalent of a second full-time job," says Andrew E. Scharlach, a USC professor.[14]

Some American employers are now realizing that eldercare is an important concern among employees. "We think this is one of the emerging issues for employers in the late 1980s and 1990s,"[15] says Keith Anderson, a spokesman for PepsiCo, Incorporated.

"Not every yuppie has a child, but every yuppie has a couple of parents," says Burke Stinson, district manager for AT&T, which has set up a ten-million-dollar fund to provide seed money for eldercare and childcare services around the country.[16]

"You have people in mid-career, trying to help their families, and they wind up with the totally unexpected dependency of a parent," says Michael Creedon, in charge of corporate eldercare programs for the National Council on Aging. "For many, it happens when you're just getting out from under child care."[17]

The toll that eldercare can take on employees includes increased absenteeism, tardiness, stress, increased telephone calls at work, and shortened hours. One study estimated that the cost to employers for workers who had to lose days at work to attend to care for aging parents was $2 million per year for a twenty-five-thousand-member work force.

Some companies now sponsor lunchtime lectures and "care fairs" in association with local social service organizations. Employees are offered flexible hours, knowing that elderly parents at home need regular care at particular hours.

A few companies are combining day care for children and elderly parents in the same building. Financial support is also offered through some employee benefit plans, including insurance coverage for long-term care. PepsiCo, Incorporated, permits employees to direct up to five thousand dollars of their salaries, tax free, toward the care of an elderly dependent or a child.[18]

Susan Johnson was a secretary at Travelers in Hartford, Connecticut. Both her parents suffered health crises within months of each other. Susan might have had to spend hours attending to their care, but thanks to an eldercare program at work, she was able to lighten her burden.

"The professionals here not only helped me find local agencies to aid my parents but also took some of the pressure off me and listened, so I could go back to work and be productive," says Johnson. She calls the eldercare program "an answer to prayer."[19]

THE IMPORTANCE OF ASKING FOR HELP

If you need help with caring for your parents, ask for it. Asking for and offering help is part of the Christian life. Someone will be delighted to help you, and to deny them the opportunity to express love through service to others is to deny them an opportunity to receive rich blessings. Don't be too proud or too rigid to reach out for help if you need it.

"Basically, it doesn't come easily for [women] to give up this idea that they should quit their job and devote everything to their parents," says Barbara Kamholz, a geriatric psychiatrist. "They need tremendous ongoing support. They often get themselves into very difficult binds, continue to work, think they should have their parents at home, get upset, angry, and don't know what the solution is."[20]

Social worker Lora Shor-Friedman helps families find solutions. "What I'm hearing more and more is that tremendous amount of guilt associated with 'Am I providing the right kind of thing for my parents?' Most people nowadays don't want a family member to move into their home, yet when you talk about placement, they disintegrate." She tells adult children to get some nurturing for themselves. "They're taking care of everyone else's needs and depleting their own," she says.[21]

YOU CAN HELP YOUR PARENTS

There is no doubt that families are still the main source of care for elderly parents, but there are all kinds of ways to help. Having an elderly parent move into an adult child's home and become part of the household is one way. But there are situations where this might not be the best idea. It depends on the specific situation as well as the people involved.

Adult children should not feel that it is their duty or obligation to have their parents move in with them. Given enough money and help, most older people prefer to live near but not with their adult children and their families. Adult children shouldn't feel guilty or inadequate if they use their energy and resources to coordinate services to help their parents continue living in their own independent housing unit.

If an elderly parent does move into the home of an adult child and the parent is ill or infirm, the child becomes the primary caregiver. This is a unique and tough role that can overwhelm anyone. Services that can help should be identified and used as much as possible to keep the caregiver from becoming physically and emotionally exhausted. Jaci Joseph has cared for her grandmother at home for eight years. "There are mornings when I stuff my pockets with Kleenex and cry it out in the park," she says. "Mostly I give myself pep talks. But it's also my praying time: 'God, if you can help, I'm open to suggestions.'"[22]

There is only so much you can do for your aged parents. Realizing this does not mean you are walking away from your responsibilities, but that you need to become aware of options for help and options for other housing arrangements.

> Ruth Berdick, 57, of Glenview, Ill., had five adults in her home, including her 88-year-old mother-in-law. "That was just too many adults in one house," she told *USA Today*. "I've learned I am not perfect. It has been a growth experience for me—and growth is painful."
>
> For five years she and her husband, Marland, have cared for his mother, Louise. "She was no longer able to cook or care for herself," Berdick says. "We never considered other options."
>
> A counselor through Marland's employee assistance plan helped the family pull together. The counselor also helped locate a state-supported adult day-care program that Louise now attends five days a week.
>
> "She calls it her work," Ruth says. "It gives her companionship, and organizes her day." In addition, the couple has joined a support group through church. "You're not in this alone," Ruth says. And she and Louise now go to church together.
>
> Her advice: "Seek professional counseling before bringing a parent into your home. It gives perspective. Take good care of yourself. Don't judge yourself too harshly. Think through your own retirement. Make plans for the future. And join a support group!"[23]

CHAPTER ELEVEN

Other Housing Options for Mom and Dad

If the old homestead is no longer the best place for Mom and Dad to live and you don't think living with you is the best option, where can they go? What type of living arrangement is best for your parents when they are in their seventies, eighties, or even nineties?

The answer depends on many factors. Carefully consider:

- your parents' health
- their ability to cook for themselves
- their ability to manage for themselves in their own living unit
- their financial situation
- the location and condition of their old home
- the level of assistance they will probably need in the next few years.

After talking it over with her daughter and son-in-law for almost a year, Ann's mother decided that her old house was not where she wanted to stay. Like many older houses, it was a large, wooden, two-story structure in an old part of town. It had poor insulation, laundry facilities in the basement, and four bedrooms and one bathroom on the second floor.

Ann's father had died three years before, and her mom lived

alone in the old house. Although the house had been paid for since 1958, it was costly to heat and maintain. Considerable work needed to be done on the electrical system, and the plumbing was far from adequate. Even if they spent the large amount of money to update the plumbing and electrical system, it would still be an old house with only one bathroom—upstairs.

Ann's mother didn't want to admit it was time to move, even though she was having a hard time climbing the stairs. Many of her friends in the neighborhood had either died or moved away, and she became even more lonely when her church moved to the suburbs.

Ann urged her mom to face the realities of her situation and look around for other housing arrangements. After much persuasion, Ann's mother finally agreed.

Where should she go? What would meet her needs and make her happy? Fortunately for Ann's mom and millions of older people like her, there are a range of housing options for older persons.

MOVING AND OLDER PERSONS

If you are going to help your parents move from one home to another or even from one geographic area to another, remember that while moving is stressful for anyone, it is perhaps especially stressful for older people.

The ease with which your parents move will depend upon their age, health status, the degree of change, and the degree of their personal involvement in the move. Studies have shown that when the move promotes independence of living, moving can be beneficial.

Why are some older persons so opposed to moving when they could greatly improve their living accommodations? The first reason that comes to mind is the expense of moving. To move into better housing costs money, and some older people don't want to spend the money to improve their housing even if they can afford it. They see it as an unnecessary expense. "Why should we move?" your parents might say. "We've been in this house for thirty years, and we can stay in it for another thirty. We own this house, so why should we spend all that money for another living arrangement?"

Some people just resist change. "I know my neighbors, and I know where to find good groceries, cheap medicine, and a good dry cleaner," one man complained. "Why should I move? I'd have to start all over again." Older people often do not have the physical or emotional resources to cope with changing life conditions.

Finally, some older people don't want to move because they are emotionally attached to the old home. They spend most of their time at home, and they don't want to leave the old neighborhood, familiar surroundings, family furniture, and old friends. One woman refused to leave her tulip beds. Familiar surroundings in old neighborhoods give older people a sense of stability and security.

Until relatively recent times, living in older residential areas of cities was often convenient for many older people because these areas were close to stores, doctors, and dentists. But as stores and services of all kinds began to move to the suburbs, many older people who lacked transportation were left behind. When services and resources become remote and inaccessible, older people are bound to feel isolated and uncomfortable.

Relocating older people involves much more than providing them with better housing units. Moving can threaten their entire world. If you are encouraging your parents to move, be particularly sensitive to their spoken and unspoken needs.

You can help your parents feel more comfortable in their new home by visiting the new place several times before the move. Look at the rooms and meet the staff (if the move is to a group living situation). Describe the situation positively and help your parents become excited about moving.

If time and circumstances permit, encourage your parents to make the decision themselves to move, where to move, and when to move. Linda and Fred were concerned about Linda's eighty-four-year-old mother, Florence. Although Florence had been on her own for some time, Linda knew the sprawling house she lived in was too much for her to keep up. So Linda came up with an innovative plan. She and Fred would sell their house, Florence could sell hers, and while their houses were on the market they would build a new house together. Florence would have a master bedroom and living room on the first floor, and there would be two bedrooms for Linda and Fred's teenage sons. Linda and Fred would have a den and large bedroom on the basement level.

The situation seemed ideal. The kitchen was located next to Florence's living room, so she didn't have to tackle stairs every time she went into the kitchen. She had a private bath, as did the boys, and Linda and Fred had privacy in their living area downstairs. With their resources combined, they were able to add a pool for exercise and a triple garage to include Florence's car.

Because the housing market was depressed, they found a builder who purchased their homes outright to resell later while he built their custom-designed home. While the home was being built, the entire family drove over each night and watched its progress. Florence was as excited as anyone in the family, and she proudly watched "her quarters" being built. There was room for her antiques, her piano, her trunks, and her memories.

As excited as Florence was, it wasn't easy for her to leave her old home. Linda once drove over to the old house and found her mother sitting alone in an empty living room. But before long, the family adjusted well to the new house.

HOUSING OPTIONS FOR OLDER PERSONS

Almost 95 percent of all elderly people in America live in some form of independent household. Only about 5 percent live in some type of group housing.[1] Of this number, about one percent live in group (congregate) housing, and the remainder are divided almost evenly between personal-care and nursing homes. Not many actually live with their children.[2]

As a person ages, however, the possibility of living in some form of congregate housing arrangement increases dramatically. For persons eighty-five and older, about 25 percent live in some group living arrangement.[3] And among this same group, 27 percent live with a relative compared to nearly 15 percent of all persons sixty-five and older.[4]

Once you've helped your parents overcome the resistance to moving, the next decision you will have to make is what type of housing unit to investigate. Would they be willing to rent a place, or is owning their home too important to them? What type of unit will meet their present physical needs as well as their needs a few years down the road? Would they be happy being around older people like themselves, or would they enjoy living among people of all ages, including children? All of these questions need to be considered to determine what type of housing situation your elderly parents need.

AGE SEGREGATED OR AGE INTEGRATED?
The question of whether a specific housing unit is "age integrated" or "age segregated" is important. Would your parents be happier living among people their own age (age segregated) or among persons of all ages (age integrated)? Many older people are happier living among other elderly people who have similar lifestyles. Most older people do not appreciate loud stereo music at any time, especially at night. Nor do they enjoy loud barking dogs or noisy cars. When the living arrangement involves close living quarters, such as a mobile home park or an apartment building, many older persons are happier among people their own age.

Other older people are happiest living among people of all

ages. This is particularly true where there is a natural interaction among the people of different ages. It is good for older persons to see babies take their first steps and watch children play. The key here, though, is that younger persons should not unduly interfere with the lifestyles of older persons. For example, older people tend to go to bed earlier than younger people. Older persons should not have to put up with loud parties after nine or ten at night. This is difficult to avoid in some age-integrated housing situations, such as mobile home parks, where people live close together.

APARTMENT LIVING

Apartment living can be an ideal option for many older people. There is a broad range of apartments in all price ranges, except in some rural areas of the nation. Like all housing markets, the apartment market varies from one community to another.

Before choosing apartment living, you and your parents should become familiar with what types of apartments are available in the area, price ranges, the tightness of the market, and market trends. This may seem like a rather difficult task, and it will be helpful to ask the advice of a realtor or a friend familiar with this market.

Apartment living can transfer the responsibilities of property ownership to someone else. A person's commitment is for a fixed time, usually a year. This can be good or bad depending on your parents' circumstances. During the year, cost obligations are fixed, so tenants can budget fixed income and resources. On the other hand, at the end of the year, the rent for the unit can go up—and it usually will in areas where apartments are in short supply. That is why it is important to know the apartment market in your area.[5]

It is helpful to know the owner of the apartment to have some long-term commitment to the price range and potential cost increases. Because many older persons live on limited or fixed incomes, often they are not able to compete financially with younger persons for apartments. As a result, they need to be in a rental situation that gives them the opportunity for long-range budgeting if it is their intention to remain an apartment dweller.

Apartments can offer older people a sense of physical security as well as the opportunity to meet and talk with others. However, some older persons feel that they lose privacy in an apartment setting. Others feel the loss of ownership or control is a major barrier to apartment living. Others simply cannot stand the idea of renting, believing that rent is money "down the drain."

For many older people, however, apartment living can be an economical way to gain tax-free profit from the equity they have gained from the sale of their old home, and to get out from under the rising costs of taxes, insurance, utilities, and maintenance associated with keeping their own home. As apartment residents, they can use the money they received from the sale of their home to add to their life savings. This will give them some added financial security for financial emergencies, and earn them interest to add to their monthly income, supplementing their retirement income to pay for their apartment rent. As long as they can take care of themselves, apartment living can be ideal for many older persons.

CONDOMINIUM LIVING
Condominiums are individual housing units in multi-family developments. The difference between a condo and an apartment is that individuals own their own condos, while apartments are only rented. Condominiums range in style and design from detached single units to apartments in high rise buildings. Although they are individually owned, they share common grounds and facilities that could include pools, tennis courts, beachfronts, clubhouses, recreation areas, and saunas. Usually the more facilities a condo complex offers, the more expensive the condominium.

Buying a condominium is just like buying a house, except that somebody else does the upkeep and repairs for a service fee, which varies depending on the condominium complex. In a properly run condominium, the management keeps the building clean, neat, and running smoothly. The resident owners are entitled to use the recreational facilities, although this may also be subject to a monthly or yearly charge.

Since owning a condominium is somewhat similar to owning a house, condominiums are assessed and taxed the same as houses. This also means that the owner can sell, lease, or mortgage a condominium.

How do you choose the right condominium? The granter, or developer, of the condominium must establish it by making certain policies in a declaration. If you and your parents are investigating a condominium, you need to be aware of any language in the declaration that permits the granter to lock the condominium into a long-term agreement or that unduly restricts owners' rights to make their own decisions.

Conditions, covenants, and restrictions in the declaration should be reviewed by an attorney representing your parents. You also need to be aware of something called "right of first refusal." It restricts the rights of owners to sell their condominium. It means that the owner cannot sell to whomever he chooses, but must first offer to sell his condo to the whole association of condominium owners. Also, you need to beware of any clause reserving the right of the association to approve of prospective buyers. This restricts your rights of disposal and is prohibited by law.[6]

Rules for governing a condominium are very important. They shouldn't restrict the owners' rights of sale, policy making, and facility use; yet they should not be so loose that anything is allowed. Certain things should be regulated, such as the level of noise and hazardous or unsanitary behavior.

For many older people, condominium ownership combines

the benefits of living in an apartment-type setting with home ownership. It does tie up a person's capital as home ownership does, but it does not involve all the personal responsibilities of a homeowner, such as landscaping and building maintenance. As with all living arrangements, it is important to weigh all the pluses and minuses of a condominium before deciding if it is a comfortable option for your elderly parents.

MOBILE HOME LIVING

Many housing experts point out that mobile home living is the only remaining relatively low-cost housing option in America.[7] This depends on the mobile home and the park in which it is located. While a person can buy a relatively low-priced mobile home, in some choice recreational areas of the South or Southwest a buyer can pay as much as fifty to seventy thousand dollars for a mobile home and lot.

Regardless of the price of the home itself, the total cost of mobile home living must be figured. In addition to the price of the mobile home, the total cost includes set-up expenses (which can be extensive), monthly rental rates, and extra fees such as water and sewage charges. The spiraling cost of rent is a big danger in mobile home parks where the spaces are rented. Since these fees tend to increase on a regular basis, often at the whim of the park owner, many older people have been forced to move because they can no longer afford the higher monthly charges.

It is often difficult, if not impossible, for older people to move their mobile homes. Mobile homes really aren't very mobile. Most parks will not accept mobile homes over a certain age, and even if your parents were to find a park that would take an older mobile home, many elderly people on fixed incomes could not afford the expenses involved in moving a mobile home.

If you and your parents are seriously considering a mobile home park, you should learn about the nature of the park and the quality of its management by talking to several residents. If your parents buy a mobile home in a park or install a new trailer in a park, it is likely it will remain there. Because of the difficulty of moving, no more than ten percent of mobile homes move once they are installed and set up.

Another economic consideration in mobile home living is that the value of any property is determined by its highest and best use. At some point, a piece of land may become more valuable for a shopping center or gas station, and the owner may sell and force the residents to leave. This is not only emotionally difficult for older people, but moving is extremely impractical.

Another major consideration for mobile home dwellers is the list of restrictions for park residents. Some parks are so restrictive that residents are not allowed to wash their cars or have visitors stay overnight.

In some cooperatively owned parks, residents own the lot on which their mobile home sits. Some, such as Trailer Estates in Manatee County, Florida, even have their own fire departments and emergency paramedical units. The elderly residents there participate directly in the decision-making processes of operating the park. Cooperatively owned mobile home parks usually keep monthly fees modest. Most important, there is no rent to pay each month beyond minimal service charges. In addition, these parks will not be sold unless there is a cooperative decision by the park's resident owners.

Resident owners of a cooperatively owned mobile home park are in a much better position to control their living situations, the environment of the park, and their costs. We strongly recommend mobile home parks that are owned and operated by the residents. Older people who live in them have much greater control over their own lives.

In the past, mobile homes often depreciated faster than many people could pay them off. This has changed. Depending on the nature and the location of the park, some mobile homes have appreciated in value.

Living in a well-managed mobile home park can be an excellent housing option for older people. The similar interests and lifestyles of people in older adult–oriented mobile home parks often provide older people with a sense of community in which they find companionship and security. If your parents are considering a mobile home, we recommend that you find a park that is focused on persons of a similar age range (fifty or fifty-five years and older) and one that is cooperatively owned or exceptionally well managed.

ACCESSORY APARTMENTS

Another form of housing that might be attractive to your parents if they own a relatively large home is something called an accessory apartment. This is a private, independent living arrangement usually consisting of a sleeping area, kitchen, bathroom, and sometimes a separate entrance in an existing home.[8] This type of housing has been called a "mother-in-law apartment." It is a separate apartment developed in a single-family home. Many big old homes can be remodeled to include this type of apartment. Some new homes are built with this arrangement included. The main advantage of an accessory apartment is that your elderly parents can have their own complete living unit in a residence occupied by someone who can look after them as the needs arise.

The arrangement of an accessory apartment can vary. The older person can live in the original house with a relative (daughter, son, daughter-in-law, etc.) occupying the accessory apartment. Or the accessory apartment can be rented out to a nonrelative who agrees to look after your mom or dad. "Looking after" an older person can range from just having someone in the same house for security to actively caring for their daily needs. Renting an accessory apartment can generate some extra income that can be used to help pay the costs of keeping up a home.

This arrangement can be a very good way to live close to your elderly relatives without intruding in their "space" or lifestyle, as well as not having them intrude in your "space" or lifestyle. As we have already seen, having one's own "space" is very important to members of all generations. It is one of the key ingredients of successful daily living when two or more generations try to live together.

Zoning laws can be a problem in developing accessory apartments in areas zoned for single family homes. This can be dealt with in different ways, depending on the community, through (1) revised zoning ordinances that allow accessory apartments, (2) zoning variances for a particular house, (3) licensing, by which local governments periodically review requests and renewal requirements for accessory apartments, and (4) special use permits, for which local governments review each application at a public hearing. In the special use permit process, the permit to develop an accessory apartment is usually granted to the individual applicant rather than for the property itself. In this case, the personal situation of the older person is important to the granting of the permit. Zoning ordinances are sometimes more lenient concerning these arrangements in rural areas.

The American Association of Retired Persons (AARP) has a free publication that describes in detail accessory apartments (*A Consumer's Guide to Accessory Apartments,* 1987), which is available by writing to AARP Fulfillment (see appendix).

ELDER COTTAGE HOUSING OPPORTUNITY (ECHO)
Another type of housing arrangement that promotes the privacy and independence of your mom and dad while you live very close to them is called ECHO housing—Elderly Cottage Housing Opportunity. This refers to a relatively small, freestanding, removable housing unit placed on the side or backyard of a single

family home to provide private, independent housing for your elderly parents. This arrangement enables you to be near to and care for your aging parents without leaving your own property.

ECHO housing enables each generation to have their own private living unit with their own "space" and privacy. Both you and your parents can follow your own lifestyles with your own habits without interfering with each other. You and your parents can listen to your own music, watch your own television programs, go to bed when you choose, and carry on with all the other activities of daily life without affecting each other. This approach enables each of you to avoid the traumas and adjustments that become necessary if your elderly parents were to move into your home.

As you might expect, the major problems with this type of living arrangement revolve around zoning laws and regulations. Developing ECHO housing units usually requires enabling legislation and procedures to process zoning applications. The American Association of Retired Persons has developed four publications that deal with ECHO housing. These can be obtained by writing AARP Fulfillment (see appendix). These publications are:

- *A Model Ordinance for ECHO Housing*
- *ECHO Housing—A Review of Zoning Issues and Other Considerations*
- *ECHO Housing—Recommended Construction and Installation Standards*
- *ECHO Housing Fact Sheet*

This type of living arrangement is not new. It has been used for some time in the rural and Southern areas of the United States in the form of mobile homes set up for elderly parents on the property of an adult child. In Australia, where this type of housing originated, they are called "granny flats." As the number of older people increases dramatically, and modular housing becomes more acceptable, this type of housing may become quite common if zoning laws can be developed to accommodate older persons living on the properties of their adult children.

CONGREGATE OR GROUP LIVING

Mary Wilson and Sally Lazarus live at Tanya Towers, a ten-story, terraced apartment complex for deaf or blind elderly people in Manhattan. Wilson enjoys her new home's proximity to museums, shows, and restaurants. "You're never lonely," Wilson signed, as Maryanne Roberto, director of residential services, translated. "I know the names of all who live here and what floors their apartments are on."

Lazarus signs that "this is the best home deaf people can have in New York. They keep us busy with art classes, bingo, captioned movies, cooking classes, dance exercises, and trips."

Tanya Towers, which offers a seventy-cent lunch on weekdays, is owned and operated by the New York Society for the Deaf. Each residence has flashing lights for doorbells, an emergency alarm system, and a grab-bar in the bathtub.[9]

Congregate living is expanding throughout the nation and takes many forms. These living arrangements have been called "homes for the aged," "retirement homes," "old people's homes," and "retirement villages."

The common factor in these facilities is a group or congregate housing arrangement with a common dining room in which meals are served on a regular basis. In the past, many of these homes for the aged were developed and operated by churches, religious denominations, and fraternal or social organizations. Most of these were, and continue to be, nonprofit. They provide rooms or apartments of varying sizes, basic supportive services, and regularly served meals.

In a sense, congregate homes are dormitories for the old. One of the authors regularly drives to work down a road which has a college and its dormitories on one side, and a home for the aged on the other. The outward similarity of both "dorms" is remarkable. Both have rooms, both have basic services, both have common rooms and space, and both serve meals on a regular basis. Inside, however, as we all know, the home for the aged is much cleaner, quieter, and more orderly.

No matter what a person's age, however, not everyone likes "dorm life." Whether the dorm is for college kids or older people, there are bound to be rules and set procedures. But for a college student, a dorm is temporary. A student spends relatively little time in his dorm because of the demands of an active college schedule.

An older person, however, spends much time in his "dorm room." It is difficult for many older people to give up being in charge of their lives and move to a group living situation. This may be particularly true for your parents if they think of homes for the aged as old, dismal, and generally depressing.

In the past, "retirement homes" were often dismal. But many of today's congregate homes provide a sparkling physical environment with a range of entertainment and recreational opportunities along with modern services: exercise classes, shuttle service, good food, and security. They are designed to attract people who can get around by themselves but who want the security of a controlled, supportive environment with operational rules and procedures that are designed to promote as much independence as possible.

If you and your parents decide to consider a congregate living arrangement, you should ask the following questions of the manager and some of the other residents:

1. Who owns the facility? Is it for-profit or nonprofit? What is its business reputation? Do you know anyone who knows the owners? Whom can you ask?

Start with the Better Business Bureau and see if any complaints have been filed against the owners or managing company. Check with a banker you know. Ask the advice of a respected business-person in your church. If it is an established facility, it should have a good track record in business and a good reputation in the community.

2. Who manages the home? Is the management competent? Does the facility have a record of sound management? If it is a new facility, who can recommend the management?

3. Is there a support base to carry the facility financially? If it is a nonprofit operation, how much money is behind the facility to ensure its long-term financial health? If it is a for-profit operation, is there enough money behind it for long-term stability without large increases in monthly rates?

4. What happens to your parents' entry fee or investment in their living unit if they change their mind before they actually move in? What happens to this money if they move in and decide they don't want to stay there?

5. What is included in the monthly fees? What costs are extra? Do the fees cover such household maintenance as clean linens changed regularly, room/apartment cleaning, cable TV, and food service to the room when the resident is ill?

6. What are the other residents like? Will your parents feel comfortable living there?

7. What are the rules and regulations of the facility? How free are the residents to decorate or furnish their own rooms or apartments?

8. Is there a choice in the food that is served? Can special diets be accommodated? How good is the food?

9. Do the residents feel happy or content living in this facility? Do they have more than the usual complaints?

Before moving your parents into a retirement facility, investigate it as thoroughly as you can. Some of the new facilities are dazzling, but keep in mind that many are basically business opportunities for profit. This does not mean that all of them are operated by get-rich-quick artists, but you need to be careful before committing your parents and their resources to a congregate living facility.

CONTINUING CARE COMMUNITIES

Many retirement villages or complexes call themselves "life-care" or "continuing care" communities. Incoming residents sign legal contracts known as life-care agreements. Housing units in these complexes can range from single rooms in a retirement home, to elaborate apartments in a retirement village with extensive recreational facilities.

Through life-care agreements, these facilities promise to provide all the needs a person may have as she continues to grow older in exchange for an entry fee and monthly fees. The amount required upon entry can range from $15,000 to more than $150,000. The monthly fees can range from $200 to $2,000—probably more if the person requires nursing care.[10]

The goal of the continuing care retirement community is to take away the older person's worry about the future. Regardless of the level of care she may someday need, once a person pays the entry fee and becomes a resident of the facility, she is to be provided the level of care she needs as long as she lives. This usually includes supportive care and nursing home care when and if the older person needs it.

In the most desirable continuing care communities, all the resources an older person might need are part of the retirement complex. Some of the newer complexes include private apartments either in duplex or townhouse arrangements, apartments in a larger building, rooms in a manor type of building, supportive care rooms, and a nursing home. As the resident's needs change, she is able to move within the same retirement community to the next level of assisted-living housing unit, all the way to nursing-home care. All of this is done within the framework of the life-care agreement.

For older persons who can afford it, a continuing care community with a life-care agreement can be a solution to the long-term care problem that most older people eventually face. But before your parents invest the proceeds of the sale of their home or their life's savings in such a facility, there are things to consider, according to Anne Harvey in an article entitled "Life-Care Contracts for the Elderly: A Risky Retirement?"[11]

1. *Long waiting lists.* There may be long waiting lists of two or more years for the best facilities. Many of these complexes have physical mobility and mental fitness requirements that make it difficult for frail older people to gain admission. Some have maximum age limitations for entry. So plan ahead if this type of retirement arrangement looks good to you and your folks. Many good facilities will place a person's name on a list, and when their name comes up they are given the option to enter the facility or continue to wait until they are ready to move. Applying for entry to these facilities usually costs somewhere between fifty and two hundred dollars. This is a modest investment to begin the admission process.

2. *Fraud.* Unfortunately, some extended-care facilities have been developed and operated fraudulently. Older people put all or most of their money into what they thought was a sound investment that would provide for them for the rest of their lives, and many have been cheated out of their money. It is important to investigate the operation thoroughly.

3. *Mismanagement.* Some life-care facilities have been mismanaged. The intentions of the operators have been good, but they simply ran out of funds to fulfill their long-term contracts with their residents. Look at the track record of a facility. If it is new, see if it is a branch or subsidiary of a similar facility that has been in operation longer. Find out who the developers are.

4. *Lack of capital.* Some facilities don't have enough money behind them. They may not have enough to begin with or they may not have projected expenses and income realistically. Again,

determine who owns the facility and what long-term capital is behind it to carry out long-term contracts.

5. *Lack of institutional financial support.* Some life-care retirement communities, even some associated with churches, lack adequate financial support from the sponsoring organizations. It is important to learn whether the life-care facility really has the support it claims from its sponsors to make up any financial shortfalls that might occur. Some of the church-sponsored facilities have long-standing support mechanisms from the churches and denominations that sponsor them. Some of these facilities are in the budgets of their churches and denominations; others do not have this built-in and ongoing support.

6. *Underoccupancy.* For financial health, some facilities depend on high occupancy rates that are never achieved. It is important to check occupancy rates in older facilities, and try to determine projected occupancy for new ones.

7. *Rising medical costs.* Some life-care facilities have not provided adequately for rising medical costs for the residents of the supportive-care sections. Try to determine how these will be covered.

8. *Unclear contracts.* Some continuing care contracts are not clear about long-term provisions. Everything needs to be spelled out in definite language before you or your parents sign the contract and invest a large sum of money in this type of facility. Not having a clear contract can result in financial loss and confusion over needs and procedures.

As you investigate a life-care facility, ask the same questions you would ask of a congregate home, as well as the following questions:

1. What happens when my parents need the next level of care? Are they guaranteed that the next level of care will be available within the facility? What will be the additional expense for the next level of care? Will there be additional costs for supportive

or nursing-home levels of care? Will the facility help in getting my parents on Medicaid if they run out of money?

2. What happens if for some reason my parents are unable to continue to pay the ongoing monthly fees, especially if the fees are continually raised? Is there some support program in the life-care facility, or in its support base, to assist long-term residents who find themselves caught in this situation?

3. How extensive are the supportive-care facilities? Can they handle the projected patient load of the residents as they continue to grow older?

4. How extensive are the nursing-home facilities of the complex? Can they meet the projected needs of the residents?

5. What happens to my parents' entry fee or investment in the facility if one of them dies? What portion reverts to the surviving spouse, children, or the estate?

SUBSIDIZED HOUSING

Many older people who need to move cannot do so because they simply don't have the money. Prominent in this group are older women who live alone.

Public housing was introduced with the passage of the Housing Act of 1937, two years after the enactment of the Social Security Act. But it was not until 1956 that the Housing Act was amended to provide public housing specifically for the elderly. Despite what you have heard, believe, or feel about public housing in general, public housing developments for the elderly have been among the most successful of all government-supported programs. Public housing for the elderly has been cooperatively developed through federal government loan programs by communities, church organizations, private investors, and various social agencies.

The concept is not so different from loans that colleges, both public and private, obtain to build dormitories and then pay off through the rental of the rooms. There is only one major problem with publicly assisted housing for the elderly—it has been and continues to be in very short supply. There have been major cutbacks in subsidized housing programs in the last few years. Most publicly assisted housing developments have long waiting lists.

SHARED HOUSING

More and more single older people are realizing the advantages of taking in a roommate, or, more accurately, a housemate. With a housemate, senior adults can cut costs, share chores, and enjoy having a companion. Bill Dafft of Dallas, Texas, found a person to share his house through Dallas's Shared Housing Center, one of a growing number of organizations springing up around the country to match people of compatible needs.

Bill needed someone in the house. He was seventy and spent most of his days in a wheelchair smoking cigarettes and watching television. He couldn't cook. Now, however, his housemate cooks, runs errands, and shares expenses. "I think it's a wonderful program," says Dafft.

Whether home sharing involves pairing two people or several in a house, it is a rapidly growing means of finding housing for older adults. The American Association of Retired Persons says that fifteen percent of its members polled in 1988 were interested in shared housing, more than twice the number in a similar survey taken in 1980. The organization estimates that about 670,000 people over sixty-five are now involved in some form of shared housing.[12]

> Real-estate developers are also building a broad range of new retirement communities. . . . "We haven't even begun to realize all the things we can do to keep people independent," says Sheldon Goldberg, president of the American Association of Homes for the Aged. "It's going to be incredible."[13]

If there is no shared housing center in your community, your mother or father could find a housemate by advertising or simply by spreading the word at church or in the community. Shared housing, of course, must be investigated carefully. You will want to make sure your parent is living with someone trustworthy. As with all cooperative arrangements, it should be clearly understood which expenses are to be shared and which are to be paid by each individual.

CHAPTER TWELVE

Nursing Homes: When and Where?

"The decision by an adult child to place Mother or Father in a nursing home is an infinitely painful one," writes Vivian Greenberg in her book, *Your Best Is Good Enough: Caring for Your Aging Parents.* "Unlike death, which is final, nursing home visits to our parents are a constant reminder of the cruel thing we have done. Every visit brings to full consciousness our sadness and pain. If we were close to our parent, the pain is unbearable."[1]

Marge was having a conversation with her sister and two brothers. Their mother was a widow, and she had been in the hospital for three weeks with a broken hip.

They hadn't thought the broken hip would cause other complications, but as Mom lay in the hospital, other problems surfaced. Now Mom would need not only physical therapy, but also someone near her all the time to help her get to the bathroom, get dressed, cook, and clean the house.

"Where can Mom go?" Marge asked. "Who can take care of her? Can one of us be there all the time if she needs something or has an emergency?"

Marge knew the others were silently hoping she would volunteer to take Mom into her house, but Marge didn't think she could handle it. Her sister and brothers, though, weren't shy about speaking up.

"Mom will be scared to death if you put her in a nursing home," Anne offered. Anne lived in another state and wasn't a good candidate for taking Mom in. "Mom has heard all kinds of horror stories about nursing homes. You just can't consider putting her in one."

"She knows your house," Jeff volunteered. "She'd feel comfortable with you."

"She can't afford a nursing home," Steve pointed out. "I don't know how much they cost, but I know it's a lot. And what if Mom spends the rest of her life in one of those places? We'd all go broke paying for it!"

Anne shook her head. "Mom is one of our family, for crying out loud. We just can't ship her off."

"Think of all the times we were sick and she took care of us," Steve said. "I think we owe her."

"Besides, she might refuse to go to a nursing home," said Jeff. "How can we overrule her? She's not mentally incompetent."

"You'd feel terribly guilty if you didn't take her in," Anne said, putting her hand on Marge's shoulder. "And we'll send monthly checks to help out so you can hire someone to sit with her if you need help. You can do it. You just can't send her to a nursing home."

Marge felt trapped. She didn't really think she was up to moving Mom into her home and being responsible for all her care. But her sister and two brothers pressured her into trying to take care of Mom and keep her out of a nursing home. She, like all daughters or daughters-in-law in similar situations, felt a range of emotions including resentment for being the one the burden fell on, guilt for thinking she really did not want to take on all the responsibility, and fear of what might happen to her mom—and to her, no matter which way she decided. It seemed like a no-win situation.

Between 80 and 90 percent of care for dependent older people is provided by family caregivers.[2] Among the most ill and frail elderly, more than twice as many are cared for by relatives than are placed in nursing homes.[3] But the stresses on adult child caregivers are tremendous. To make matters worse, only about 20 percent of caregivers in the home use any of the available community-based services.[4]

REASONS TO TURN TO A NURSING HOME

Marge decided to try to take care of her elderly mother by moving her into her home. She thought she had to give it a try. She thought she owed it to her mom, and she couldn't hold out against the urging of her siblings. But in spite of all the pressures on Marge to care for her mother in her home, after several months she got to the point where she had to place her mother in a nursing home. She did this for two reasons: her mother's health continued to deteriorate, and the strain and exhaustion of caregiving was too much for Marge to handle.

People who are placed in nursing homes after being cared for by their families have an average of four chronic health problems.[5] These multiple conditions are difficult for the home caregiver to manage. When Marge's mom developed health problems in addition to her broken hip, caring for her at home became an impossible situation.

The average home caregiver spends four to five hours a day, seven days a week, in direct hands-on care for the elderly patient in her home.[6] When the amount of care needed goes beyond these numbers and gets to fifteen or more daily hours of care, other arrangements need to be made to prevent the collapse of the caregiver.

Marge didn't know how to properly care for her mother's health problems. When professional medical skills are needed on an ongoing basis, in fairness to the patient and to the caregiver, nursing home placement needs to be considered. Some older people have a combination of physical and mental problems that untrained family members just cannot handle.

Marge didn't want to admit it, but she really couldn't handle her mother's loss of bladder and bowel control. She wasn't prepared to assume the level of care needed to provide for her mother. She was afraid she might snap in anger or frustration. Her brothers and sister who supported keeping Mom at home weren't around to change Mom's diapers.

After a few months, Marge was exhausted. She felt she had neglected her own family. After all, her teenage children needed help too, but Marge was too tired or too busy with her mother to be there for her own kids. She and her husband had grown distant, and caring for Mom was expensive, too. They had bought medicine, special equipment, and hired a sitter for Mom when Marge had to go out to run errands. And now that Marge wasn't working because of Mom, there was no extra money for the extra needs. The small checks her sister and brothers sent each month didn't go very far.

Marge did investigate community services, but Mom didn't like strangers coming in to care for her, and Marge couldn't afford any of the private agencies. In addition, Marge felt it wasn't right to ask a stranger to do things for her mother that she thought she ought to do herself.

Marge needed to get out of her situation. All the things her brothers and sister had told her seemed downright stupid. "Mom doesn't care about being here with me," Marge told herself one afternoon. "She often gripes and complains about everything I do for her. And I'll admit at times I've been horrible to her, too. I just don't think we can stand any more of this."

CHOOSING A NURSING HOME

It is no surprise that dutiful daughters like Marge literally run out of steam. It is amazing they last as long as they do in their multiple roles of spouse, mother, homemaker, employee, volunteer, and primary caregiver of the elderly in their family. Often sheer exhaustion of the primary caregiver finally leads to nursing-home placement—exhaustion that comes from too much work, stress, worry, depression, and guilt. In cases like Marge's, a nursing-home placement is best for everyone.

If you make a decision to place your elderly parent in a nursing home, how should one be chosen? If you live in a small town with only one or two facilities, your choices are very limited. But in most areas of the country, there are many nursing homes from which to choose.

What should you look for in a nursing home? Your role in the selection process is very important. First, you should choose the home that will best serve your parent's needs and wants. Needs are obvious and apply to the medical/physical/mental needs of the patient. *Wants* refers to the particular personality and lifestyle of your parent. There are some places that will be more comfortable for your parent than others.

Second, your active participation in the selection process of the nursing home can ease the guilt you may feel about placing your parent in a home. You should take some comfort in knowing you have weighed the important factors in selecting a nursing home and chosen the best home for Mom or Dad.

A variety of pamphlets, books, and experts offer advice as to what to look for in selecting a nursing home. One of the best outlines for selecting a nursing home is in Salamon and Rosenthal's book, *Home or Nursing Home: Making the Right Choices.*[7] They point out that a nursing home is not a hospital. Even though the nursing home will be providing a range of personal care services, the emphasis should be on the home aspect of a nursing home.

Salamon and Rosenthal tell of a confused elderly woman who loved to play the piano. Her relatives found her a home with a piano in the dayroom, and the staff encouraged the residents to play. This was important because it made the patient feel much better about being in that home.

To begin finding the right home for your parent, get a list of the types of homes in your area that have facilities, services, and resources appropriate to your parent's needs. These lists can be obtained from some doctors, discharge planners in hospitals, professional health care associations, the state regulatory agency that licenses nursing homes and other health care facilities (which can be contacted by calling the operator for the state government in your area), and your local long-term care ombudsman program.

An ombudsman program can play an important role in your continuing relationship with the nursing home. These programs were established under the Older Americans Act all across the country. They are designed to assist elderly or handicapped people and their relatives with a range of issues, questions, and problems that can arise in long-term care situations. Some ombudsman programs help people select a nursing home. All help residents and their loved ones with questions and complaints that may arise once a person is in such a facility.

Your minister may be a good source of information about nursing homes in your area. Quite often a minister is a regular visitor to long-term care facilities. Friends and relatives who have had loved ones in nursing homes can also be very good resources.

The next step in selecting a nursing home is to visit those that seem appropriate. It is helpful to visit as often as you can and at various times of the day. While visiting, try to talk with a variety of people including patients, relatives of patients, the administrator, nurses, aides, and others who may have a hand in the care of patients. This is the time to ask questions. It is important to ask a lot of questions to get the information you need to help make the right decision.

Vivian Greenberg advises children to take their parents with them when they visit nursing homes. "It is your parent's right to help choose his final home," she says. "The greater the role a parent can play in the selection process, the less powerless she will feel over her life."[8]

QUESTIONS TO ASK

Experts in the nursing-home field suggest asking the following questions:[9]

- Is the facility licensed?
- Who owns and manages the home?
- Is it a for-profit or nonprofit home?

  Is it part of a chain?

  Does the administrator have more than one home to manage?

  Who is in charge when the administrator is away?

  Is the administrator licensed?

  Does the administrator seem friendly?

- Is the home eligible for Medicare and Medicaid reimbursement?
- Does the home have Medicaid residents?

  Is the home restricted to private-pay patients?

  What happens to private-pay patients when their funds run out?

- What are the basic costs of the home?

  What do these costs include?

- Does the home make extra charges for special diets or feeding a patient?
- Are there special charges for walkers, crutches, or canes?
- Are bills itemized?
- What about physician services?

  Which physician services are included? Which are extra?

  Are there charges to hold a bed while the resident is in the hospital?

- What are the visiting policies?

  What are the limitations?

- What are the living arrangements?

  Do residents share rooms?

  Are private rooms available?

  How much privacy is there for a patient?

Is the facility clean?

How does it smell?

- What is the food like?

Is there any choice?

Are special diets accommodated?

Do the patients enjoy the food?

- Are private physicians allowed?
- Who provides eye care, dental care, and mental health care?
- Is there a staff social worker?

Is there a recreation staff?

- Are rehabilitation services available?
- Are clergy encouraged to visit?

Does the facility recognize and support the religious needs of the patient?

Is there a chapel or prayer room in the facility?

- What is the ratio of staff to patients?
- What are the rules concerning personal possessions, including some personal furniture?
- Is the location convenient?

Is it close to the family?

Is it in an area that is generally pleasing?

- What happens to a resident when he becomes ill?

How ill must he become before he is hospitalized?

Does the facility work with a local hospital in the case of ill residents?

- Does the staff try to get to know the resident?

Do staff members show respect for the patient?

How does the staff address patients?

- Does the home encourage the participation of a resident council?

What are the rights of the resident council?

- How are suggestions, questions, and complaints handled?

Is there a way to effectively address the questions and
complaints of residents and relatives?

Obviously it isn't necessary to ask all these questions for each
home you visit. It would be helpful, however, to look at a
prospective nursing home from the following basic standpoints:

1. *Overall impression.* What is your overall impression of the
facility? Does it look and smell clean? Is the atmosphere cheery
and bright or dull and dingy? Are staff members courteous to
the residents, family, and visitors? You can get a pretty good
impression of the place by simply looking all around and talking
to people.

2. *Ownership.* Who owns the facility? Is it a nonprofit or
for-profit operation? Who operates it in either case? Is it licensed? Is it supported by or affiliated with a church or denomination? Is it a stable operation? Does it appear it will be in
operation for a long time? Ownership and management affect
the total operation of the facility.

3. *Costs.* How much does it cost to be in the home? What do
the costs cover? Are there extra costs? If so, what are they, and
when do they apply? Is this a self-pay facility only? Does it accept
Medicaid patients? What happens if and when we run out of
money?

4. *Treatment of residents.* How well are the residents cared for?
What is the training of the various staff who care for patients?
How much freedom do residents have? What restrictions are
placed on residents? Are they restrained? To what extent are they
medicated? Do they have any choice of roommates? Are there
any private rooms? How are problems and complaints handled?
Is there a resident's council? How are patient and family concerns
handled?

Choosing a nursing home is not easy. The whole process of
placing a loved one in a nursing home is usually very difficult.
But if you are creatively involved in helping your parent find the

best situation for her, you will know you have done your best. That's all you can do.

PAYING FOR NURSING-HOME CARE

In the United States, there is no adequate support system, private or public, to help families finance long-term care for their elderly parents. This may not be the case in the future, but for those who are already elderly, there are no adequate answers. Only about 16 to 20 percent of Americans can afford long-term care, primarily in the form of nursing-home care.

Two-thirds of older people who are single and one-third of married people fall into poverty after being in a nursing home just thirteen weeks.[10] And the average older person has enough resources to pay for only seven months in a nursing home. This is because Medicare, the primary health insurance for people sixty-five and older, only pays 2 percent of nursing-home costs in America.[11] As it is administered, Medicare does not pay for the custodial care of older people.[12] Medicare only pays for skilled care—daily medical attention from a licensed health professional such as a registered nurse or physical therapist working under orders from a doctor.

Medicare only pays for acute or curative care. Acute care coverage refers to the costs associated with an illness or injury that requires hospitalization. As we all know, these costs can be enormous, and Medicare does a pretty good job of covering them. However, it is important to have something called "medigap" insurance to cover what Medicare doesn't cover for acute illnesses requiring hospitalization. Curative care refers to the type of treatment prescribed by a physician and performed by a health professional and is intended to improve a condition an older person has.

Medicare does not cover custodial, chronic, or continual care, which describes the situation of most older people in nursing homes. With nursing-home costs varying between twenty-five and thirty-five thousand dollars each year, only the wealthy can afford an extended stay.

Are there alternatives in paying for nursing-home placements and stays? For the present generation of older people, not really. One solution being suggested is private insurance for long-term care. Private long-term insurance may be important for future generations of older people. But for those who are already old, private long-term insurance is no solution at all because it is not available after a certain age. And for those who have some form of long-term insurance, many of the early policies did not allow for inflation. Most older people who are still eligible to buy a long-term care policy would find such a policy unaffordable.

According to the Health Care Financing Administration, only one percent of current nursing-home costs are covered by private insurance.[13] This leaves millions of Americans in the financial "no care zone."[14] This is part of the national health-care financing crisis we face. With private insurance nonexistent or unaffordable for the current population of older Americans, and with the Medicare system only covering 2 percent of nursing-home costs, how can the average hard-working family pay up to thirty-five thousand dollars or more per year to keep one of their loved ones in a nursing home? The answer is, they can't. They are forced to spend down to poverty to qualify for Medicaid.

Medicaid is a program designed to help people with low incomes and limited assets to pay for medical-related costs. Medicaid has become a major way for the elderly in America to pay for long-term care. Unfortunately, Medicaid is an "alternate" way to pay for nursing-home costs, not a "supplemental" way. Older people who need financial assistance to help pay for the high costs of a nursing home get none unless and until they are poor enough to qualify for Medicaid.

The amounts of resources a person can keep before they qualify for Medicaid vary. Michigan, for instance, lets a person keep a minimal amount of cash or liquid assets: her home, one car, personal belongings and household goods, a burial plot, a prepaid irreversible funeral contract for a limited amount (two thousand dollars or less), and assets that the person has been unable to sell for at least thirty days.[15]

The above list of assets is not complete; it only suggests the kind of resource limitations. Complete and current lists of limitations are available from a local long-term care ombudsman program, a local Department of Social Services office, or by calling a local Area Agency on Aging to find out where you can get regulations that apply to your state.

Local attorneys, either in private practice or those available from legal hot lines or lawyer-referral services, can provide help in qualifying for Medicaid. In Michigan, for example, free legal services are provided for persons age sixty and over to help them with Medicaid eligibility.

Knowing the specific eligibility requirements for Medicaid is important, especially if you and your parent are considering disposing of your parent's assets below their reasonable value to their children or people other than a spouse. Since January 1991, Medicaid reviews all assets transferred during the thirty-month period before a Medicaid application. If a person does give away resources and belongings to become eligible for Medicaid nursing-home coverage, the person probably will not be eligible for coverage for the period of time the assets would have paid for the costs of the nursing home. For example, if an older person gave away six thousand dollars within the thirty-month period before entering a nursing home, and if the home charged two thousand dollars per month, the person would not be eligible for three months of Medicaid nursing-home coverage.

The reality for so many older people is that in order to qualify for assistance in nursing-home coverage, they have to "spend down" their savings and resources to a level that qualifies them to apply for assistance. This is demeaning for older people who worked hard all their lives to be self-sufficient and independent.

But nearly four out of five Americans cannot afford extended stays in a nursing home.[16]

Is there any solution? In his book, *Avoiding the Medicaid Trap: How to Beat the Catastrophic Costs of Nursing-Home Care,*[17] Armond Budish suggests that older people establish a Medicaid trust. He says such a trust works best for persons with relatively modest nest eggs whose investment income does not cover the entire costs of the nursing home.

The trust removes assets from the reach of the nursing home and results in Medicaid's picking up more of the bill. In order for this to work, at least thirty months before applying for Medicaid, a person must place his assets (cash, certificates of deposit, stocks, etc.) in an irrevocable trust. The person can live on the trust's interest.

When a person is admitted to a nursing home, the interest goes for expenses. If the individual is discharged from the nursing home, the trust assets still produce income for expenses. But if not in the trust, the assets would have been consumed by the expenses of nursing-home care. When the individual dies, the trust assets go to a spouse, children, or other beneficiary.[18]

Social Security was designed to help older people pay basic bills. Medicare covers all of an older person's hospital costs for the first sixty days after a copayment of $592 (as of 1990), with a copayment of $148 per day for days sixty-one through ninety. But long-term health care is the unfinished part of a triangle that represents the basic resources older people need to survive financially with some degree of dignity and self-esteem. With the fastest-growing group of Americans eighty-five and older, the problem is not going to go away.

BEING A CAREGIVER FOR
PARENTS IN A NURSING HOME

After Marge found a place for her mother at a nearby nursing home, she tried hard to relieve her guilt by being the best caregiver she could be from outside the home. She discovered there were positive steps she could take to make her mother's stay more enjoyable.

VISITING

One of the most important things an adult child can do is visit. You don't have to visit twice a day, or even every day. Maybe once a week is all you can manage because of your job, distance, or other responsibilities. But meaningful visits are important.

A delightful but little-known film is *Peege*. It is the story of a family who visits Grandma in a nursing home. Mom, Dad, and the children go together to visit Peege, the grandma, who is not lucid. She sits in her chair and merely stares at them.

The family members all talk about their busy lives—lives that Peege really doesn't comprehend. They ramble on about school activities and business trips. Their small talk goes over Peege's head. After a relatively short time everybody leaves Peege except one of the sons, who stays to talk with Peege.

He talks about the good times they had together in the past. Memory of those times really gets through to Peege, and a beautiful smile lights up her face. She remembers with love her zest for life in years past and the fun she had with her grandson. It is a beautiful time, a beautiful visit.

MONITOR CARE

Another important thing you can do for your parent in a nursing home is to monitor the care she is receiving. This is important, and it must be handled delicately. You should know whom to talk to when you don't think something is right.

"After placement, be assertive in verbalizing your grievances and complaints," advises Vivian Greenberg. "The spinoffs of such efforts are enormous. You will experience less helplessness and guilt and consequently be a more loving, meaningful, and effective care-giver to your institutionalized parent."[19]

It is a good idea to talk first to the person who can do

something about the situation. This may be an attending staff person, a nurse, a supervisor, or the administrator. If you are in doubt about a condition or situation and don't really know how to handle it, it might be a good idea to ask someone in the long-term care ombudsman program in your local area how to proceed. Describe the problem and get his advice on whom to address and how to proceed. He may handle it for you.

In some states the ombudsman programs have some enforcement powers. In some states they have semiregulatory authority. In most states, they help to resolve complaints. In this respect, if they or the family can't resolve an issue or complaint, the ombudsman can refer the situation to the state agency that regulates nursing homes. In the case of abuse or neglect, the case is referred directly to the state regulatory agency. In cases other than abuse or neglect, attempts are made on a local level to resolve the issue.

The long-term care ombudsman programs are important resources in educating patients and their families. Very often they work closely with the facility in resolving problems. They also work with the homes and the families to obtain Medicare or Medicaid coverage for patients. They know how to apply for the rights of nursing-home residents, as guaranteed by federal and state laws. In short, they are an excellent resource of information as well as an excellent ally in resolving complaints, issues, and problems.

ACQUAINT THE STAFF WITH YOUR PARENT
Another way you can help your parent in a nursing home is to talk to the staff of the home and let them know something about your mother's or father's life. Help them understand your parent as a whole person.

One older man was placed in a nursing home and immediately caused problems because he slept much of the day and tried to wander around the home at night. The staff didn't know what to do with him. They tried various medications to help him get his nights and days straightened out, but nothing worked. Then one day his daughter explained that her father had been a night watchman most of his adult life. He was used to being up all night. This information greatly helped the staff in caring for him.

A suggestion has been made by the ombudsman in our area that a short biography be placed by each resident's bed so all of the staff has a better understanding of the person they are caring for. Knowing something about the person personalizes a patient. It makes her a real person instead of just another occupant of a bed.

NURSING-HOME RIGHTS

You can also obtain copies of the rights of nursing-home residents as guaranteed by the federal government and the state in which you live from local ombudsman programs, Area Agencies on Aging, or a State Office on Aging (whose telephone number and address can be obtained from the directory of state offices in your state). These rights are updated from time to time, and it is important to have the latest versions. These rights relate directly to the quality of care and the quality of life of nursing-home residents.

RESIDENT AND FAMILY COUNCILS

Another way to assist your parent in a nursing home is to become familiar with something called a "resident council" for the residents, and something called a "family council" for family members of the residents.

Resident councils are important for information for the residents, and for ongoing resident input into the operation of the nursing home. Not all nursing homes have family councils, but it is important to know how to have ongoing input into the life of the nursing home. The availability of these councils, and the role they play in the life of the nursing home, could be one of the determining factors in choosing a nursing home.

Irene and her mother had always been close. They talked about the possibility of nursing home placement three years before it actually happened. Although they were open and able to talk freely, still Irene's mother became depressed at the thought of leaving her home.

"In her heart, Mother hoped that with aides and companions she could remain in her own home until death. In Irene's heart rested the same wish. In the end it was Mother, in fact, who called Irene one evening to tell her she felt it was time to 'say goodbye to my home.' The hardest decision of all had been made in a matter of minutes over the telephone—not by Irene, but by Mother herself."—Vivian Greenberg[20]

PART FOUR

PART FOUR

CHAPTER THIRTEEN
Dealing with Frustration, Anger, and Guilt

The Scriptures tell us that children are responsible for their aging parents.

> If [widows] have children or grandchildren, these are the ones who should take the responsibility, for kindness should begin at home, supporting needy parents. This is something that pleases God very much. . . . Anyone who won't care for his own relatives when they need help, especially those living in his own family, has no right to say he is a Christian. Such a person is worse than the heathen. (1 Timothy 5:4, 8)

We are told in Exodus 20:12:

> Honor your father and mother, that you may have a long, good life.

The Bible does not give us details about how we are to care for and honor our parents. God's Word does not deal with nursing homes, group living situations, pensions, Social Security payments, Medicare provisions, or Medicaid. There is no commandment in the Bible that says you must take your parents into your home. Neither does the command to honor our fathers and mothers say that children must allow themselves to be manipulated and controlled by overly authoritative parents. In addition, there is no command that says a person must accept responsibility for the full cost of having his or her parent in a nursing home.

The biblical mandates are clear, though, that elderly parents are not to be ignored, shunned, left to their own devices, or neglected in a time of need. Elderly parents are to be loved, honored, and helped.

The problem for Christian children is knowing how to fulfill these biblical guidelines. We want to help our aging parents, and often we are filled with guilt because we can't solve every problem.

Providing care for aging parents is not easy. It is tough work. People who automatically say, "Oh, I would take my mother in without a second thought," probably should have second thoughts. It is difficult to give the type of constant loving care that many parents need. If the care provider does not get enough rest and help, the result can be anger, depression, anxiety, and resentment. And often after these negative feelings comes a crushing load of guilt.

Today's children are doing more to provide for frail aging parents than those of any previous generation. Too often, though, we have an unrealistic concept of caregiving. In the past, parents did not live as long as they do today, and "the old person's friend," pneumonia, brought death to many folks before they deteriorated into totally dependent individuals.

As an aging parent develops conditions that require more and more care, the caregiver will often begin to scold herself for her negative thoughts. She may want to give of herself freely, but when she is tired she begins to feel unloving and selfish. Daughters often torture themselves for not loving more, for not working harder, and for not having more energy. They must cope not only with their aging parents but with a spouse and children who need time and attention.

The Christian family should have no illusions about the

difficulty of providing for aged parents. Although we are promised God's strength and grace, we still have weaknesses and are prone to failures. If you care for your parents, you may at times feel angry, frustrated, exhausted, and guilty. It is all right to have those feelings. You are not abnormal, hateful, or unappreciative.

It is very helpful to have someone to talk to, so try to find a support group for children of aging parents in your area. After discussion, tears, and practical answers to specific problems, you will often find ways to continue to cope within your limits. Then you will be able to say to your parent, "I love you, and I want to do what is best for you."

Aged parents can make our job difficult by their irritability, demands, confusion, and anger. That is why the fourth commandment, "Honor your father and mother," was directed at middle-aged adults to remind them to care for elderly parents, not to small children to obey their parents. Often these negative attitudes are complicated by relationships from the past.

SITUATIONS THAT CAN RESULT IN STRESS, FRUSTRATION, AND TENSION

UNRESOLVED TENSIONS

It is possible that you and your parent never resolved problems that once existed between the two of you. Your parent may have been too domineering, too smothering, too demanding, or too immature. Perhaps your parent was abusive or neglectful. Your parent may have had a significant problem that kept him from being a good parent.

The passing of time by itself does not resolve these kinds of problems. If this is your situation, you need to make a real effort to lovingly confront your parent with your feelings, experience an emotional release, and attempt to move the relationship to a more positive basis. This may require professional help.

"The illness of an aging parent brings all the unresolved issues to the surface," says Leonard Felder, coauthor of *Making Peace with Your Parents* (Random House). "Remember you cannot change your parents. But you can become more assertive. You can forgive them."[1]

ROLE REVERSAL
If you were especially dependent upon your parents, you may find it extremely hard to make decisions for your parents when necessary. In addition, your parents may resist this role reversal.

A RESCUE FANTASY
Some children imagine that they will be able to rescue their parent from illness or other difficulties. These children might take their sick parent to hospital after hospital, trying to find a doctor who will give a more hopeful diagnosis. They may even submit their parents to medical quacks who promise quick relief for arthritis, Parkinson's disease, Alzheimer's disease, etc.

The movie *Dad,* starring Ted Danson and Jack Lemmon, featured a man who convinced himself that his father was getting no better in the hospital, so he literally pulled him out of the hospital bed and took him home. Dad did no better at home, though, and the son was forced to admit reality—he couldn't rescue his father from a lingering illness.

DEALING WITH NURSING-HOME STAFF
If your parent is placed in a nursing home, make sure you do not try to relieve your own possible guilt feelings by becoming too demanding of the nursing-home staff. People in nursing homes work under very difficult conditions. They are usually under-paid and work with tremendous tension. They need to be praised for their work. Children of parents in a nursing home need to show appreciation for the care given to their parents.

THE GENERATION GAP
Some children experience tension in their relationship with their parents because they do not understand their parents' perception of music, entertainment, money, and even the roles

of men and women in church and society. Don't let these differences lead to conflict and anger. Respect your parents' opinions. They grew up in a different time than you, and they have been molded through years of life experiences that were different from yours.

SIBLING RIVALRY

Sibling rivalry, which may have been dormant in your family for years, may unexpectedly rear its ugly head while you are caring for an aging parent. Both you and your siblings want love and approval from your parents. It is not unusual, even in middle age, for an adult child to try to prove to his parents that he loves them more than the other children do.

Friction often arises between brothers and sisters when one child is left to provide primary care for the aging parent. This overburdened child may give 100 percent physically and emotionally while the other children drop in for small talk occasionally or send checks in the mail.

Marsha lives near her mother. Her sister lives nearby, too, but because Marsha was always close to her mother, she found herself nominated to become the primary caregiver for their mother. A brother lives out of state and isn't expected to contribute much. "If I don't do it or at least direct it, it doesn't get done," Marsha told a reporter from *Newsday*. "No one picks up the slack, and this is where the resentment comes in."[2]

Sara, another woman who cares for an aging mother, has a similar story. "My sister does what she's told, when she's told, if she can," says Sara, whose sixty-eight-year-old mother lives alone in a Brooklyn apartment. "She makes the call as if it's a gesture to do me a favor, but she never takes responsibility alone. I've told many people I'd prefer to be a single child."[3]

Unresolved issues come up in sibling relationships, too.

"You were always the favorite, so you handle it."

"You never have gotten over the fact that I got piano lessons and you didn't. No wonder you don't care about her."

"You girls never did a thing for us boys. We're the only ones who care about Dad now."

Marsha's sister frequently tells her that she has left their mother to die in a nursing home. "Quite the contrary, I put her there to live," Marsha says.

Marsha visits her mother several times each week and takes her out whenever she can. Her sister visits occasionally, but took their mother to the beach for two weeks. "She always thinks it's a contest," says Marsha. She imitates her sister: "'Did you ever take Mama for two weeks?'"[4]

If you find yourself feeling resentful or squabbling with your siblings, call a family meeting and invite a neutral third party to mediate. Often your pastor or a family friend can serve in this role. Let each child have his or her say, and air your feelings and frustrations. Remind each other that you aren't caring for your parent in order to please each other, but in order to do *what is best for your parent*.

At your family meeting, select one child who can have a durable power of attorney in case your parent becomes incompetent. Arrange for the power of attorney as soon as possible. Ideally, it should be a child who lives near your parent.

Also lay out what needs to be done for your parent and which of you are best equipped to handle those needs. It is not fair to expect one child to do everything. If the primary caregiver cannot handle everything and distance limits the other brothers and sisters, they should arrange outside help through the variety of private and public social service agencies available in most communities.

Don't be afraid to ask your siblings for the help you need. "You have to do it," says Jane Bardavid, director of a community advisory program for the elderly in New York. "You have to put yourself through the pain. It's better to know what the realities are than to live with assumptions."[5]

Avoid accusing your siblings. Don't play the martyr and list all you do for your parent. Instead, explain that your parent requires a great deal of care and you are feeling burned out or exhausted. Ask what others can do to help ease your load.

Bardavid says it is easier to involve other siblings if the parent can ask for help themselves. For instance, if your mother needs to go to the doctor and you can't take her, have your mother call your sister. This will not only give you a break, but it will reduce your mother's dependence upon you.

Whatever you do, be aware of one paradox: The more you do for your parent, the less you may be appreciated. The less your siblings do, the more they may be portrayed as saints. Don't let this eat away at you. Your parents may be attempting to rationalize the lack of attention by your brother or sister by picturing them in a rosier light than is realistic.

If a daughter has to quit her job to provide care for a parent, her brothers or sisters should offer to help her with financial support or be willing to see that she gets a larger share of the estate for being the one who provides most of the hands-on care.

CARING FOR YOUR PARENTS FROM FAR AWAY

Gary lives in Florida; his sister, Vicki, lives in Louisiana. When their father fell ill last year, they strained their family budgets to fly to Ohio several times to visit. They both felt frustrated by distance.

"We had no one to talk to," Gary recalls. "I called the doctor a couple of times just to get a report on Dad's condition, but I felt like we really didn't know what was going on. We were just too far away."

"Caregiving is not only hands-on but involves coordination, financial backup, and emotional assistance," says Lucy Steinitz, executive director of Jewish Family Services in Baltimore. "Long distance, it's very frustrating."[6]

If your parent falls ill far away from you, you may have to:

- communicate with a hospital, nursing home, or other busy medical specialists
- judge medical treatment—or conflicting medical judgments—from a distance
- plan for medical emergencies
- arrange for your parent to seek medical care or go into a nursing home when he or she is against it
- know when it's time to drop everything and go to the sick person's bedside
- redefine your relationship with your parent once you become a long-distance caregiver
- balance day-to-day concerns with the pressing medical needs of the far-away person[7]

Often children of older parents are tempted to physically move their parents out of their home after a medical emergency has struck. This is usually not a good idea, however, because a move requires greater planning. "Don't kidnap the parent and geographically bring them away from where they live," says Janet Kurland of Baltimore's Jewish Family Services. "If there's any possibility, help them stay."[8]

You can help your parent by getting his or her medical care information down on paper. Learn what hospitals are nearby. Know what medications your parent is taking and how the medical bills are being paid. Find out who is in your parent's support system: his lawyer, banker, pastor, neighbor, and best friend. Establish a friendly relationship and ask them to call you if something seems amiss.

If your parent enters a hospital or nursing home at a distance from you, it is helpful to appoint one family member—either yourself or a sibling—to be the family representative and keep the others informed. If your parent is in the hospital, try to have at least one family member there at all times. Split travel times if possible.

If your parent is having major surgery, don't forget that he will need someone at home after he is released from the hospital. Many times children crowd at the hospital for a parent's operation, only to disperse at the time when they are most needed.

"If you are the primary contact for the family," says Cristine Russell, "don't be afraid to ask questions of doctors and hospital personnel. If you have concerns about the care, encourage the patient to get a second opinion or even to switch doctors. Most hospitals and medical facilities have a social worker or patient advocate to help work with the hospital system and arrange follow-up care after discharge."[9]

Routine care for aging parents must sometimes be handled from a distance, too. One Midwestern businessman hired a woman in Los Angeles to look after his parents. His "surrogate sister," as he calls her, is Judith Tobenkin, a gerontologist.

Tobenkin's job is to visit the homes of older folks and see that they are safe and appropriately equipped. She finds household workers and coordinates medical, legal, and financial services. She even buys food and clothes and on occasion acts as chauffeur.

"When Judy came into my life, I had enormous problems," said the businessman. "Those problems haven't gone away, but at least they are manageable."[10]

If you hire a private care manager such as Judith Tobenkin, for a fee ranging from $150 to $500, he or she will visit your parent and make a report. For additional fees ranging from $50 to $120 an hour, private care managers will find home health care workers, recommend nursing homes, make regular visits, and handle emergencies. For referrals, you may call the National Association of Private Geriatric Care Managers in Tucson, Arizona, at (602) 881-8008.

But heed Jane Bryant Quinn's warning: "This field is utterly unregulated. So check every claim on the manager's resume to see if it's true. Interview at least three clients, get a written plan of action, plus costs, and don't choose anyone who rubs you wrong."[11] You can also get a free booklet from the American Association of Retired Persons, *Miles Away and Still Caring*. Write to AARP Fulfillment (see appendix).

UNDERSTANDING YOUR PARENTS IN CONFLICT

In his book *You and Your Parents: Strategies for Building an Adult Relationship*, Harold Ivan Smith points out that parents react to conflict in the following ways:[12]

1. Some parents are *avoiders* of conflict. At the first hint of trouble, they retreat because they just don't want to make trouble.

2. Some parents are *exploders*. At the first hint of confrontation, conflict, or disagreement, they explode in anger. As a result basic issues can't be resolved, and children either stay away or try to pacify their parents.

3. Some parents are *victors*. These parents will argue because they believe they must win. They cannot tolerate the fact that their child might be brighter, more educated, or more insightful than they are. Their daughter might have a degree in nutrition, but they still insist that they know more about food than their daughter.

4. Other parents are *extinguishers*. These parents deny that a conflict exists. When a troublesome topic comes up, they will change the subject.

You may feel tension between you and your parent because your father or mother is rigid and demanding. Perhaps you simply hide behind a wall of silence and listen to your parents talk. The thought of going to visit your parent may be enough to give you an upset stomach. You may be suppressing anger that can be overcome by professional counseling.

Why are your parents rigid and critical? It is possible that your parents were ill-equipped for parenting and not prepared to face the realities that life dealt them. Perhaps one of their children did something to bring "shame" on the family. Your parents may dwell on some real or imagined pain and turn away children who could be supportive. Sometimes this behavior is the result of undiagnosed depression.

If you are unable to make changes in your relationship with your folks or your siblings, you should talk to your pastor or seek professional counseling. We should all try to make our parent-child relationships more like the biblical ideal.

GUILT: THE SILENT SHADOW OF CAREGIVERS

"Guilt is such a primary emotion among care-givers," says Lynn Osterkamp, founder and editor of the Parent Care newsletter at the University of Kansas Gerontology Center. "Most people, no matter how much they do, never feel it is enough."[13]

"Guilt is the gift that keeps on giving," agrees psychologist Marilyn Bonjean. "And there is not one care-giver who doesn't feel it. . . . Our emotions are not rational on this issue. It is human to resent our parents for getting older and frail."[14]

OVERCOMING GUILT

As Christians, many of us are familiar with overpowering feelings of guilt. But guilt is taken away by the Cross. Too often guilt is excess baggage many of us carry around through life. We need to shed guilt that keeps us from living a victorious Christian life.

We need to keep our responsibilities to our parents in perspective. You are not likely to abandon your parents. Finding alternative care for your folks is not abandonment. Neither is placement in a nursing home. To continue to feel guilty after you have done your best to provide for your folks is not realistic and will only lead you into depression.

But how can you plan to live happily and victoriously while your parents grow older and sicker? How can you plan your own life when your emotional and physical limits are taxed to the utmost? The answer lies in examining your priorities and what God indicates is important in your life.

WHERE SHOULD YOUR PRIORITIES LIE?

One priority is *your marriage.* The biblical concept of marriage includes the independence of children from their parents. You and your spouse each left your father and mother to form a new family. You developed a oneness that results in an emotional, intellectual, physical, and spiritual togetherness

Aged parents should not be so demanding that they threaten your relationship with your spouse. Some manipulative parents develop an illness or have an emergency just when their child is about to go on a vacation, get a new job, or become involved in community or church activities. At that point, these children should lovingly, firmly, and clearly insist that they are going to go ahead with their plans, explaining that alternative care will be provided.

The needs of *teenage or young adult children* often come ahead of the needs of parents. There will be times when you cannot be with your parents because your children need you. Your parents need to understand that you have a responsibility to be available for the moral and emotional development of the new generation.

Married or single, your care for your aging parent should not jeopardize *your own health.* Many caregiving children themselves are older and do not have the strength to provide for an elderly parent. A recent study reported that 65 percent of fifty-year-old women in the U.S. had living mothers as compared to 37 percent a generation ago.[15] The average age of caregivers surveyed was fifty-seven, with one-third of them over sixty-five. Over 30 percent rated their health as fair to poor.[16] About 75 percent of the caregivers are females who devote an average of four to five hours a day providing care. Some do it around the clock.[17]

KEEP YOUR ROLE AS A
CAREGIVER IN PERSPECTIVE

"I realized the vital role of the caregiver recently when I became ill and found I had to keep going on with the tasks of personal care like preparing meals when I couldn't even look at food," says Ethel Sharp, who cares for her eighty-seven-year-old mother. "The physical fatigue from the daily work routine and the mental fatigue from role reversal, frustration, loss, and concern are just a few emotions not to be taken lightly."

Sharp gives practical pointers for caregivers:

- Know your limitations and provide for adequate rest
- Exercise and concentrate on proper nutrition
- Reach out for help and use the community service resources available
- Make time to do those things that bring pleasure and relaxation
- Work at having fun and enjoy yourself
- Maintain communication between family members and involve them in activities
- Have ongoing contact with health care providers
- Keep your spiritual life alive

Put yourself first, advises Sharp, because if you don't take care of yourself, "you will not be any good to anybody."[18]

Joan Conway, a nurse who works the night shift in a nursing home, is quoted in *Newsweek:*

The unseen guests at each bedside are the persons who were chosen to admit the aging parents who, 99 percent of the time, are unwilling and incapable of admitting themselves. Long after the patients are comfortable in their new beds, the tortured children are left standing bereft in the hall, trembling with fear, dreading the consequences of the act, afraid that what they have just done to their mother will someday be done to them. We are taught early in life that the care we give our parents when they get old is the care our children will give us when we are past caring for ourselves. Nursing homes have taken on the color and reputation of the old-fashioned asylum or poorhouse that was the dread of everyone 50 years ago.

Last week, I stood in the hall talking to the daughter of one of our new patients when she returned with her mother's medicine. I realized when I saw her so shaken and weeping that her guilt caused her to be my major concern. "How is she?" the daughter asked, trembling. Then she began to cry. "Did she sleep last night?" "Yes," I said, "she slept like a baby. She is in better shape than you are."[19]

In all of the concern, anxiety, guilt, and anger that often result from a crisis of extended care, love remains. It can be expressed by word, touch, and deed. Even if your parents have severe physical and mental conditions, they can respond to a hug, a touch, a kiss from you. Many people who have lost short-term memory can recall the past. If you sit with your parents, touch them, and help them recall an earlier, less-confusing time, you will be giving your parents the love they need. Try to overcome your hesitancy to ask for help. You might like to think you are self-sufficient and a pillar of strength, but God made us to relate to others. We need each other, and you will need help from other people.

Don't let yourself become angry or embarrassed over strange behavior, obscene language, and weird attitudes of mentally incompetent older people. Strange behavior in confused and ill people does not mean that the ailing person is controlled by evil. If the person's brain is deteriorating, he or she is not responsible for strange behavior or thoughts. Family members might find it very useful to get professional help in coping with the strange and different behavior of their loved ones. Helene McLean's book, *Caring for Your Parents: A Source Book of Opinions and Solutions for Both Generations,* is a helpful source here.[20]

TIPS TO IMPROVE VISITS WITH AGING PARENTS OR GRANDPARENTS

Loneliness can be devastating. Your parents, institutionalized or not, would appreciate your visits. Your parents would also enjoy visiting their friends; if you can provide the opportunity or transportation, you will be helping a great deal.

When visiting your parents, touch them, hug them, give them a kiss, put your arm around them, and put your hand on their arms. All human beings need the touch of people who love them. A touch can frequently be much more powerful and important than words. If your family has not been a touching family, have the courage to break that pattern.

Before you visit, think of topics for conversation that your parent would enjoy discussing. Don't just run in, say hi, make small talk, and leave. Adult children and the grandchildren need to spend enough time to make the visit worthwhile. Occasionally children could bring a present such as flowers, chocolates, a book, a record, or a magazine. Everybody enjoys presents.

Birthdays and anniversaries should be celebrated. Don't assume that because your parents have had many birthdays they don't enjoy celebrating them. Celebration can include cards, calls, and visits.

Family reunions are important. Old people enjoy seeing their relatives. Family members can "pay their respects" and spend some time talking to their elderly relatives about the past as well as current topics. The Scriptures tell us that wisdom resides with the elderly, and younger family members can learn from their aged relatives.

It is helpful to assist your aged parents in their religious life. Help your folks attend a worship service if they are still able and wish to, provide religious music they enjoy, have religious publications available, and don't be afraid to talk about their assessment of their lives as Christians.

> The care of the elderly will teach you more about yourself than anything you've ever done.
>
> You'll feel noble, and then realize that nobility is pretty hollow. You'll feel humble, and wonder just how much humility you can swallow; you'll feel exhausted and find out the road ahead is still uncharted; you'll feel angry, and learn that rage will get you nowhere.
>
> How well you manage will depend on the health of everyone involved and the money that's available, but mostly it will depend on your attitude.[21]

Your attitude in this process is key. Although a positive attitude is essential, it can be difficult to maintain. But without a positive attitude, you may find that eldercare has four levels: "hard, harder, hardest—and overwhelming. Caring for the elderly is a bit like caring for children: You have to expect less, give more, laugh when you can and, above all, you have to let your anger go."[22]

CHAPTER FOURTEEN
Honoring Your Parents as Their Years Increase

"There are a lot of cases where alcohol, drugs, or caregiver stress have nothing to do with abuse," says Ms. Wolf, president of the National Committee for the Prevention of Elder Abuse. "A case in one of our studies involved a 55-year-old son who was living with his elderly mother because he was out of a job. He was living off her money and living in her house. One time he hit her because the food was cold when she served it to him."[1]

Unfortunately, too many Americans see older people as less vital and less important members of the community. Some people think that too many of our resources are used for old folks. Already we hear complaints that medical costs for the old are too high. As Christians we need to point out the contributions people of all ages can make. Our old people are old "spirits" who need to be loved, cared for, respected, and recognized as contributing members of our communities.

The Christian life is a journey of faith for persons of every age. The peak of the mountain is not reached until death, when a new reality begins. Our society's concept of being "over the hill," that is, having reached the top at sixty-five or so and then sliding down the other side of the mountain, is not correct, nor is it healthy to think of life that way. It is better to see retirement as a milestone, a marker on the journey to the top of the mountain. It is a pause for refreshment, a time for regrouping and reconsidering a person's life goals.

WALKING IN AN OLD PERSON'S SHOES

Pat Moore aged from her mid-twenties to eighty-five in a matter of hours. She put on a gray wig and latex wrinkles. She applied baby oil to her eyes to blur her vision, wore splints and bandages under her clothing to stiffen her joints, and put plugs in her ears to dull her hearing. As an "old" woman she traveled for three years in 116 cities in 14 states and 2 Canadian provinces.

She didn't don her disguise as a prank, on a dare, or to defraud businesses who offer a senior's discount. She did it out of altruism and a desire to honestly see how society perceives its elders.

When Pat was only seventeen, she left home for the first time as a promising student at the Rochester Institute of Technology. As she rode a bus through downtown Rochester, trying to balance her homesickness with her strong drive and ambition, her thoughts were momentarily diverted by an old man who walked on the sidewalk. "He was disheveled, but clean," recalls Moore, "and he carried two loaded shopping bags, one under each arm. I could see the deliberateness of each step and the strain of his load. I just sat there in tears, watching. Seeing him was like ice water in the face for me."

During her numerous forays into the world disguised as an old person, Pat learned what it is like to be ignored, shoved, mugged, cheated, and ostracized. Once she was mugged and badly beaten. Often she was treated rudely. "When I was in character, if I got a smile or a hello from a passerby, I felt like I'd received a hug from God himself," she recalls.

Moore has recently received great pleasure from "finally seeing so much of what I've been talking about involved in the business sector. People are beginning to realize the large number of older people in our society, and this is resulting in many products and services for elders and their caregivers."

Although Moore sees progress in the way businesses are beginning to perceive older adults, she still is often frustrated by society's attitude toward old people. "I've seen things that made me pull the car over and weep. I see things and I can't believe they don't hit other people the way they hit me. Witnessing the exchange of a store clerk with an elder when the clerk is condescending, cruel, patronizing; seeing someone 'put one over' on an older person; the overtness of speaking rudely to an older person; people who honk at older people who are slowly crossing the street—these things are still there. We're approaching the tenth anniversary of the experiment, but it saddens me to think there are bullies and brutes who are still racist, sexist, and ultimately ageist."

Through her experiment and her work, Pat Moore has learned that aging is not a cause for fear. "I tell people to relax. There is nothing to be frightened about. We have made aging fearful because of our cultural press, advertising, and the media. We have made a mockery of our elders, but we can undo that. If you are going to be blessed with a long life, rejoice! It saddens me that people will do anything to stave it off. . . . We should be happy for what and who we are and celebrate aging with grace."[2]

HELP YOUR PARENT FIND MEANING IN LIFE

Do not cast me away when I am old; do not forsake me when my strength is gone. (Psalm 71:9, NIV)

How can you help your aging parent "celebrate aging with grace"? Life needs to have meaning in the "golden years" as well as in mid-life. If we isolate the elderly, we cheat both them and ourselves. The older people in your life—your parents, older aunts and uncles, and even your grandparents—can still make a contribution to your life and the lives of your family members.

Tim Stafford tells the story of a depressed woman in a nursing home. Stafford's father asked the woman why she was discouraged, and she replied that she couldn't do all she used to do for others.

"What is it that you used to do?" Stafford asked.

"I used to bake pies for people. Then I would smile and cheer them up."

"Well, you can still smile," Stafford told her.

The woman didn't believe Stafford. What was the use of a smile without a pie to go along with it?

But one day Tim Stafford's father visited her again with his father, a resident in the same nursing home. Tim Stafford's grandfather could not say an intelligible word, but he greeted the woman and said, as clear as a bell, "You always have the nicest smile."

"After that," writes Tim Stafford, "no more intelligible words came out of him. But from this small miracle the woman seemed to draw encouragement and stopped struggling with a sense of purposelessness. She began to smile."[3]

We all struggle with the question of what gives meaning to life. Material things seem to be important in our earlier years, but those things do not really bring happiness and contentment. Rather, inner peace, understanding, and love for others bring true joy. Your parents, who are out of the race for material possessions and status, probably realize this.

Your parents may not be able to do all the things they used to do for you. They probably don't have large amounts of money; they may not have much strength. But they have other qualities. Find the strengths that your parents have and encourage them. Perhaps your mother can baby-sit the children. Maybe your father tells stories like no one else.

Your parents, no matter what their condition, can help bring balance to your life. Listen to them and respect what they have to say. They deserve honor for the progress they have made in their journey through life. Older people can teach us that there is glory in Christian community, joy in the spiritual life, and lasting value in being in touch with God's love.

HELP YOUR PARENT FIND HONOR IN AGE

Gray hair is a crown of splendor; it is attained by a righteous life. (Proverbs 16:31, NIV)

Some older people see aging only as a losing struggle against terrible losses. They see aging only as pain. This attitude is a result of our youth-oriented society. Although the losses and pain are too often real, the Bible tells us we can gain wisdom, insight, and grace as we age.

Different traditions have different interpretations of what it means to be old. In some cultures, age brings great honor. In ancient Israel, the term *old* meant having wisdom, insight, knowledge, and serenity of spirit. In America, we try to avoid using the word *old* by calling our older people a variety of names such as "third-agers," "golden agers," "senior citizens." For too many the term *old* means that one is, or will soon be, dependent on others, a condition most Americans cannot accept. For many others it means decline, lack of energy, and poverty.

This negative view of aging stems from our emphasis on present gratification. Many of our older citizens know that there is a reality beyond materialism. They know that life has an end and that people should plan ahead for an eternity to come.

God loves us for "being," not for "having." He cares for us regardless of our position or status in life. We are not abandoned because of our lack of accomplishment. Our value does not depend on a wrinkle-free face, a lack of gray hair, a paid-off mortgage, large bank accounts, successful businesses, or status in our community. If the value of life is defined by physical attractiveness, financial status, and personal fame, growing older will be a sad time for many of us.

So tell your mother that you admire her for the way she managed your home. Make your father feel like your hero for supporting his family. Ask them what lessons they've learned in life. Then listen with your heart to what they have to say.

HELP YOUR PARENTS MAINTAIN THEIR DIGNITY

Teach the older men to be temperate, worthy of respect, self-controlled, and sound in faith, in love and in endurance. (Titus 2:2, NIV)

There are many programs for older people that were begun with the best of intentions but are patronizing and degrading. Programs that keep older people busy while ignoring their decision-making capabilities or that cater to their limitations send negative messages about older people. Do not encourage your parents to participate in these programs if they will offend their dignity.

Discrimination against the old, "ageism," is part of American life. It is the result of a value system that reveres the attributes of youth but not the values of the old. For instance, a mandatory retirement age seems to suggest that after a certain age, a person is not worthy of employment. How unfair! The question in employment should be whether or not a person can do the job. Older people should not be dismissed, refused promotion, put off to other tasks, or given lesser positions simply because of their age.

After decades of employment, older people have a right to enjoy leisure, take a "break," participate in enjoyable activities, and just "goof off." But Christians never have to retire from serving God. And they can get real satisfaction from serving their fellow citizens. So encourage your parents to use their free time in service to others if they are willing and able.

The Bible's view of aging is one in which older mothers and fathers can continue to have responsibilities, make important decisions, and stay active in life. The wisdom that comes from years of living the Christian life can be shared with others, used by the church and the community, and valued by people around them who are in difficult circumstances.

REALIZE THAT WE ALL ARE DEPENDENT

On the contrary, those parts of the body [of Christ] that seem to be weaker are indispensable, and the parts that we think are less honorable we treat with special honor. . . . Now you are the body of Christ, and each one of you is a part of it. (1 Corinthians 12:22-23, 27, NIV)

Many people fear growing old because they worry about becoming dependent upon others. Your parents have no desire to become a burden to you or to the community. Dependence on God, however, is part of the Christian life.

None of us is truly independent. We depend not only on God, but on others, too. We should all accept that independence and dependence shift over time. Because we are dependent does not mean we are weak in character, strength, or fortitude. It means, rather, that we acknowledge that we need help. Our dependence allows others to receive a blessing by helping us.

There is no doubt that some dependent people make unreasonable demands upon others. Your parent may try to load you with undeserved and unrealistic guilt. But by now you should know what you are capable of handling. You can only do what you are capable of. No more. You should not feel guilty because you can't do everything. If your parents are truly unreasonable, they may need psychiatric diagnosis and treatment. They may be suffering from physical changes in the brain. They may be depressed or continuing a lifelong pattern that gets worse in their later years.

Don't let your parents cling to the notion that if they lose independence they are not worthy people. The Christian community is a mutual support network in which there is a continual shift between giving and receiving, dependency and caregiving. We can no more ignore those who want to help us than we can ignore those who need our help.

> Rise in the presence of the aged, show respect for the elderly and revere your God. I am the Lord. (Leviticus 19:32, NIV)

CHAPTER FIFTEEN
When You Must Say Good-bye

Early in the evening of March 28, I received a call from
the Powhatan Nursing Home in Arlington saying that my
mother had died. Her name was Margaretta Warden, she
was 87 years old, and she had been living in the shadow
of death for more than a year. As anticipated as that call
was, there are no words to describe the sense of loss I felt
then, and feel to this day. The closest physical sensation I
can think of is having the wind knocked out of you,
again and again and again.[1]

Very few families have meaningful discussions about death and
dying. Even children whose parent has a terminal illness are
reluctant to bring up the subject. Some people may be able to
discuss funeral arrangements, but few dwell on their thoughts
and feelings about death.

Death is an eventual reality for all of us. The very old realize
that each day may be their last, and they come to grips with this
idea. This enables some to enjoy every day and to rejoice in every
sunrise. Others view the passing of time with despair and insecurity.

Many older folks are comfortable about talking about death.
Don't think it morbid if your Christian parent begins to talk
about death; it is an event for which he is well-prepared. Older
Christians may want to talk of their hope in the resurrection,

their faith in God's promises, and the joy they will experience when they are reunited with loved ones. Your parent may want to give you advice or testify about God's mercy. Don't ignore or silence him if he wishes to talk about death. Instead, rejoice in your parent's peace of mind and spirit.

Where, O death, is your victory?
Where, O death, is your sting? (1 Corinthians 15:55, NIV)

Thanks be to God, who has given us the victory over death! Anyone who works in a nursing home knows that some older people are unhappy that they survived the night. They are eager to quit this life, and they look forward with great anticipation to heaven. One eighty-five-year-old man sat upright on his bed at the moment preceding death and pointed upward. "The angels are here," he announced. Then he died.

THE FEAR OF THE DYING PROCESS

The evidence is clear that older people fear the dying process more than death itself. They worry about the possibility of a long period of illness, of being hooked up to tubes, of being kept alive artificially by machines. Some worry that they will leave their loved ones with large emotional, physical, or financial losses.

Too often we hide the dying. People die in hospitals and nursing homes, away from the curious, and even from family members. In the early 1900s death was more visible because half of all deaths were among children. Today most deaths occur among people over sixty-five, and because these people who die are in institutions, our tendency is to read the obituaries with a disinterested eye. We expect old people to die, and if they die out of sight, they are out of mind.

It is ironic that what should be a powerful, semipublic ending to one's pilgrimage has become a hidden finish to one's journey.

Just as we are prepared for death by life, we can be prepared for life by death. The death of others forces us to realize that life is temporary and that things done for eternity should take highest priority. In addition, as we face death, we realize that we should give attention to the life to come.

The Bible is clear that the presence of God and the joys of heaven wait for the Christian. We have this assurance. This is not to deny that for many Christians the dying process consists of continuing physical pain or depression as the result of illnesses.

For some elderly people despair is the result of the side effects of prescription drugs, hormonal imbalances, or other physical changes in the brain. Some are struggling over distorted memories of past events. A supportive pastor, loving relative, and caring professional can be important for these suffering persons.

John Bunyan's book *The Pilgrim's Progress* portrays the constant struggle of the Christian life. It reminds us that as Christians we can claim God's grace and move forward in life even though we are buffeted by trials. We can all look back in triumph on shortcomings and failures.

In sickness, and as the result of prescription drugs, hormonal imbalances, or changes in the brain, your parent may be tempted to neglect God's repeated assurances of forgiveness, grace, eternal joy, and peace. When this happens, you and other family members need to remind your parent of the hope and joy of the Bible's assurances that God's grace is sufficient for all our conditions, even the conditions brought about by serious illnesses.

MODERN MEDICINE AND DYING

Dying isn't easy today, especially in a hospital. With the technological advances of modern medicine, doctors often reach for every possible means to prolong life, even if the life they are prolonging is spent in pain, discomfort, and indignity. Only if a family member specifically tells medical personnel not to undertake "heroic measures" or "do not resuscitate" are these measures avoided. Family members must be sure to make their wishes plain—once a patient is put on a respirator, it often takes a court order to get it turned off.

Helen Reynolds, sixty-three, was dying. Her legs were amputated to prevent gangrene, and she was hooked up to a ventilator that helped her breathe. After two months of living in a hospital room, Helen asked for a piece of paper and wrote that she no longer wanted to "live like this."

Gayle MacPherson, her eldest daughter, said, "She told me she'd just like to go to sleep. She's tired. She's had it."

The doctors unhooked the ventilator, and Helen Reynolds lived three more days. Then she drifted off to sleep, and death.[2]

The issue of "death with dignity" raises many questions for the Christian.[3] When do we have the right to refuse treatment that may be slightly helpful but will not be a cure? May we refuse extraordinary means to try to prolong life if that life will be filled with added pain and confusion? Do we have the right to say "enough" to treatment? Can we decide when our parents are ready to die?

It is our opinion that we should have the right to refuse heroic means to keep our parents alive if that longer life is without dignity and is one of pain and anguish. We believe that if elderly parents tell their adult children they do not want any extraordinary means used to keep them alive, that wish should be granted. This can be accomplished by a "durable power of attorney" and/or "living will." We believe that when there is no likelihood that a person will return to clear thinking, heroic means need not be used. Christians should not take actions to end life, but neither should they use mechanical or chemical means to prolong life artificially against a person's wishes and when the person will not recover.

If your parents have expressed their desire not to live in a vegetative state, a living will can speak for them if they are unable to express these views at a time of medical crisis. The living will expresses their wishes, and a durable power of attorney can appoint someone to make medical decisions on their behalf. For forms to help you write a living will or to assign power of attorney, contact your local Area Agency on Aging, one of your state legislators, a retirement home, or a pastor or denominational leader.

The National Living Will Registry will store your parents' living will in its original form. With a single phone call from a health care provider, a copy of the living will will be delivered in minutes, at any time of the day or night. For more information call (800) 336-9999 or write the National Living Will Registry, 720 Goodlette Road North, Suite 304, Naples, FL 33940.

DYING AT HOME

The National Institute on Aging examined the circumstances of a cross-section of elderly Connecticut residents over sixty who died. More than half of the people in the survey died in their sleep, without pain, and with family and friends nearby. More than half were in good or excellent health a year before death. More than half spent time with their relatives during the last days of their lives.[4]

If your parent lives with you and is facing death, you may want to seriously consider allowing your parent to die at home.

In medieval times in Europe, many religious orders established a hospice at river crossings, mountain passes, and country crossroads. These hospices provided the ill, weary, and lost with food, medical care, and instruction.

In 1967 in London, Dr. Cicely Saunders founded St. Christopher's Hospice, a special treatment center for the dying that emphasized pain control and provided the dying with sympathetic support staff.[5] Her emphasis was on organizing the dying person's family and others as a care unit so the patient did not feel that she was dying alone. The patient's pain was controlled, but she was not too drugged to relate to family members and friends.

Most dying persons prefer to die at home. Some medical personnel tend to interact less and less with dying persons, at times isolating them. Some have not been trained to interact with the dying and prefer to spend their time and energy on patients who will get well.

The hospice program founded by Dr. Saunders is thriving in the United States. By 1986 there were about seventeen hundred hospice programs in our country, most of which involve home care supported by a team of doctors, nurses, health aides, social workers, and volunteers.[6]

If there is a hospice care program in your area, you can arrange for medical care while your parent stays in your home. Dying at home is more personal. Barbara Deane writes, "One of the blessings of a terminal illness spent at home is that it gives the dying person time to reflect on his life, to make peace, to ask forgiveness if necessary, and to say good-bye to loved ones. This is impossible if he's in intractable pain or if his mind is clouded by pain medication. Hospice, by supporting families who care for the dying at home and controlling their pain, has allowed many to experience a 'good death.'"[7]

To receive hospice services, patient, family, and doctors must agree that the patient has six months or less to live. After admission, the hospice team cares for the family's needs, not just the patient's, around the clock. Other professionals help the family through the bereavement period. Medicare and some private health insurance companies now cover hospice services.[8]

FACING EMOTIONS

The apostle Paul wrote, "Brothers, we do not want you to be ignorant about those who fall asleep, or to grieve like the rest of men, who have no hope" (1 Thessalonians 4:13, NIV). Paul is not saying that Christians do not grieve; we do. But we can go through the stages of grief with hope. We know that our Christian parents go to an eternity with God. Their suffering and pain is over and done, never to be experienced again.

Psychiatrist Elizabeth Kubler-Ross, in her book *On Death and Dying,* has indicated that your parent probably will go through five stages in the process of dying: shock and denial, anger, bargaining, depression, and finally, acceptance.[9]

According to Kubler-Ross, in the first stage, shock and denial, your parent may not believe he has a terminal illness. He may seek a second or third opinion. He may refuse to talk about death and claim that he will "lick" the disease. He may claim that his faith is so strong God will heal him.

When your parent can deny the reality of his illness no longer, he may become angry. This anger may be directed toward God, loved ones, doctors, or at life in general. He may feel that God has been unfair, vindictive, or punishing. Often the anger will be directed at those closest to your parent.

If your parent works through his anger, he may go on to the process of bargaining in which he promises that if he can get well, he will devote his life to religious work . . . or never smoke again . . . or he'll start exercising . . . or be a better husband. He will make apologies for past mistakes and try to start again.

Once it is clear the bargaining will not work, your parent may become depressed. This may not be related to fear of death but rather the sorrow that comes from leaving loved ones or not being able to support or assist the family.

Finally, your dying parent will accept his impending death. Acceptance doesn't mean he is happy about dying, although many come to see death as relief, but he has accepted it. He is at peace with God, himself, and others.

Kubler-Ross does not claim that all persons go through all of these stages in sequence in the dying process. Some may be in two or more stages at the same time. Some persons may die in great anger while others may die quite quickly and still be in the stage of denial. Death, like all human behavior, is highly individualized. However, Kubler-Ross's research is important because it does indicate that there is a process of dying for many persons. Her writings help us relate to our parents who are in the dying process. It also enables us to understand better the various moods our parents have during the dying process. In whatever stage of dying you find your parent, it is important to be present to give support, to listen, to love, to grieve, and to share the hope for that future we have in paradise.

Not only will a terminally ill patient go through some variation of the grieving process, but his spouse and children will grieve, too. Everyone will work through the stages of grief on their individual timetables.

Tom Tugg was never able to move past the stage of shock and denial, and consequently, his wife's death devastated him. Tom and Brenda Tugg were a prosperous couple in their mid-fifties when doctors diagnosed inoperable cancer in the walls of Brenda's lungs. Their son, Jim, watched their personal drama unfold before him.

"My dad had always been self-sufficient and prosperous," Jim said. "For the first time he faced a problem he couldn't solve himself. He tried buying mother everything she had ever wanted until she asked him to stop. He wanted to try every medical option available. But neither Mom or Dad ever admitted that Mom's 'sickness' was cancer. He could not face the fact that Mom was dying."

At the funeral, Jim's father bore everything with equanimity until the time came to close the lid of the casket. He couldn't bear to take his eyes off the face of his beloved wife, and when his sons urged him to leave, his legs buckled under him and his sons carried him from the room. It was many months before Tom reached acceptance.

Ron Hunt passed through the stages of grief successfully, but not without wounding those he loved. When the doctors told Ron there was no further hope for his wife, Jean, he battled anger and despair. Jean only grew quieter and more reflective, finding comfort in prayer. But Ron turned his anger toward his children who lived hundreds of miles away. When they called home, he demanded that they come and visit their mother. When they did visit, he was moody and unpredictable. Jean was quietly dying; Ron was raging at those who loved them both.

"Jean was never angry," Ron recalled later. "I think she became sweeter in the last year of her life. I was angry at God. You expect rough things from life, but you never expect this. I questioned God—why was this allowed to happen?"

One hot day at home Jean became quiet and slipped into a coma. "I was beside her," Ron recalls. "Even in the coma her face was marked by pain. An hour after she went into the coma, her face suddenly relaxed and brightened. She was more beautiful than I had ever seen her in my life. She had passed away. I've seen a lot of people die, but even if I did not believe in heaven, I would have seen the change in her and known that she had gone to a place where she was not suffering."

Those who live with a dying parent must not only endure the dying, but also the living that follows. Logically, those who believe in life after death take comfort in believing they will someday be reunited with their loved ones, but that knowledge does not always help fill the void of the feeling of mortality that grips a child whose parent has died.

But always remember that living with a dying parent is still *living*. When doctors told Orville Kelly he had terminal cancer, he felt life could not be more unfair. He was only forty-two, a good churchgoing man, and the father of four children. He was frightened and depressed, and he contemplated suicide.

Driving home from a chemotherapy treatment, Kelly turned to his wife and said, "Let's talk about it. I'm going to die from cancer unless something else kills me, but I'm not dead yet. So let's start enjoying life again. Let's go home tonight and have a barbecue just like old times."

Kelly's change in attitude and his decision to accept each day as a gift from God encouraged his family and strengthened them throughout his remaining seven years. He shared his encouragement with others, too.

Kelly once said, "After all, none of us really knows when he is going to die. We are all 'terminal' in a sense." His manner of coping with cancer was to begin each day "not as another day closer to death, but as another day of life. I accept each day as a gift from God to be appreciated, enjoyed, and lived to its fullest."

MAKING FUNERAL ARRANGEMENTS

The funeral industry has been charged with taking advantage of people who are in a state of shock after the death of a loved one. Undoubtedly some funeral directors have overcharged clients and sold unnecessary items and services, but there are ethical funeral directors who are very helpful during a difficult time.

It makes a great deal of sense for older people to plan their funeral with a director they respect and trust. Many older people are buying preburial agreements and prepaying their funerals. Years before death, people can purchase a cemetery plot, a casket, and indicate what type of funeral they prefer.

If possible, try to make some initial arrangements before the shock of death. If you do not, you will be making decisions during a period of intense grief. Shopping for a funeral is not like buying a car—you can't always compare products and prices, and you will probably not be in the mood to dicker over the price. You can be at a distinct disadvantage if you wait until the last minute to make funeral arrangements.

Some people feel that they need to have a showy, expensive funeral for their loved one in order to show how much the deceased was loved or respected. Others feel their families must maintain their social status by arranging for an expensive funeral. Try not to be drawn into either trap. A funeral is for the family, and whatever suffices for the family will work best.

When James Lewis learned he had cancer as well as rheumatoid arthritis, he went right to work settling his affairs. He called the Social Security office, picked out a casket, and arranged for his funeral. Although his children had misgivings at first, James made plans to give his body to medical research. "I've got two diseases for which there is no cure," he told them. "Maybe this can be used to help someone else."

"His whole life was giving," his daughter says. "That was his biggest delight. I didn't feel I had the right to take that from him at his death."

At some point you might want to sit down with your parents and ask them what they want for a funeral service. Do they want to be buried or cremated? Perhaps they want to donate their bodies to science. This discussion does not have to be morbid. It can be a thoughtful way to find out what your parents really want.

The AARP has developed three free publications that are useful in planning a funeral:

Product Report: Funeral Goods and Services: This is a guide providing product and price information on traditional funerals and alternatives.

Product Report: Prepaying Your Funeral?: This guide gives funding options for various pre-need funeral plans and describes costs, price increases, portability (the ability to use the prepaid funeral in other locations), and other factors involved in funeral prepayment.

Cemetery Goods and Services: This guide deals with how to plan for and buy cemetery goods and how to recognize deceptive practices.

You can write to AARP Fulfillment (see appendix) for copies of these publications.

HANDLING BEREAVEMENT

Bereavement is an individual process. Not all people grieve in the same way, but all people do go through a grieving process, even if their relationship with the deceased was not a happy one. If you lose one parent, you may find that your remaining parent needs help to get through the grieving process. Let your surviving parent talk through her feelings of loss, fear, loneliness, and uncertainty.

It is usually best for the grieving spouse not to make important decisions about what to do with the old home or the estate for at least a year, until she is clearly through the grieving process. If your parent insists on making decisions, you can help by offering support and guidance.

It is not helpful for you to let your surviving parent grow dependent on you. Don't be too protective of your parent. Try to help your surviving parent to become as independent as possible without appearing to be insensitive or cold.

Support groups are often very helpful for those who grieve. In a support group, your surviving parent can find people who have gone through similar experiences and make new friends who will help her work through her loneliness.

The American Association of Retired Persons offers publications for the recently widowed. *On Being Alone* is a free publication that offers information on grief, housing concerns, finances, and adjustment to loss. *Widowed Persons Services Directory* (this publication costs one dollar) lists programs and services for widowed persons in the United States and Canada. Both publications can be obtained by writing to the AARP address listed in the appendix. Although these publications are designed for people who lose a spouse, they can help you as well if your parent has recently died.

Toward the end, when mother seemed to be sleeping most of the time, my father visited her every afternoon and read her poetry. He took her roses. He spent the last evening with her. My family and I have taken comfort in the idea that the last year was a way of letting us prepare for mother's death. Father could not have handled it a year ago. He was not ready to let go until a couple of days before the very end. We think of the last year as her final gift, her way of giving us time to get ready."[10]

None of us knows when we will die. Death may come quickly and unexpectedly. It may come after a lingering illness. But Christians have the assurance of Easter. We know that death is the doorway into heaven. It is the beginning of our eternal life.

APPENDIX

Organizations for Caregivers

This is a list of national organizations you can write to or call for specific interests, concerns, and needs. Often these organizations can refer you to local agencies, organizations, or chapters that can be of service to you. (Note: The addresses and telephone numbers of these organizations were accurate when this book was written. Some may have changed since that time.)

Alzheimer's Disease and Related Disorders Association
919 North Michigan Street
Suite 1000
Chicago, IL 60611
(800) 272-3900
Develops family support systems for the relatives and victims of Alzheimer's disease.

American Academy of Home Care Physicians
4660 W. 77th Street
Suite 200
Edina, MN 55435
An organization of physicians who deliver home care services.

American Association of Homes for the Aging
1129 20th Street NW
Suite 400
Washington, DC 20036
(202) 296-5960
Has a national listing of nursing homes which provide respite care for families of home care clients.

American Association of Retired Persons
601 E Street NW
Washington, DC 20049
(202) 434-2277
Dedicated to helping older Americans achieve lives of independence, dignity, and purpose. Provides a wide range of benefits, services, and community service programs and activities.

American Cancer Society
19 West 56th Street
New York, NY 10019
(212) 586-8700
Provides information about special services to cancer patients.

American Diabetes Association
National Service Center
1660 Duke Street
Alexandria, VA 22313
(703) 549-1500
Provides information about 200 local groups and 62 regional groups and supports research and education.

American Foundation for the Blind
15 W. 16th Street
New York, NY 10011
(212) 620-2000
Maintains referral and lending library. Records and talking books. Directory of agencies serving the blind and visually impaired in the U.S.

American Heart Association
7320 Greenville Avenue
Dallas, TX 75231
(214) 373-6300
Supports research and education about cardiovascular diseases and strokes.

American Lung Association
1740 Broadway
New York, NY 10019
(212) 315-8700
Supports research and education and has local groups.

American Mobile Home Association
12929 West 26th Avenue
Golden, CO 80401
(303) 232-6336
An association of manufactured home owners designed to promote their interests.

American Parkinson Disease Association
60 Bay Street
Staten Island, NY 10301
(800) 223-2732
Has regional groups and subsidizes patient information and referral centers.

Arthritis Foundation
1314 Spring Street NW
Atlanta, GA 30304
(404) 872-7100
Provides information to the public and has 71 local groups.

As Parents Grow Older
Institute of Gerontology
University of Michigan
Ann Arbor, MI 48109

Association for Brain Tumor Research
3725 N. Talman
Chicago, IL 60618
(312) 286-5571
Supports research and patient education.

Children of Aging Parents (CAPS)
1609 Woodbourne Road, Suite 302A
Levittown, PA 19057
(215) 345-5104
Has support groups for children of aging parents across the country. They also provide a newsletter, publications, and counseling, and are a clearinghouse for information on caring for aging parents. When looking for help with caring for aging parents, call CAPS first.

Commission on Legal Problems of the Elderly
American Bar Association
1800 M Street NW
Washington, DC 20036
(202) 331-2297
Concerned with legal issues of older persons. Makes available a number of publications.

Community Associations Institute
1630 Duke Street
Alexandria, VA 22314
(703) 548-8600
Assists in establishing and the ongoing management of homeowners' associations run by owners of condominiums, co-ops, and other types of units.

Department of Veterans Affairs
810 Vermont Avenue NW
Washington, DC 20420
(202) 233-4000
Administers laws authorizing benefits for former members of the Armed Forces and their dependents, including compensation for disabilities or death related to military service, pensions for disabled veterans or certain survivors, education and rehabilitation, home loan mortgages, burial, and a comprehensive medical program involving nursing homes, clinics, and medical centers.

Directory of National Self-Help/Mutual Aid Resources
American Hospital Association
840 North Lake Shore Drive
Chicago, IL 60611

Epilepsy Foundation of America
4351 Garden City Drive
Landover, MD 20785
(301) 459-3700
Offers referrals, assistance, and counseling for patients and their families and provides a low-cost pharmacy program.

Interreligions Liaison Office
Program Department
American Association of Retired Persons
601 E Street NW
Washington, DC 20049
Helps churches and synagogues develop programs to meet the needs of the vulnerable elderly.

Joint Commission on Accreditation of Health Care Organizations
875 N. Michigan Avenue
Chicago, IL 60011
Provides accreditation for home care agencies.

Legal Council for the Elderly
1909 K Street NW
Washington, DC 20049
(202) 662-4933

Love, Inc.
PO Box 1616
Holland, MI 49422
(616) 392-8277
Local chapters link up needy individuals and families with church outreach programs and services. There are 150 active and developing chapters in several states. Call to find a chapter in your area.

Love Thy Neighbor
PO Box 386
Camby, OR 97013
(503) 678-2228
A nursing home ministry that trains and provides volunteer chaplains to visit nursing homes.

National Academy of Elder Law Attorneys
655 N. Alvernon Way
Suite 108
Tucson, AZ 85711
(602) 881-4005
Organization of lawyers who specialize in problems of the elderly.

National Alliance of Senior Citizens
2525 Wilson Blvd
Arlington, VA 22201

(703) 528-4380
Informs members of the programs and policies of the government and other agencies for the benefit of older people. Lobbies state and federal legislatives.

National Association for Home Care
519 C Street, NE
Stanton Park
Washington, DC 20002-5809
(202) 547-7424
Represents home health, hospice, and homemaker service providers and maintains a list of home health care organizations.

National Association of Private Geriatric Care Managers
655 N. Alvernon Way
Suite 108
Tucson, AZ 85711
(602) 881-8008
Publishes a directory of private care managers for families involved in the home care of an elderly relative who lives at a distance.

National Association of Retired Federal Employees
1533 New Hampshire Avenue NW
Washington, DC 20036
(202) 243-0832
Protects the interests of present and future retired federal employees.

National Caucus and Center on Black Aged
1424 K Street NW
Suite 500
Washington, DC 20005
(202) 637-8400
Sponsors an employment program for older people and advocates to improve the lives of low-income older persons.

National Center for Home Equity Conversion
1210 E. College Drive
Room 300
Marshall, MN 56258
(507) 532-3230
Organization dedicated to promote widespread availability of home equity conversion.

National Center for Housing Management
1275 K Street NW
Suite 200
Washington, DC 20005
(202) 872-1717
Promotes professionalism and excellence in managing and developing senior housing facilities.

National Citizens' Coalition for Nursing Home Reform
1424 16th Street NW
Washington, DC 20036
(202) 797-0657
Organization of local and state nursing home advocacy groups and individuals to improve long-term care services and the quality of life of nursing home and assisted facility residents.

National Consumers League
815 15th Street NW
Suite 928-N
Washington, DC 20005
(202) 639-8140
Encourages participation in decisions of industry and government.

National Council of Senior Citizens
1331 F Street NW
Washington, DC 20004-1171
(202) 347-8800
Provides a referral source of adult day-care centers and home health agencies.

National Council on Alcoholism
12 W. 21st Street
New York, NY 10010
(212) 206-6770
Provides information and programs on alcoholism and coordinates telephone hot lines in many communities. Has local groups.

National Council on the Aging
Family Caregivers of the Aging Program
409 3rd Street SW
Washington, DC 20024
(202) 479-1200
Promotes contact between people who want to start caregiving programs and experts who can help them.

The National Displaced Homemakers Network
1411 K Street NW
Suite 930
Washington, DC 20005
(202) 628-6767
Addresses the concerns of women who have been homemakers for years and suddenly lose their financial support through death, divorce, separation, or disability.

The National Hispanic Council on Aging
2713 Ontario Road NW
Washington, DC 20009
(202) 265-1288
Provides for the well-being of Hispanic elderly with particular emphasis on self and mutual help.

National Hospice Organization
1909 W. Fort Meyer Drive
Suite 307
Arlington, VA 22209
Provides information about local hospice programs.

National Indian Council on Aging
6400 Upton Boulevard NE
City Center West, Suite 510
Albuquerque, NM 87110
(505) 888-3302
Provides information about native Indian and Alaskan aging programs.

National Interfaith Coalition on Aging
P O Box 1924
Athens, GA 30603
(404) 353-1331
Provides information and advocacy for quality of life and spiritual well-being of the elderly.

National Low Income Housing Coalition
1012 14th Street NW
Suite 1200
Washington, DC 20005
(202) 662-1530
Promotes decent housing, suitable environments, adequate neighborhoods, and housing choices for low-income people.

National Multiple Sclerosis Society
205 East 42nd Street
New York, NY 10017
(212) 986-3240
Provides services to people with MS and related diseases and their families; has local groups.

National Pacific/Asian Resource Center on Aging
Melbourne Towers Suite 914
1511 3rd Avenue
Seattle, WA 98101
(206) 624-1221
Promotes the delivery of health and social services to elderly Pacific/Asians.

National Parkinson Foundation
1501 NW Ninth Avenue
Miami, FL 33136
(305) 547-6666
Sponsors regional patient self-support groups and distributes educational literature.

National Resource Center on Health Promotion and Aging
American Association of Retired Persons

601 E Street NW
Washington, DC 20049

National Self-Help Clearinghouse
City University of New York
33 West 42nd Street
New York, NY 10036
(212) 840-7606

National Shared Housing Resource Center
6344 Greene Street
Philadelphia, PA 19144
(215) 848-1220
Provides information on shared housing.

Older Woman's League
730 11th Street NW
Suite 300
Washington, DC 20001
(202) 783-6686
Provides leadership and advocacy for issues of concern to middle-aged and older women.

The Retired Officers Association
201 N. Washington Street
Alexandria, VA 22314-2529
(703) 549-2311
Assists current and former commissioned or warrant officers of the U.S. uniformed services and their dependents and survivors with retirement issues and benefits.

RVICS Ministries
1499 Wedgewood Ranch Road
Orlando, FL 32811
(407) 293-4170
Roving Volunteers in Christ's Service are retired Christians.

Services Corps of Retired Executives
1825 Connecticut Avenue NW
Suite 503
Washington, DC 20009
An organization of retired and professional persons provide technical assistance to small businesses in local communities.

U.S. Congress. House of Representatives, Select Committee on Aging
Room 712
House Office Building Annex I
300 New Jersey Avenue SE
Washington, DC 20015
(202) 226-3375

A fact-finding body that informs the House and its committees of the problems of older Americans. Available are publications concerning legislation and the elderly.

U.S. Congress. Senate, Special Committee on Aging
G-31 Dirksen Bldg
Washington, DC 20510-6400
(202) 224-5364
Studies all issues affecting older people and informs and makes recommendations to other Senate committees for legislative action. Also has some publications available.

The Well Spouse Foundation
c/o Joanne Watral
PO Box 58022
Pittsburgh, PA 15209
For spouses and family members of the chronically ill.

Widowed Persons Service
Program Department
American Association of Retired Persons
601 E Street NW
Washington, DC 20049

Recommended Reading

Brody, Elaine M. *Women in the Middle: Their Parent Care Years*. New York: Springer, 1990.

Brown, Robert N. *The Rights of Older Persons*. 2d ed. Carbondale and Edwardsville, Ill.: Legal Counsel for the Elderly, Southern Illinois University Press, 1989.

Deane, Barbara. *Caring for Your Aging Parent*. Colorado Springs, Col.: NavPress, 1989.

Fries, James M. *Aging Well: The Life Plan for Health and Vitality in Your Later Years*. Reading, Mass.: Addison-Wesley, 1989.

Gelfand, Donald E. *The Aging Network: Programs and Services*. 3d ed. New York: Springer, 1988.

Gillespie, Ann E., and Katrinka Smith Sloan. *Housing Options and Services for Older Adults*. Santa Barbara, Calif.: ABC-CLIO, 1990.

Gordon, Harley, with Jane Daniel. *How to Protect Your Life Savings from Catastrophic Illness and Nursing Homes*. Boston: Financial Planning Institute, 1990.

Gordon, Michael. *Old Enough To Feel Better: A Medical Guide for Seniors*. Baltimore: Johns Hopkins University Press, 1989.

Haber, David. *Health Care for an Aging Society*. New York: Hemisphere Publishing Corporation, 1989.

Maves, Paul B. *Faith for the Older Years: Making the Most of Life's Second Half*. Minneapolis: Augsburg Fortress, 1986.

Nouwen, Henri J., and Walter J. Gaffney. *Aging: The Fulfillment of Life*. New York: Doubleday, 1976.

Ortlund, Ray and Anne Ortlund. *The Best Half of Life*. Dallas: Word, 1987.

Rossman, Isadore. *Looking Forward: The Complete Medical Guide to Successful Aging*. New York: E. P. Dutton, 1989.

Salamon, Michael J., and Gloria Rosenthal. *Home or Nursing Home: Making the Right Choices*. New York: Springer, 1990.

Shelley, Florence D. *When Your Parents Grow Old*. New York: Harper Collins, 1988.

Shulman, Bernard H., and Raeann Berman, *How to Survive Your Aging Parents*. Chicago: Surrey Books, 1988.

Sommers, Tish, and Laurie Shields. *Women Take Care: The Consequences of Caregiving in Today's Society*. Gainsville, Fla.: Triad, 1987.

Stafford, Tim. *As Our Years Increase*. Grand Rapids, Mich.: Zondervan, 1989.

Zuckerman, Connie, et al., eds. *Home Health Care Options: A Guide for Older Persons and Concerned Families*. New York: Plenum, 1990.

Free Publications from the AARP

The following are free publications from the American Association of Retired Persons. To obtain one or more that pertain to your interests and needs, write to:

AARP Fulfillment
601 E Street NW
Washington, DC 20049
Allow 6-8 weeks for delivery.

Activities and Exercise

Staying Well—D12763
Pep Up Your Life—D549
Activities with Impact—D12642

Caregiving and Long-Term Care

A Checklist of Concerns/Resources for Caregivers—D12895
A Handbook about Care in the Home—D955
A Path for Caregivers—D12957
Long-Term Care—D13078
The Nursing Home Regulatory System—D13716
The Ombudsman Program—D13717
Making Wise Decisions for Long-Term Care—D12436
Miles Away and Still Caring: A Guide for Long Distance Caregivers—D12478
Nursing Home Life: A Guide for Residents and Families—D13063
New Protections of Nursing Home Residents' Rights—D13713
Home Is Where the Care Is—D12892
Tomorrow's Choices—D13479
Caregivers Reports Executive Summary—D13203
Before You Buy: A Guide to Long-Term Care Insurance—D12893
Caregivers in the Workplace—D12933
Coping and Caring: Living with Alzheimer's Disease—D12441

Consumer Information

A Consumer's Guide to Probate—D13822
Older Consumer Behavior—D13975
Consumer Guide to Advertising—D12583
Five Ways to Cut Your Phone Costs—D12175
Older Bank Customers—D12347
Meeting the Need for Security and Independence—D12905
Deferred Payment Loans (DPLs) for Home Repairs and Improvement—D12518
How to Right a Wrong—D1126

State Specific Benefits Guide for Older Citizens (benefits available to older persons)
D13594—Connecticut
D12962—Georgia
D12615—Nebraska
D12617—New Hampshire
D12614—Oklahoma
D12964—South Carolina
D12616—Wyoming

Home Equity

Home-Made Money—D12894
Borrowing against Your Home—D12987
Home Equity Conversion Fact Sheet—D13722
Home Equity Conversion for the Elderly: An Analysis for Lenders—D12504
Toward a Better Understanding of Home Equity Loans and Home Equity Conversions—D12881

Legal Issues on Housing

Legal Issues: Accessory Apartments—Zoning Covenants Restricting Land to Residential Use—D1187
Legal Issues: ECHO Housing—Restrictions on Manufactured Housing—D1186
Legal Issues: House Sharing—What is a Family?—D13290

Senior Consumer Alert

Senior Consumer Alert: Credit Discrimination: Knocking Down Barriers—D13497
Senior Consumer Alert: Home Equity Scams—D12842
Senior Consumer Alert: Investment Fraud—D13915
Senior Consumer Alert: Life Care Contracts—D12579
Senior Consumer Alert: Medigap Insurance Fraud—D13572

Crime Prevention

How to Conduct a Security Survey—D396
How to Protect You and Your Car—D393
How to Protect Your Home—D395
How to Protect Your Neighborhood—D397
How to Protect Your Rural Homestead—D12244
How to Report Suspicious Activities—D12779
How to Spot a Con Artist—D394
The Criminal Justice System: A Guide for Citizens—D682
Older Americans and the Criminal Justice System—D1054
AARP National Study on Volunteers Augmenting Law Enforcement Agencies
D12620
Citizen Volunteers in Law Enforcement Agencies—D12586
Crime Prevention: Whose Duty? Whose Responsibility?—D12098
Have You Thought of Older Volunteers with Law Enforcement?—D12097

Revitalizing Your Crime Prevention Group: Ten Points on Maintaining a Neighborhood Organization—D12595

Neighborhood Dispute Resolution: Helping Seniors—Seniors Helping—D13068

Domestic Mistreatment of the Elderly: Towards Prevention—D12810

Domestic Mistreatment of the Elderly: Towards Prevention—Some DOs and DON'Ts—D13707

Educational and Community Service Resources

All About AARP—D12335

AARP Educational and Community Service Programs 1991—D990

Acronyms in Aging—D747

AARP Audiovisual Library—D12218

A Change for the Better: How to Make Communities More Responsive to Older Residents—D13395

Think of Your Future Information Flyer—D12486

Think of Your Future/AARP Retirement Planning Program and Services for Employers and Organizations—D12789

Using the Experience of a Lifetime—D13353

AARP Works Fact Sheet—D12821

Preparing a Directory of Long-Term Care Services—D12488

Establishing a Nursing Home Community Council—D13385

Learning Opportunities for Older Person—D171

Social Outreach and Support Fact Sheet—D13790

Making America Literate: How You Can Help—D12755

Widowed Persons Service—D1152

Growing Together: An Intergenerational Sourcebook—D12342

Truth about Aging—D301

Wish You Had Finished High School?—D13048

Community Television: A Handbook for Production—D12761

Reminiscence

Reminiscence Fact Sheet—D12602

Reminiscence: Reaching Back, Moving Forward—D13186

End of Life Information and Funeral Planning

Product Report: Funeral Goods and Services—D13496

Health Care Powers of Attorney—D13895

D12644—Alabama

D12645—Alaska

D12646—Arizona

D12647—Arkansas

D12648—California

D12649—Colorado

D12650—Connecticut

D12651—Delaware

D12652—District of Columbia
D12653—Florida
D12654—Georgia
D12655—Hawaii
D12656—Idaho
D12657—Illinois
D12658—Indiana
D12659—Iowa
D12660—Kansas
D12661—Kentucky
D12662—Louisiana
D12663—Maine
D12664—Maryland
D12665—Massachusetts
D12666—Michigan
D12667—Minnesota
D12668—Mississippi
D12669—Missouri
D12670—Montana
D12671—Nebraska
D12672—Nevada
D12673—New Hampshire
D12674—New Jersey
D12675—New Mexico
D12676—New York
D12677—North Carolina
D12678—North Dakota
D12679—Ohio
D12680—Oklahoma
D12681—Oregon
D12682—Pennsylvania
D12683—Rhode Island
D12684—South Carolina
D12685—South Dakota
D12686—Tennessee
D12687—Texas
D12688—Utah
D12689—Vermont
D12690—Virginia
D12691—Washington
D12692—West Virginia
D12693—Wisconsin
D12694—Wyoming
Product Report: Prepaying Your Funeral?—D13188
Cemetery Goods and Services—D13162
Model Law for Prepaid Funeral Arrangements—D12643

Free Publications from the AARP

Finances, Financial Services, and Financial Planning

A Guide to Understanding Your Pension Plan: A Pension Handbook—D13533
Look Before You Leap: A Guide to Early Retirement Incentive Programs—D13390
Social Security: Crucial Questions and Straight Answers—D13640
A Primer on Financial Management for Midlife and Older Women—D13183
Your Credit: A Complete Guide—D13286
Money Matters—D12380
What To Do If You're Denied Credit—D13285
A Woman's Guide to Pension Rights—D12258
Planning Your Retirement—D12322

Health Care and Costs

Product Report: Hearing Aids—D13766
Organizing Educational Seminars—D12220
Strategies for Good Health—D12261
The Eyes Have It—D12460
Aging and Vision: Making the Most of Impaired Vision—D12363
How Does Your Nutrition Measure Up?—D12994
Have You Heard?—D12219
Healthy Questions—D12094
Eating for Your Health—D12164
Effective Physician Oversight—D12907
Action for a Healthier Life: A Guide for Midlife and Older Women—D13474

Health Care Campaign

AARP Health Care Volunteers in Action—D12961
Payment Record for Health Insurance Policies—D13561
The Smart Consumer's Guide to Prescription Drugs—D13579

Housing Alternatives

A Change for the Better: How to Make Communities More Responsive to Older Residents—D13395
Understanding Senior Housing for the 1990s—D13899
A Home Away from Home: Consumer Information on Board and Care Homes—D12446
Your Home, Your Choice—D12143
Congregate Housing—D12141
Continuing Care Retirement Communities—D12181
The Doable, Renewable Home—D12470
The Board and Care System: A Regulatory Jungle—D13396
Housing Publications List—D12173

CHISS (Consumer Housing Information Service for Seniors)

Introducing CHISS—D12449
CHISS Information Pack—D12877
CHISS: Consumers Guide to Homesharing—D12774

CHISS: Local Housing Resources Guide—D12785
CHISS: Resource Guide on Accessory Apartments—D12775
CHISS: Resource Guide on Rental Housing—D12773

ECHO (Elder Cottage Housing Opportunity)

A Model Ordinance for ECHO Housing—D13791
ECHO Housing: A Review of Zoning Issues and Other Considerations—D1023
ECHO Housing Fact Sheet—D1006

Insurance

Insurance (Policy Wise) Checklist—D1032
Before You Buy: A Guide to Long-Term Care Insurance—D12893

Medicare and Medicaid

Knowing Your Rights—D12330
Medicaid Discrimination and Consumer Rights—D13715
Medicaid: What It Covers, What It Doesn't—D13133

Legislative Advocacy

Making Your State Government Work for You—D13268
Mental Health
I Wonder Who Else Can Help—D13832
If Only I Knew What to Say or Do—D13830
Now Where Did I Put My Keys—D13829
So Many of My Friends Have Moved Away or Died—D13831

Older Workers

Social Security: Questions and Answers—D13761
The Age Discrimination in Employment Act Guarantees You Certain Rights. Here's How—D12386
A Woman's Guide to Pension Rights—D12258
Look Before You Leap: A Guide to Early Retirement Incentive Programs—D13390
A Guide to Understanding Your Pension Plan: A Pension Handbook—D13533

Work Force Education

Planning Your Retirement—D12322
AARP Works Fact Sheet—D12821
Working Options: How to Plan Your Job Search, Your Work Life—D12403
AARP Retirement Planning Fact Sheet—D13260

Pensions

A Woman's Guide to Pension Rights—D12258
A Guide to Understanding Your Pension Plan: A Pension Handbook—D13533
Look Before You Leap: A Guide to Early Retirement Incentive Programs—D13390

Free Publications from the AARP

Religion and Aging

Interreligious Liaison Activities—D750
The Church/Synagogue and Aging—D88

Resources For Professionals

Guidelines for Pastoral Care of Older Persons in Long-Term Care Settings—D13574
Aging Society: A Challenge to Theological Education—D13161
A Matter of Choice: Planning Ahead for Health Care Decisions—D12776
Spousal Bereavement and Primary Health—D13418

Retirement Planning

AARP Retirement Planning Fact Sheet—D13260
Planning Your Retirement—D12322

Safety

Safety Steps for Pedestrians—D12757
Dangerous Products, Dangerous Places—D13050
What Smart Shoppers Know about Nightwear Safety—D12838

Taxes and Tax Assistance

Tax Facts for Tax-Free and Tax-Deferred Investments—D13812
Are My Social Security Benefits Taxable?—D13812
Tax Aide Fact Sheet—D12609

Transportation, Traffic, and Driver Safety

Getting Around—D13849
55 ALIVE Information Sheet—D934

Volunteering

To Serve, Not to Be Served—D12028
Older Volunteers: A Valuable Resource—D12025
Volunteer Opportunities for Your Congregation—D12612
Museum Opportunities for Older Persons—D12211
Becoming a School Partner—D13527
Volunteer Now!—D13417

Widowed Persons

On Being Alone—D150
Grief Has No Color—D13152
Widowed Persons Service Bibliography—D435
Widowed Persons Service Directory—D13402
Widowed Persons Service Fact Sheet—D12601

Women

Divorce After 50: Challenges and Choices—D12909
Facts About Older Women: Income and Poverty—D12993
Facts About Older Women: Housing and Living Arrangements—D12880
Helping Women Turn Longer Lives into Better Lives—D12887
A Primer on Financial Management for Midlife and Older Women—D13183
Your Credit: A Complete Guide—D13286
Action for Healthier Life: A Guide for Midlife and Older Women—D13474

Notes and Sources

INTRODUCTION
1. Kent S. Collins, *Philadelphia Inquirer,* 16 January 1991, E2.
2. "Caregivers Need to Find Time for Themselves," *USA Today,* 19 April 1989, 5D.
3. Ibid.
4. Ibid.
5. Ibid.
6. Karen S. Peterson, "Adult Kids in Crisis: What to Do with Mom, Dad? Hard Times for 'Sandwich Generation,'" *USA Today,* 18 April 1989, 1A.
7. William E. Smart, "Caught Between the Generations: Middle-Aged and Caring for Young and Old," *Washington Post,* 5 December 1986, C5.
8. Ibid.
9. Karen S. Peterson, "A Push to Help Care-givers of Aging Parents," *USA Today,* 11 May 1989, 1D.
10. Ibid.
11. Karen S. Peterson, "Adult Kids in Crisis."
12. Ibid.

CHAPTER 1—WHAT'S HAPPENING IN AMERICAN FAMILIES?
1. Bureau of the Census, *Selected Population and Housing Characteristics: 1990,* (Washington: Government Printing Office, June, 1991), table 1.
2. Bureau of the Census, *Current Population Reports,* series P-25, no. 1018 (Washington: GPO, 1989).
3. Karen S. Peterson, "Adult Kids in Crisis."
4. Neill A. Borowski, "The 65-Plus Population Soared in Last Decade—Advances in Health Care and a More Active Lifestyle Boosted the Population and in 20 Years, Baby Boomers Will Start Turning 65," *Philadelphia Inquirer,* 7 July 1991, B1.
5. Cheryl Simon, "The Myth of Abandonment," *Psychology Today,* April 1988, 47.
6. Barbara Vobejda, "Caring for Three Generations: Families Juggle Needs of Elderly, Young," *Washington Post,* 24 November 1990, A1.
7. E. M. Brody, *Women in the Middle: Their Parent Care Years* (New York: Springer, 1990), xi.
8. J. K. Footlick, "What Happened to the American Family?" *Newsweek Special Edition: The 21st Century Family,* Winter/Spring 1990, 14–20.
9. Barbara Vobejda, "Caring for Three Generations."
10. Ethel Shanas et al., *Old People in Industrial Societies* (New York: Atherton, 1968); Cary Kart, *The Realities of Aging,* 3d ed. (Boston: Allyn and Bacon, 1990), 217–245; Louis Harris and Associates Poll, 1975; Ethel Shanas, "The Family as a Social Support in Old Age," *The Gerontologist* 19 (1979): 169–174; Ethel Shanas, "Older People and their Families: The New Pioneers," *Journal of Marriage and Family* 42 (1980): 9–14.
11. Neill A. Borowski, "The 65-Plus Population."

12. "Chinese Turning to Contracts as Children Lose Respect for Age," *Detroit News,* 23 December 1990, A4.

Sources

Harris, D. K. *Sociology of Aging.* 2d ed. New York: HarperCollins, 1990.

Hooyman, N. R., and N. A. Kiyak. *Social Gerontology: A Multidisciplinary Perspective.* Boston: Allyn and Bacon, 1988.

CHAPTER 2—UNDERSTANDING THE AGING PROCESS

1. Dana Parsons, "Aging Baby Boomers Find New Wrinkle in Old Story," *Los Angeles Times,* 16 June 1991, B1.

2. J. G. Saxe, "I'm Growing Old," in *Dictionary of Quotations,* Bergen Evans, ed. (New York: Avenel, 1978), 13.

3. T. R. Holmes and R. Rahe, "The Social Readjustment Rating Scale," *Journal of Psychosomatic Research* 11 (1967): 213–218.

4. Darrell Sifford, "Mining the Pleasures of the Golden Years," *Philadelphia Inquirer,* 28 June 1990, E5.

5. "Stengel, Casey," in *The Little, Brown Book of Anecdotes,* Clifton Fadiman, ed. (Boston: Little, Brown, 1985), 523.

6. S. Bould, B. Sanborn, and L. Reif, *Eighty-Five Plus: The Oldest Old* (Belmont, Calif.: Wadsworth, 1989), 77–94; I. Rosenwaike, *The Extreme Aged in America* (Westport, Conn.: Greenwood, n.d.), 145.

7. "Chesterfield," in *The Little, Brown Book of Anecdotes,* 116.

8. R. C. Atchley and S. J. Miller, "Older People and Their Families," *Annual Review of Gerontology and Geriatrics,* vol. 1 (New York: Springer, 1980), 337–369; R. C. Atchley, *Aging: Continuity and Change,* 2d ed. (Belmont, Calif.: Wadsworth, 1987), 81.

9. J. C. Morgan, *Becoming Old* (New York: Springer, 1979); N. R. Hooyman and H. A. Kiyak, *Social Gerontology,* 233–236.

10. Ben Jonson, "Homeri Ulysses," *Explorata,* quoted in *Dictionary of Quotations,* Bergen Evans, ed. (New York: Avenel, 1978), 12.

11. D. B. Preston and P. K. Mansfield, "An Explosion of Stressful Life Events, Illness, and Coping Among the Rural Elderly," *The Gerontologist* 24 (1984): 490–494.

12. S. M. Crown, "Friendship in Old Age," in *Personal Relationships 2: Developing Personal Relationships,* S. Duck and R. Gilmour, eds. (New York: Academic, 1981), 231–246.

13. N. F. Mouser et al., "Marital Status and Life Satisfaction: A Study of Older Men," in *Social Bonds in Later Life,* W. A. Peterson and J. Quadango, eds. (Beverly Hills, Calif.: Sage, 1985), 71–90; P. M. Keith et al., "Confidants and Well-Being: A Note on Male Friendships in Old Age," *The Gerontologist* 24 (1984): 318–320; W. J. Dickens and D. Perlman, "Friendship Over the Life-Cycle," in *Personal Relationships 2* (New York: Academic, 1981), 91–122.

14. Darrell Sifford, "Mining the Pleasures of the Golden Years."

15. Barbara Deane, "Why Can't You Be the Parents I Knew?" *Discipleship Journal,* July/August 1990, 32.

16. Richard Johnson, quoted by Barbara Deane, "Why Can't You Be the Parents I Knew?"

17. E. Brody, et al., "A Woman's Changing Roles and Help to Elderly Parents: Attitudes of Three Generations of Women," *Journal of Gerontology* 33 (1983): 597–607.

18. E. Brody and M. Kieban, "Day to Day Mental and Physical Health Symptoms of Older People: A Report of Health Lags," *The Gerontologist* 23 (1983): 75–85.

19. M. H. Cantor, "Strain Among Caregivers: A Study of Experience in the United States," *The Gerontologist* 23 (1983): 597–604.

20. Dana Parsons, "Aging Baby Boomers Find New Wrinkle in Old Story."

Sources

Atchley, R. C. "Respondents vs. Refusers in an Interview Study of Retired Women." *Journal of Gerontology* 22 (1969):42–47.

Atchley, R. C. *Social Forces and Aging.* 5th ed. Belmont, Calif.: Wadsworth, 1988.

Borzan, N. "The Sandwich Generation." *Aging.* Eleanor Goldstein, ed. Social Issues Series, 1980, article 52.

Cox, H. *Later Life.* 2d ed. Englewood Cliffs, N.J.: Prentice Hall, 1988, 156–168.

Depner, C., and B. Ingersoll-Dayton. "Conjugal Social Support and Patterns in Later Life." *Journal of Gerontology* 40 (1975): 761–766.

Glasser, P., and L. Glasser. "Role Reversal and Conflict Between Aged Parents and Their Children." *Marriage and Family Living* 24 (1962): 46–51.

Hancock, B. L. *Social Work with Older People.* Englewood Cliffs, N.J.: Prentice Hall, 1987.

Schulz, R., and R. B. Ewen. *Adult Development and Aging.* New York: Macmillan, 1988.

CHAPTER 3—PHYSICAL CHANGES AND THE AGING PROCESS

1. "Barrymore, John," *The Little, Brown Book of Anecdotes,* 41.

2. "Fontenelle, Bernard de," *The Little, Brown Book of Anecdotes,* 211.

3. Dr. Michael Freedman, "It's Disease, Not Age, That Kills," *St. Petersburg Times,* 27 August 1991, Seniority, 21.

4. D. Albanes, A. Blair, and P. R. Taylor, "Physical Activity and Risk of Cancer in the WHANESI Population," *American Journal of Public Health* 79 (1989): 744–750; Ilene Springer, "A New Miracle Cure," *NRTA Bulletin,* vol. 31, no. 11 (December 1990).

5. Research at Tufts University, reported in Ilene Springer, "A New Miracle Cure"; Richard Cranall, *Gerontology: A Behavioral Science Approach* (New York: McGraw-Hill, 1991), 176–180.

6. Jim Melvin, "The Fit Bones Are Connected to Your Lifestyle," *St. Petersburg Times,* 25 August 1991, G1.

7. W. Utian, *Managing Your Menopause* (New York: Prentice Hall, 1990); Jean Seligman et al., "Aging: Not Past Their Prime," *Newsweek,* 6 August 1990, 66–68.

8. J. A. Livingston, "The Graying of America," *Philadelphia Inquirer,* 19 February 1989, G1.

9. E. Norden, "The Mormon Advantage," *Longevity,* September 1990, 72.

10. Sharon Lynch, "Seniors Catch Weightlifting Fever," *Grand Rapids Press,* 22 September 1991, B4; Maria A. Fiatarone et al., "High-Intensity Strength Training in Nonagenarians: Effects on Skeletal Muscle," *The Journal of the American Medical Association* (13 June 1990), 3029–3034.

11. JoAnn Manson et al., "A Prospective Study of Obesity and Risk of Coronary Heart Disease in Women," *The New England Journal of Medicine* (29 March 1990), 882–889.

12. "Walking a Tightrope: Hidden Population of Older Drinkers Worries Experts," *NRTA Bulletin*, vol. 32, no. 2 (February 1991), 2.

Sources

Andres, R., E. L. Bierman, and W. R. Razzare, eds. *Principles of Geriatric Medicine.* San Francisco: McGraw-Hill, 1985.

Barbagallo-Sangliorgi, G., and A. N. Exton-Smith, eds. *The Aging Brain: Neurological and Mental Disturbances.* New York: Plenum, 1980.

Behnke, J. A., C. E. Finch, and G. B. Moment, eds. *The Biology of Aging.* New York: Plenum, 1978.

Bender, B., and G. Caranasos. *Geriatric Medicine.* Philadelphia: W. B. Saunders, 1989.

Bittles, A. H., and K. J. Collins, eds. *The Biology of Human Aging.* Cambridge: Cambridge University Press, 1986.

Burke, E., ed. *Exercise, Science and Fitness.* Ithaca, N.Y.: Movement Publications, 1981.

Cooper, K. M. *The Aerobics Program for Total Well-being.* New York: Bantam, 1982.

Dietz, A. A., ed. *Aging—Its Chemistry.* Washington, D.C.: American Association for Clinical Chemistry, 1980.

Dychtwald, K., ed. *Wellness and Health Promotion for the Elderly.* Rockville, Md.: Aspen Systems Corp., 1986.

Finch, C. E., and E. L. Schneider, eds. *Handbook of the Biology of Aging.* New York: Van Nostrand Reinhold, 1985.

Fries, J. F., and L. M. Crape. *Vitality and Aging.* San Francisco: W. H. Freeman, 1981.

Hampton, John K., Jr. *The Biology of Human Aging.* Dubuque, Ia.: W. C. Brown, 1991.

Hazzard, W. R., et al. *Principles of Geriatric Medicine and Gerontology.* New York: McGraw-Hill, 1990.

Hsu, J., and R. Davis, eds. *Handbook of Geriatric Nutrition.* Park Ridge, N.J.: Neyes, 1981.

Kart, C. S., and S. P. Metress. *Nutrition, the Aged, and Society.* Englewood Cliffs, N.J.: Prentice Hall, 1984.

Kermis, M. *Mental Health in Late Life: The Adaptive Process.* Boston: Jones and Barlet, 1986.

Pagliare, L. A., and A. M. Pagliare, eds. *Pharmacological Aspects of Aging.* St. Louis: C. V. Mosby, 1983.

Rowe, J. W., and R. W. Besdine, eds. *Health and Disease in Old Age.* Boston: Little, Brown, 1982.

Scheff, S. W., ed. *Aging and Recovery of Function in the Central Nervous System.* New York: Plenum, 1984.

Sekular, R., D. Kline, and K. Dismukes, eds. *Aging and Human Visual Function.* New York: Alan R. Liss, 1982.

Simonson, W. *Medications and the Elderly.* Rockville, Md.: Aspen Systems Corp., 1984.

Whitbourne, S. K. *The Aging Body: Physiological Changes and Psychological Consequences.* New York: Springer-Verlag, 1985.

Young, E. A., ed. *Nutrition, Aging and Health.* New York: Alan R. Liss, 1986.

CHAPTER 4—MENTAL HEALTH AND AGING

1. Barbara Sorid, "When Aging Parents Need Assistance," *Philadelphia Inquirer,* 27 July 1988, B2.

2. Steve Padilla, "Those Struggling with Aged Parents Find a Circle of Support," *Los Angeles Times,* 26 January 1991, B5.

3. D. Blazer, *Depression in Later Life* (St. Louis: C. V. Mosby, 1982); Cary Kart, *The Realities of Aging,* 126.

4. Sandy Rovner, "Dementia Care Takes a Toll on Families," *Washington Post,* 27 March 1990, Z17.

5. Ibid.

6. Barbara Sorid, "When Aging Parents Need Assistance."

Sources

Belsky, J. K. *The Psychology of Aging.* Monterey, Calif.: Brooks/Cole, 1984.

Birren, J. E., and K. W. Schaie, eds. *Handbook of the Psychology of Aging.* New York: Van Nostrand Reinhold, 1977.

Butler, R. N., and M. Lewis. *Aging and Mental Health.* 3d ed. St. Louis: C. V. Mosby, 1982.

Clausen, J. *The Life Course: A Sociological Perspective.* Englewood Cliffs, N.J.: Prentice Hall, 1986.

Cohen, D., and C. Eisdorfer. *The Loss of Self.* New York: Penguin, 1986.

Kaplan, O. *Psychopathology of Aging.* New York: Academic, 1979.

Kermis, M. D. *Mental Health in Late Life.* Boston: Jones and Bartlett, 1986.

Maddox, G. L., ed. *The Encyclopedia of Aging.* New York: Springer, 1987.

Miller, M. *Suicide after Sixty: The Final Alternative.* New York: Springer, 1979.

Neugarten, B., ed. *Middle Age and Aging.* Chicago: University of Chicago Press, 1980.

Poon, L. W., ed. *Aging in the 1980s: Psychological Issues.* Washington, D.C.: American Psychological Association, 1980.

Powell, L. S., and K. Courtice. *Alzheimer's Disease: A Guide for Families.* Reading, Mass.: Addison-Wesley, 1983.

Richard, S., F. Livson, and P. G. Peterson. *Aging and Personality.* New York: Wiley and Sons, 1962.

Zarit, S. M. *Aging and Mental Disorders.* New York: Free Press, 1980.

CHAPTER 5—PLANNING AHEAD FOR THE GOLDEN YEARS

1. Anne C. Roark, "Elder Care: Caring for California's Aging Population," *Los Angeles Times,* 20 May 1990, 13.

2. Lori Durso, "Preparing to Care for Aging Parents," *Philadelphia Inquirer,* 28 August 1988, J7.

3. Erin Kennedy, "What if You Can't Care for Yourself?" *Philadelphia Inquirer,* 7 June 1990, H4.

4. D. K. Harris, *Sociology of Aging,* 2d ed. (New York: Harper and Row, 1990), 32–35.

5. E. R. Kingson, B. S. Hirschorn, and J. M. Cornman, *Ties that Bind: The Interdependence of Generations* (Washington, D.C.: Seven Locks, 1986).

6. U.S. Senate Special Committee on Aging, *Aging America: Trends and Projections (1985–86)* (Washington, D.C.: Department of Health and Human Services, 1986).

7. S. Bould, B. Sanborn, and L. Reif, *Eighty-Five Plus: The Oldest Old,* 32.

8. U.S. Bureau of the Census, *Current Population Reports,* series P-23, no. 153, *America's Centenarians* (Washington: GPO, 1987).

9. T. N. Monga, M.D., "Geriatric Rehabilitation," *Center on Aging,* vol. 5, no. 3 (Winter 1989–1990), 1–2.

10. M. Beck et al., "Be Nice to Your Kids," *Newsweek,* 12 March 1990, 72–75.

11. D. Gelman et al., "The Brain Killer," *Newsweek,* 18 December 1989, 54–56.

12. Ibid.

13. Ibid.

14. Frank Devlin, "Aiding Those Caring for an Aged Parent," *Philadelphia Inquirer,* 11 June 1989, H4.

15. Ibid.

16. Ibid.

17. Erin Kennedy, "What if You Can't Care for Yourself?"

18. Ibid.

19. S. Bould, B. Sanborn, and L. Reif, *Eighty-Five Plus: The Oldest Old,* 33.

20. Erin Kennedy, "What if You Can't Care for Yourself?"

21. Ibid.

22. Ibid.

Sources

Atchley, R. C. *Social Forces and Aging.* 5th ed. Belmont, Calif.: Wadsworth, 1988.

United Nations Demographic Year Book: 1977. New York: United Nations.

United Nations Demographic Year Book: 1984. New York: United Nations.

CHAPTER 6—WHY DOES MONEY GROW SHORT AS PEOPLE GET OLDER?

1. Andrea K. Hammer, "For the Elderly, the Journey Is a Difficult One," *Philadelphia Inquirer,* 4 July 1990, A11.

2. H. G. Cox, *Later Life: The Realities of Aging,* 2d ed. (Englewood Cliffs, N.J.: Prentice Hall, 1988), 256.

3. Ibid.

4. Louis Harris and Associates, *The Myth and Reality of Aging in America,* 2d ed. (Washington, D.C.: National Council on the Aging, Inc., 1975).

5. Bureau of the Census, *Statistical Abstract of the United States* (Washington: GPO, 1990); R. C. Crandall, *Gerontology: A Behavioral Science Approach,* 2d ed. (New York: McGraw-Hill, 1991), 359–364.

6. U.S. Senate, Special Committee on Aging, *Developments on Aging,* vol. 3 (Washington: GPO, 1986), table 2-4.

7. Bureau of the Census, *Statistical Abstract.*

8. Andrea K. Hammer, "For the Elderly."

9. N. R. Hooyman and H. A. Kiyak, *Social Gerontology,* 501–505.

10. Ibid.

11. Ibid.

12. S. Bould, B. Sanborn, and L. Reif, *Eighty-Five Plus: The Oldest Old,* 137; Bureau of the Census, "Characteristics of the Population Below the Poverty Level: 1985," Current Population Reports Series—60, no. 158 (Washington: GPO, 1987).

13. Karen S. Peterson, "Financial Planning," *USA Today,* 18 April 1989, 4D.

14. Susan Dentzer, "America's Scandalous Health Care," *U.S. News and World Report,* 12 March 1990, 25–30.

15. C. Matthiessen, "Bordering on Collapse," *Modern Maturity,* October/November 1990, 30–38.
16. Melinda Beck et al., "The Geezer Boom," *Newsweek Special Edition: The 21st Century Family,* 66.
17. Andrea K. Hammer, "For the Elderly."

Sources

Hollonbeck, D., and J. C. Ohls. "Participation among the Elderly in the Food Stamp Program." *The Gerontologist* 24 (6): 616–621.

CHAPTER 7—HOW TO HELP AGING PARENTS COPE WITH FINANCES

1. Karen S. Peterson, "Financial Planning," *USA Today,* 18 April 1989, 4D.
2. "Woman Specializes in Untangling Medicare Rules," *St. Petersburg Times,* 25 August 1991, 22A.
3. Cary Kart, *The Realities of Aging,* 268–269.
4. A. L. Kahn, "Program and Demographic Characteristics of Supplemental Security Income Recipients," *Social Security Bulletin* 50 (December 1985): 23–57.
5. Cary Kart, *The Realities of Aging,* 269; C. Estes, *The Aging Enterprise* (San Francisco: Jossey-Bass, 1979).
6. C. S. Kart, *The Realities of Aging,* 268–269.
7. D. Hollonbeck and J. C. Ohls, "Participation Among the Elderly in the Food Stamp Program," *The Gerontologist* 24 (1984): 616–621; The Commonwealth Fund Commission, *Old, Alone and Poor* (Commonwealth Fund: Baltimore, 1987), 30.
8. L. Drazaga, M. Upp, and V. Reno, "Low-Income Aged: Eligibility and Participation in SSI," *Social Security Bulletin* 45 (May 1982): 28–35.
9. Compilation of the Older Americans Act of 1965 (Washington: GPO), 1–2.
10. G. Thompson, "Pension Coverage and Benefits: Findings from Retirement History Study," *Social Security Bulletin* 41 (1978): 3–17.
11. Cary Kart, *The Realities of Aging,* 271–275.
12. D. Colburn, "Health Frauds: Quackery Thriving Among Elderly Ill," *Washington Post,* 18 July 1985, 1ff.
13. Ibid.
14. Jane Bryant Quinn, "Old, Sick, and Far Away," *Newsweek,* 26 August 1991, 39.
15. "Physicians to Fill Medicare Forms but Up to a Year to File Them," *Grand Rapids Press,* 3 September 1990, C3.

Sources

Schultz, J. *The Economics of Aging.* 4th ed. Dover, Mass.: Arburn House, 1988.
Schulz, R., and R. B. Ewen. *Adult Development and Aging: Myths and Realities.* New York: Macmillan, 1988.

CHAPTER 8—HOW CAN CHRISTIANS HELP OLDER PEOPLE?

1. Material from *Growing Old in the Country of the Young* quoted from Angela Elwell Hunt, "Senior Saints: Loved or Lonely," *The Fundamentalist Journal,* July/August 1985, 14.
2. A. Bieler, *The Social Humanism of Calvin* (Richmond, Va.: John Knox, 1964), 25, 29–30.
3. Billy Graham, *Peace With God* (Garden City, N.J.: Doubleday, 1953), 190.

4. Billy Graham, "My Answers," *St. Paul Dispatch*, 23 July 1964, 20.

5. Carl F. H. Henry, *The Uneasy Conscience of Modern Fundamentalism* (Grand Rapids, Mich.: Eerdmans, 1947), cited in David Moberg's *Inasmuch: Christian Social Responsibility in the Twentieth Century* (Grand Rapids, Mich.: Eerdmans, 1965), 15.

6. Earle Cairns, *Saints and Society* (Chicago: Moody Press, 1960).

7. David Moberg, *Inasmuch*, 38.

8. C. Sanyte, "One Day at a Time," *The Church Herald*, October 1991, 12–13.

9. P. Nordstrom, "Coming Home," *The Church Herald*, October 1991, 13.

10. J. Boehm, "Model A's and Black Crayons," *The Church Herald*, October 1991, 14.

11. H. VanWyk, "Dedicated to Each Other," *The Church Herald*, October 1991, 16–17.

12. H. Lenters, "Keeping in Touch," *The Church Herald*, October 1991, 16.

13. P. Kranendonk, "Breaking Down the Myth," *The Church Herald*, October 1991, 11–12.

14. Chet Vanscoy, interview with Angela Elwell Hunt, November 1990.

CHAPTER 9—SHOULD MOM AND DAD LEAVE THEIR HOME?

1. Amanda Spake, "When Children Become Parents to Their Parents: 'Nursing Home' Were the Two Words I Dreaded Most to Hear," *Washington Post*, 13 March 1990, Z14.

2. Barbara Sorid, "Making It Easier to Face Later Years," *Philadelphia Inquirer*, 22 March 1989, B28.

3. U.S. Department of Health, Education and Welfare, PHS, "Home Care for Persons Aged 55 and Over in the U.S. July 1966–June 1968," *Vital and Health Statistics*, series 10, no. 73 (July 1972); E. M. Brody, *Women in the Middle: Their Parent Care Years* (New York: Springer, 1990), 32.

4. J. K. Belsky, *The Psychology of Aging: Theory, Research, and Interventions*, 2d ed. (Pacific Grove, Calif.: Brooks/Cole, 1990), 89–90.

5. M. W. Bozian and H. M. Clark, "Counteracting Sensory Changes in Aging," *American Journal of Nursing* 80 (1980): 473–476.

6. E. D. Huttman, *Housing and Social Services for the Elderly: Social Policy Trends* (New York: Praeger, 1977).

7. Karen S. Peterson, "Your Words of Wisdom and Sorrow," *USA Today*, 18 April 1989, 4D.

8. Don Campbell, "What's Best for Seniors," *Los Angeles Times*, 12 May 1991, K4.

9. B. L. Hancock, *Social Work with Older People* (Englewood Cliffs, N.J.: Prentice Hall, 1987), 246–248.

10. Erin Kennedy, "What if You Can't Care for Yourself?" *Philadelphia Inquirer*, 7 June 1990, H4.

11. Janet Nassif, *The Home Health Care Solution: A Complete Consumer Guide* (New York: Harper and Row, 1985).

12. Victor Cohn, "The Patient's Advocate: Home Care: Where to Turn," *Washington Post*, 28 October 1986, Z8.

13. Don Campbell, "What's Best for Seniors."

14. A. Harvey, "Life-Care Contracts for the Elderly: A Risky Retirement?" *USA Today Magazine*, July 1988, 27–29.

15. Barbara E. Sorid, "Making It Easier to Face Later Years."

Sources
Cox, H. G. *Later Life: The Realities of Aging.* 2d ed. Englewood Cliffs, N.J.: Prentice Hall, 1988.
Hooyman, N. R., and N. A. Kiyak. *Social Gerontology: A Multidisciplinary Perspective.* 2d ed. Boston: Allyn and Bacon, 1991.

CHAPTER 10—SHOULD MOM AND DAD MOVE IN WITH ME?
1. Jean Redstone, "For the Frail but Unfulfilled, Social Day Care Offers Help," *Philadelphia Inquirer,* 5 August 1990, G8.
2. Sherry Angel, "Stumbling Into a Hidden Parent Trap," *Los Angeles Times,* 20 February 1991, E3.
3. Ibid.
4. C. Tibbits, "Some Social Aspects of Gerontology," *The Gerontologist* 8 (1968): 131–133; Cary Kart, *The Realities of Aging.*
5. J. Demos, "Notes on Life in Plymouth Colony," *William and Mary Quarterly* (Third Series) 22 (1965): 264–286.
6. P. Greven, "Family Structure in Seventeenth Century Andover, Mass.," *William and Mary Quarterly* (Third Series) 23 (1966): 234–356.
7. J. Demos, "Families in Colonial Bristol, Rhode Island: An Exercise in Historical Demography," *William and Mary Quarterly,* (Third Series) 25 (1968): 40–57.
8. J. S. Greenberg and M. Becker, "Aging Parents as Family Resources," *The Gerontologist* 28 (1988): 786–791.
9. E. M. Brody, *Women in the Middle: Their Parent-Care Years* (New York: Springer, 1990), 32.
10. Jean Redstone, "For the Frail but Unfulfilled, Social Day Care Offers Help."
11. Ibid.
12. M. S. Caserta et al., "Caregivers to Dementia Patients: The Utilization of Community Services," *The Gerontologist* 27 (1987): 209–214; J. K. Belsky, *The Psychology of Aging: Theory, Research, and Interventions,* 2d ed. (Pacific Grove, Calif.: Brooks/Cole, 1990), 103–105.
13. L. Osterkamp, "Family Caregivers: America's Primary Long-Term Care Resource," in *Annual Editions, Aging,* 180–183.
14. Anne C. Roark, "Elder Care: Caring for California's Aging Population."
15. Jane Bryant Quinn, "Staying Ahead: More Employers Helping Out People Who Care for Elderly Parents," *Washington Post,* 7 December 1987, F67.
16. Cindy Skrzycki, "Family Blessings, Burdens: Employees Struggle to Balance Work with Care of Aging Relatives as Well as Children," *Washington Post,* 24 December 1989, H1.
17. Ibid.
18. Linda Loyd, "Firms, Workers Face New Problem: Caring for Elderly," *Philadelphia Inquirer,* 25 April 1988, D1.
19. David Streitfeld, "Seniors: Balancing Work and Eldercare," *Washington Post,* 29 July 1986, C5.
20. Shelly Phillips, "The Stress of Balancing a Career with Caring for an Elderly Parent," *Philadelphia Inquirer,* 4 February 1990, I4.
21. Ibid.

22. Karen S. Peterson, "Caring for Aging Relatives Is a Trying Labor of Love," *USA Today,* 1 November 1990, 4D.

23. Karen S. Peterson, "Counseling Pulls Troubled Family Together Again," *USA Today,* 18 April 1989, 4D.

Sources

Shanas, E. "The Family as a Social Support System in Old Age." *The Gerontologist* 19 (1979): 169–174.

Shanas, E. "Family Help Patterns and Social Class in Three Countries." *Journal of Marriage and Family* 29 (1967): 257–266.

CHAPTER 11—OTHER HOUSING OPTIONS FOR MOM AND DAD

1. R. C. Atchley, *Social Forces and Aging,* 6th ed. (Belmont, Calif.: Wadsworth, 1991), 34.

2. C. F. Longingo, Jr., *The Oldest Americans: State Profiles for Data Base Planning* (Coral Gables, Fla.: University of Miami, Center for Social Research on Aging, 1986).

3. R. C. Atchley, *Aging: Continuity and Change,* 2d ed. (Belmont, Calif.: Wadsworth, 1987), 142.

4. Bureau of the Census, "Detailed Population Characteristics. Part 1, U.S. Summary," chapter D in *Census of the Population,* vol. 1, *Characteristics of the Population,* tables 265–266 (Washington: GPO, 1980).

5. Norman Foley lectures (Grand Rapids Junior College, 1980, 1982).

6. *Understanding Your Changing World: A Manual for Grand Rapids Senior Citizens* (Grand Rapids, Mich.: Calvin College–Grand Rapids Junior College Consortium on Aging, 1976).

7. Norman Foley lectures (Grand Rapids Junior College, 1980, 1982).

8. A. E. Gillespie and K. S. Sloan, *Housing Options and Services for Older Adults* (Santa Barbara, Calif.: ABC-CLIO, 1990), 82–88.

9. Betty Ommerman, "Life Over Sixty: In Short, Living the Good Life," *Newsday,* 22 April 1989, 5.

10. A. Harvey, "Life-Care Contracts for the Elderly: A Risky Retirement?"

11. Ibid.

12. J. Michael Kennedy, "Shared Housing: Growing Answer to Costly Living," *Los Angeles Times,* 20 November 1988, A12.

13. Melinda Beck et al., "The Geezer Boom," *Newsweek Special Edition: 21st Century Family,* 62–68.

Sources

Bould, S., B. Sanborn, and L. Reif. *Eighty-Five Plus: The Oldest Old.* Belmont, Calif.: Wadsworth Publishing Company, Belmont, 1989, 34.

CHAPTER 12—NURSING HOMES: WHEN AND WHERE?

1. Vivian Greenberg, quoted by Darrell Sifford, "The Pain of Putting a Parent in a Nursing Home," *Philadelphia Inquirer,* 25 March 1990, J1.

2. A. T. Day, *Who Cares? Demographic Trends Challenge Family Care for the Elderly,* no. 9, Population Trends and Public Policy (Washington, D.C.: Population Reference Bureau, Inc., 1985); Cary Kart, *The Realities of Aging,* 229.

3. E. Shanas, "Social Myth as Hypothesis: The Care of Family Relations of Old People,"

The Gerontologist 19 (1979): 3–9; R. Schulz and R. B. Ewen, *Adult Development and Aging* (New York: Macmillan, 1988), 256.

4. L. Osterkamp, "Family Caregivers,"180–183.

5. Ibid.

6. Ibid.

7. M. J. Salamon and G. Rosenthal, *Home or Nursing Home: Making the Right Choices* (New York: Springer, 1990), 63–78.

8. Vivian Greenberg, quoted by Darrell Sifford, "The Pain of Putting a Parent in a Nursing Home."

9. M. J. Salamon and G. Rosenthal, *Home or Nursing Home*, 63–78; the booklet *How to Choose a Nursing Home*, Detroit, Mich.: Citizens for Better Care, and Institute of Gerontology, University of Michigan, 1989).

10. U.S. House Select Committee on Aging, "Long-Term Care and Personal Impoverishment: Seven in Ten Elderly Living Alone Are at Risk" (Washington: GPO, 1987), 100–631.

11. D. L. Rabin and P. Stockton, *Long-Term Care for the Elderly: A Factbook* (London: Oxford University Press, 1987).

12. J. K. Belsky, *The Psychology of Aging: Theory, Research, and Interventions*, 2d ed. (Pacific Grove, Calif.: Brooks/Cole, 1990), 100.

13. *Long-Term Care* (Washington, D.C.: American Association of Retired Persons).

14. J. Hendricks and C. D. Hendricks, *Aging in Mass Society: Myths and Realities*, 3d ed. (Boston: Little, Brown, 1986), 282.

15. *Medical Nursing Home Eligibility for Residents with a Spouse at Home* (Detroit, Mich.: Citizens for Better Care, September 1990).

16. U.S. House Select Committee on Aging, "Long-Term Care and Personal Impoverishment: Seven in Ten Elderly Living Alone Are at Risk," 100–631; N. R. Hooyman and H. A. Kiyak, *Social Gerontology*, 548.

17. A. Budish, *Avoiding the Medical Trap: How to Beat the Catastrophic Costs of Nursing Home Care* (New York: Holt, 1989).

18. Mal Schechter, "As You Get Older: Eight Decades a 'Realizable Goal' if You Manage Your Body Well," *Washington Post*, 9 January 1990, Z8.

19. Vivian Greenberg, quoted by Darrell Sifford, "The Pain of Putting a Parent in a Nursing Home."

20. Ibid.

CHAPTER 13—DEALING WITH FRUSTRATION, ANGER, AND GUILT

1. Leonard Felder, quoted by Karen S. Peterson, "Easing the Emotional Transition," *USA Today*, 18 April 1989, 4D.

2. Joan Kelly, "When Parents Need Parenting: Friction is Almost Inevitable When Siblings Share in the Care of an Aging Parent," *Newsday*, 25 February 1989, part 2, 1.

3. Ibid.

4. Ibid.

5. Ibid.

6. Cristine Russell, "Long Distance Medicine; Coping with a Crisis from Miles Away," *Washington Post*, 23 October 1990, Z12.

7. Ibid.

8. Ibid.

9. Ibid.

10. Anne C. Roark, "Elder Care: Caring for California's Aging Population," *Los Angeles Times,* 20 May 1990, Home Edition, 1.

11. Jane Bryant Quinn, "Old, Sick, and Far Away," *Newsweek,* 26 August 1991, 39.

12. Harold Ivan Smith, *You and Your Parents: Strategies for Building an Adult Relationship* (Minneapolis: Augsburg, 1987), 14.

13. Lori Durso, "Preparing to Care for Aging Parents," *Philadelphia Inquirer,* 28 August 1988, J7.

14. Karen S. Peterson, "Easing the Emotional Transition," *USA Today,* 18 April 1989, 4D.

15. E. M. Brody, *Women in the Middle: Their Parent-Care Years* (New York: Springer, 1990), 10.

16. U.S. House of Representatives, Select Committee on Aging, "Exploding the Myths: Caregiving in America" (Washington: GPO, 1987).

17. L. Osterkamp, "Family Caregivers," 180–183.

18. Ethel Sharp, "Caregivers Must Guard Their Own Health as Well," *St. Petersburg Times,* 27 August 1991, Seniority, 22.

19. Joan Conway, "The Guilt Factory," *Newsweek,* 22 May 1978, 5.

20. H. McLean, *Caring for Your Parents: A Sourcebook of Opinions and Solutions for Both Generations* (Garden City, N.Y.: Doubleday, 1987).

21. Marguerite Kelly, "Caring for Elderly Kin," *Washington Post,* 3 May 1990, D5.

22. Ibid.

CHAPTER 14—HONORING YOUR PARENTS AS THEIR YEARS INCREASE

1. Gene Yasuda, "Abuse of Elderly Cases Triple in a Five-Year Period," *Los Angeles Times,* 15 January 1990, B1.

2. Angela Elwell Hunt, "Pat Moore Celebrates Life and Aging," *Fundamentalist Journal,* April 1989, 36–37.

3. Tim Stafford, *As Our Years Increase* (Grand Rapids, Mich.: Zondervan, 1989), 209–210.

CHAPTER 15—WHEN YOU MUST SAY GOOD-BYE

1. Judy Mann, "Watching a Parent Slip Away, a Little at a Time," *Washington Post,* 21 April 1989, B3.

2. Sharon Begley and Mark Starr, "Choosing Death," *Newsweek,* 26 August 1991, 44–45.

3. An excellent discussion of these questions can be found in Hessel Bouma III, et. al., *Christian Faith, Health and Medical Practice* (Grand Rapids, Mich.: Eerdmans, 1989).

4. "The Last Days of Life" (National Institute on Aging, 1991). The study involved the deaths of 1,227 selected residents of Fairfield County, Conn.

5. M. R. Leming and G. E. Dickinson, *Understanding Dying, Death, and Bereavement,* 2d ed. (Fort Worth, Tex.: Holt, Rinehart and Winston, 1990), 174–175.

6. Ibid.

7. Barbara Deane, *Caring for Your Aging Parent* (Colorado Springs, Col.: NavPress, 1989), 236.

8. Barbara Deane, *Caring for Your Aging Parent,* 236-237.

9. Elizabeth Kubler-Ross, *On Death and Dying* (New York: Macmillan, 1969).

10. Judy Mann, "Watching a Parent Slip Away."

Sources

Bouma, Hessel, III, et. al. *Christian Faith, Health and Medical Practice.* Grand Rapids, Mich.: Eerdman's, 1989.

Gallahan, D. *Setting Limits: Medical Goals in an Aging Society.* New York: Simon and Schuster, 1987.

Garfield, C., ed. *Psychological Care of the Aging Person.* New York: McGraw-Hill, n.d.

Kalish, R. A. *Death, Grief, and Caring Relationships.* Pacific Grove, Calif.: Brookes/Cole, 1985.

Kastenbaum, R. "Dying and Death: A Life Span Approach." In J. E. Biren and K. W. Schaie, eds. *Handbook of the Psychology of Aging.* New York: Van Nostrand Reinhold, 1985.

Kubler-Ross, Elizabeth. *On Death and Dying.* New York: Macmillan, 1969.

Schneidman, E. S. *Voices of Death.* New York: Harper and Row, 1980.

Stemphenson, J. S. *Death, Grief, and Mourning: Individual and Social Realities.* New York: Free Press, 1985.

Wass, H., et. al., eds. *Dying: Facing the Facts.* New York: Hemisphere, 1988.

Index